✠ ON GOD AND DOGS

⊠ ON GOD AND DOGS

A Christian Theology of
Compassion for Animals

Stephen H. Webb

With a Foreword by Andrew Linzey

New York   Oxford
OXFORD UNIVERSITY PRESS
1998

Oxford University Press

Oxford   New York
Athens   Auckland   Bangkok   Bogota   Bombay   Buenos Aires
Calcutta   Cape Town   Dar es Salaam   Delhi   Florence   Hong Kong
Istanbul   Karachi   Kuala Lumpur   Madras   Madrid   Melbourne
Mexico City   Nairobi   Paris   Singapore   Taipei   Tokyo   Toronto   Warsaw

and associated companies in
Berlin   Ibadan

Copyright © 1998 by Stephen H. Webb

Published by Oxford University Press, Inc.
198 Madison Avenue, New York, New York 10016

Oxford is a registered trademark of Oxford University Press

Library of Congress Cataloging-in-Publication Data
Webb, Stephen H., 1961–
    On God and dogs : a Christian theology of compassion for animals /
Stephen H. Webb; with a foreword by Andrew Linzey.
     p.   cm.
Includes bibliographical references and index.
ISBN 0-19-511650-X
1. Animal welfare—Religious aspects—Christianity.   2. Dogs—
Religious aspects—Christianity.   I. Title.
BT746.W42   1998
241'.693—dc21   97-23342

9 8 7 6 5 4 3 2 1

Printed in the United States of America
on acid-free paper

Acknowledgments

While I was writing this book, my wife, Diane Timmerman, gave birth to our first child, Charis, and I could not have finished it without the caring help of my parents and my parents-in-law. The arrival of this wonderful gift, in the midst of my project, kept turning my thoughts to a story my mother has occasionally told about me. It is one of my earliest memories, although memory and story are too intermingled to be separated now. We were in a post office, and she turned away from me for a moment, only to be startled by loud cries that she knew were mine. When she found me, a woman apologized to her, explaining that she had accidentally stepped on a ladybug that I had been following across the floor, and that had sent me into tears. Children often identify with animals in ways that amuse and frustrate us, spending emotion with an abandon that adults, with their thrifty investments and prudent decisions, cannot afford. Something inevitably happens to warn us off such displays of sympathy, but the inevitable is not necessary, just as the sophisticated is not equivalent to the true or the frugal to the good. Indeed, I tend to think that all care is overreaching, that all compassion has a childlike aspect and thus risks the mawkish and ridiculous. My book tries to take seriously the gift children have of relating to animals, a gift we adults should cherish and return by changing our lives accordingly.

The writing of this book, like the subject of my reflections, is the product of much leisure and even self-indulgence, and I want to thank Wabash College for a sabbatical and the McLain-McTurnan-Arnold Fund for a grant that made this labor possible and enjoyable. I also want to thank Deborah Polley, of the Wabash Library, for essential and graceful help in obtaining necessary materials. William C. Placher, as always, read this manuscript at a crucial stage in its development, and I am happy to say that my debt to him continues to grow. Michael J. Brown made several helpful suggestions about my use of scripture and my references to the early church. Diane gave the manuscript its final reading, which resulted in a lot of rewriting I did not realize I needed to do. A very brief version of my thesis was first published in essay form, "Pet Theories: A Theology for the Dogs," in *Soundings* 78 (1995): 213–37, and subsequently developed in "Ecology vs. the Peaceable Kingdom: Toward a Better Theology of Nature," in *Soundings* 79 (1996): 239–52, and I am grateful to that journal's editor, Ralph V. Norman, for his encouragement and suggestions. I presented my thesis to a wonderful group, the Association of Disciples for Theological Discussion, and many of their comments were helpful, especially the response by Larry Bouchard. I also want to thank Jay McDaniel, Andrew Linzey, and Carol Adams for insightful comments and constructive suggestions. This book was conceived in a brief conversation with the late Eric Dean, Professor of Religion and Philosophy at Wabash College, who once told me (and I never had the opportunity to tell him that I too had this desire) that he had always wanted to write a theology about dogs. I do not know what he had in mind, but I hope I got the spirit of it right.

This book is dedicated to Charis. It is also, of course, for my dachshund Marie, whose own praxis of giving—she still insists on sitting on my lap when I spend too much time writing—is daunting and relentless.

Crawfordsville, Indiana   S. H. W.
May 1997

Contents

Foreword: Voyage to the Animal World

Andrew Linzey

Stephen Webb has boldly gone where no one has gone before. His mission is ambitious: to search out the nonhuman world and to bring back an account that is both morally and spiritually satisfying.

Of course it is an exaggeration to say that Webb has gone where *no one* has gone before. Truth to tell, there have been many theological voyagers of one sort or another. The classic figures in the Christian tradition have all paid short-term, rather perfunctory, visits to the animal world.

Most dominantly, these theological travelers have viewed the animal world like the discovery of new continents or islands: as collections of vast resources for human use—indeed, divinely made so. On this account—and such an account has been pervasive throughout Christian history—the animal world is just *there*—for us—as are any other material objects in the cosmos that God has made. "O rejoice!," exclaim these theologians, "that the Lord has provided such a bounteous storehouse for our sustenance."

These voyagers, whilst feasting on the inhabitants of the animal world, have noted with reassurance their apparent, even self-evident, inferiority. As they see it, the animal world provides sumptuous evidence of the supposed supremacy of *their own*, that is, the human world. The citizens of the animal world are by nature and providence extensions of the human larder, and we know this by the fact that these creatures can be so enslaved, hunted, and manipulated. It is God's very graciousness, they declare, that the inferior are to be eaten by the superior, not merely as a by-product of territorial conquest but by divine design. (And so, incidentally, it has remained: the most characteristically human activity in relation to animals has been to eat them.)

Other, more thoughtful travelers have been struck variously by the beauty, the magnificence, and the awe-inspiring nature of the animal world and have constructed stories of a Creator God whose creativity knows no bounds. Some have even questioned a God seemingly preoccupied with the welfare of the human species when in fact divine creativity encompasses so vast a multitude of creatures. Doctrinal courtesy alone has required some account of the Creator God whose world combines worlds within—and without—our own human world.

But the overriding feature of these accounts, even in their more awe-struck moods, has been predominantly one of unadventurousness, even neglect. While some notions of fellow-feeling and kinship have been reported in the accounts of more thoughtful theological voyagers, such expressions have not unusually been derided as misplaced, even taken as evidence of species disloyalty.

More recently, a new breed of voyagers has emerged determined to include this animal world within the moral world that humans themselves inhabit. Old maps have been torn up. The animal world, it is claimed, is not merely to be interpreted as an adjunct to the human one; its purpose is not simply to serve and feed the human species. Divine providence, if it is truly gracious, requires more than a humanly gastrocentric view of the animal world. Far from leaving theology behind, these new pioneers insist that God's own interest—and justice—is not served by progressive colonization; that God has a stake in each and every sentient creature from whatever world. The view that Jesus Christ is of immense significance for the human world but of no consequence for the rest of the cosmos is challenged as theologically parochial.

Webb's voyage is naturally an heir to these more recent voyages—not least in their widening moral concern and even their scholarly sources. He graciously acknowledges his debt to John Cobb Jr., Jay MacDaniel, Stephen Clark, Gary Comstock, and myself and our various expeditions, past and present.

What is it then that Webb discovers, and why is his discovery worthy of our attention? Webb is led to nothing less than the discovery of the animal world as a world of divine grace. Grace is "the inclusive and expansive power of God's love to create and sustain relationships of real mutuality and reciprocity." What particularly excites Webb is not just the existence of the animal world but its capacity to create relationships of joyful giving with humankind. Pet relationships are—for Webb—the moral pivot of our entire relations with the animal world. It is precisely in these relationships of "excess" that we see prefigured and actualized the self-giving God. At one stroke the traditional instrumentalist and utilitarian framework is severed. "Although animals can be traded, processed, and consumed," writes Webb, "I want to insist that, from a theological perspective that takes pets seriously, animals are more like gifts than something owned, giving us more than we expect and thus obliging us to return their gifts."

Webb's bold thesis will not be music to the ears of all his fellow travelers—and I am one of them. For those of us who have championed moral solicitude for the animal world, the existence of "pets" kept for human companionship, comfort, and control only ambiguously betokens the gospel of grace. While not denying the moral rectitude of respectful, friendly, and affectionate relations with animals, our attitude is colored by an appreciation that behind such encounters lies the modern pet industry where animals are bred, reared, sold, and traded as consumer products for human enjoyment. Moreover, a large population of dogs and cats means inevitably the destruction of other species (including whales, kangaroos, seals, cows, rabbits, turkeys, and horses) as food. The pet industry—as we see it—is part of the problem, not part of the solution.

To be fair, Webb sees that not all pet relations are "model" ones, and that they are as ambiguous and complex as any loving, devoted human relations can be. I am with him in rejecting the idea that interspecies relationships are cranky or abnormal. *At their best*—and with this all-important caveat—they can be signs of a kind of self-giving and mutuality that Christians have claimed to be true of the very sociability of God. After centuries of exploitation, harm, and abuse, a little interspecies bonding could go a long way.

The lesson of Webb's book is that we must not overlook our "domestic" relations with animals as indicators of our spiritual health. In my view Webb moves too hard against the rhetoric of rights: I doubt whether the spiritual and moral status of animals can be secured without a discourse of strong moral limits, which is what in practice a rights rhetoric entails. But voyagers and pioneers see things differently, and this needs to be so. The best way, I suggest, is not to see Webb's work as displacing other notions of duties, reverence, and rights but to see it as building upon them. Theologically, notions of moral limits are parasitic on a notion of grace, and vice versa.

But whatever disagreements there may be, the new voyagers are all agreed on one thing: Animals are not just machines, commodities, tools, resources, utilities here for us, or means to human ends; rather they are God-given sentient beings of worth, value, and dignity in their own right. This is a moral and spiritual discovery as objective and as important as any other fundamental discovery, whether it be the discovery of stars and planets or the discovery of the human psyche. One day, theologians will be altogether astonished that it took us so long to see so little.

Webb's book is certainly bold, definitely audacious, lucidly written, and—most nourishingly of all—full of spiritual insight. It will help us rethink and cherish our kinship with the animal world that we have neglected for so long. I welcome him to that growing band of animal theologians who are determined to change once and for all the character of humanocentric theology.

Mansfield College, Oxford
April 1997

ON GOD AND DOGS

Introduction: Pet Theories

This book is for two different audiences, groups that ordinarily do not read the same books: people who are interested in animal rights and people who study Christian theology. My goal is to show that these two groups have more in common (and more to say to each other) than they usually think. For the first group, those who already know the nuts and bolts of the animal rights literature, I am offering two distinctive perspectives. First, my guiding concern, Christian theology, is a voice often silent in the debates over animals and ethics. Confessing that theology has been slow to respond to the demands and challenges of the animal rights movement and confronting the contributions of Christianity to the mistreatment of animals nonetheless do not erase the important practical fact that the churches are a potential ally of great power and influence that cannot be ignored. I will argue that significant theological resources exist for both a critique of and a contribution to animal liberation. Second, from the perspective of a feminist reevaluation of the importance of feeling in the moral life, I will be unafraid to talk about animals with emotion, something that animal rights advocates too frequently resist or denounce. In fact, I will argue that the emotional bond with companion animals should play a central role in the way we think about animals in general. Thus, instead of promoting a reverence for the wild and the distancing of humans from animals, I will defend the inevitable intermingling of the human and animal worlds, an intermingling about which pets can be very instructive. The desire to protect animals, in other words, can emerge from intimacy as well as from separation.

For the second group, my theological readers, I am offering an introduction

to issues about animals that will not only survey the relevant theological options and biblical materials but also examine the way the Christian notion of
grace can illuminate our relationship with animals. I will try to imagine what
it would be like to treat animals as a gift from God. Indeed, I will argue that
animals not only are a gift to us but also give to us, so that we need to attend
to their giving and return their gifts appropriately. This relationship of giving
between humans and animals I call grace. Of course, not all interactions with
animals are full of grace, but I insist throughout this book that what Christians
call grace is present in our relations with animals just as it is in our relations
with other humans. Grace is the inclusive and expansive power of God's love
to create and sustain relationships of real mutuality and reciprocity, and I will
pursue the implications of the recognition that animals too participate in God's
abundant grace.

For both audiences, I offer a final perspective that is usually used against the
animal rights movement, namely, rhetoric. Animal defenders are often charged
with being overly rhetorical; my interest in rhetoric lies elsewhere. I am convinced that how we talk about the animals closest to us shapes the way we treat
all animals, so that an investigation into the language of petkeeping is a necessary prerequisite to the activity of animal compassion. Interesting parallels between rhetoric and pets make this investigation even more intricate. Indeed,
both rhetoric and dogs, topics I frequently treat as twins in this book, conjure
the intimate and the emotional; both appear to have only relative, contingent
value. Rhetoric adds flourish to the stable structure of language, just as the dog
signifies a conspicuous indulgence for the otherwise frugal economy of the
private household. Both involve forms of communication that, in terms of efficient, goal-driven activity, accomplish very little, referring in the end more to
the speaker or the owner than to anything objective in the public realm. Adding
religion to the discussion, subject matter that is often marginalized and privatized in modern culture, does little to change the tone of my topic. It seems
appropriate, therefore, to begin a book about such potentially idiosyncratic issues with a personal confession.

In previous work, I have tried to illuminate what I call the category of *excess*,
a linguistic construction of experience that is both aesthetic and religious, encompassing events and activities that call us out of ourselves and break the grip
of calculative rationality and utilitarian decision making. Rhetoric has been my
principal tool in analyzing the excessive because extravagant words and deeds
can be approached as forms of the figure of speech named hyperbole, more
commonly known as exaggeration. For many years, I have been interested in
showing how certain key facets of the religious life can be examined according
to the contours of the trope that both embellishes and provokes, amplifying
possibilities and revealing impossibilities. More specifically, I have tried to show
how the Christian understanding of God's grace as both a powerful intrusion

into our lives and something we share with each other through improvisational and spontaneous acts of giving conforms to and thus can be illuminated by the structural features of the rhetoric of hyperbole.

I developed my work on hyperbole in the company of a companion animal who was constantly at my side, and often on my lap, during my reading and writing. The more I thought about excess, the more I thought that pets, especially dogs, are eminently emblematic of that phenomenon; the more I thought about my theological and philosophical development—about the postmodern demand for narrative in even the most rigorous arguments and delight in the idiosyncratic and the different—the more I wanted to write from (and to some extent about) my own particular situation, in a confessionalistic mode.[1] I started to think a lot about the time I was spending with my dog, wondering about the value of activities and relationships that a certain (and dominant) strand in our culture considers to be useless and nonserious. It became increasingly clear to me that the most personal and relevant application of my theories of excess necessitated an investigation into the very common and personal world of pets.

Then I read three books that deepened my interests and channeled my wandering thoughts into an urgent and somber context. In 1990 I read Peter Singer's *Animal Liberation* (1990), and though I was not attracted to his use of utilitarian ethical theory, the fundamental value of vegetarianism and the overwhelming problem of cruelty to animals did immediately grip me. Later, I read Carol Adams's *The Sexual Politics of Meat* (1990), and her demonstration of the parallels between the way men typically talk about meat and the way they frequently talk about women led me to begin investigating the ways in which both pets and women are related to rhetoric. Why is compassion for animals considered a "soft" emotion, for example, and why is the genre of domesticated animal stories often connected to children and women (but not men)? Why are more women than men vegetarians? Finally, I read Andrew Linzey's seminal work, *Christianity and the Rights of Animals* (1987), and I realized that theology had much more to contribute to the animal liberation movement than most people think. I knew my life had to change and that I had to write about religion and dogs.

Of course, telling people that you are a vegetarian is one thing, but telling them that you are writing a theology for (rather than about) dogs is quite another. Indeed, two interrelated questions immediately arise in trying to speak theologically and philosophically about dogs. First, is the subject too frivolous and self-indulgent? Indeed, is the institution of petkeeping an expression of middle-class decadence or an index of the increasing loneliness and isolation people feel in the twentieth century? People love their pets inordinately; in fact, that is what it seems pets are for. Any work on companion animals has to account for this emotional dimension, either by bracketing it, explaining it, or, as I have chosen to do, embracing it, albeit with a bit of irony and playfulness. Although too much sentimentalism can be tedious, and some think that such emotions always should be kept private, out of the public eye, I think that there is something philosophically significant about sentimentalism itself, something that dogs can teach us by their very ability to affect us so deeply and completely.

Second, can we ever come to terms with animal otherness? It might seem easier to talk about the integrity and autonomy of animals in terms of wild animals, creatures who certainly differ from us and yet, precisely because they keep their distance from us, can strike us with their own power and purpose. Sometimes, however, the otherness that is closest to home is the most intriguing and difficult. Because domesticated animals are a sign of the inextricable intermingling of the human and the animal world, it is plausible to argue that they raise the issue of the relationship between comprehension and domination in the most pressing way. The twin motives of curiosity/sympathy and control/exploitation in our relationship to nature are, after all, difficult to separate. Among the domesticated animals, dogs have shared their world with ours longer and more intensely than any other animal. The social structure and hunting techniques of canines enabled our ancestors to redirect the kinship ties of canines to the human circle, making them a mixture of the human and the wild, a something in between, neither completely other nor totally the same as ourselves. Dogs are, literally and figuratively, what we have made of them, but it is precisely that fact that gives the question of otherness its urgency and difficulty. Can the closeness of dogs enable us to see their very otherness? Can their similarity shed light on difference? Can dogs be both our "best friends" and an intrusion of something persistently other, demanding respect and attention on their own terms? Are they more than what we need from them?

My primary thesis is that the very excess of the human-dog relationship is the key to a way of relating to animals that is often overlooked or dismissed in serious, scholarly treatments of animals. Although animals can be traded, processed, and consumed, I want to insist that, from a theological perspective that takes pets seriously, animals are more like gifts than something owned, giving us more than we expect and thus obliging us to return their gifts. Giving, in fact, is the structure of the excessive relationship between humans and dogs that makes it so important for philosophical and theological reflection. A kind of covenant, or contract, exists between the human and the dog that transcends the self-interests of isolated individuals and the calculation of the utilitarian mentality.

I am interested in this relationship for its own sake. In a world obsessed with economics, and driven by the maximization of resources and the bottom line of profits, relationships that defy cost-benefit analysis are rare and inherently valuable. I am also interested in how this relationship of mutual giving can enable us to reform our treatment of other animals, how, that is, our capacity to receive what is other and give more than we take can help us to treat all animals with more kindness and compassion. I do not mean to commit the category mistake of substituting dogs for all animals, nor do I suggest the idea that the model of the pet is literally the best way for dealing with all animals. Yet I do want to argue that the human-dog relationship can engender a kind of valuing that is appropriate, in various ways, to our relationship with other animals as well. The human-dog relationship reveals clues to understanding how we can approach the world both as an inevitable extension of our own plans and projects and as something unpredictably and surprisingly valuable in itself.

The language of mutual giving is deeply consonant with religious rhetoric about grace and compassion, yet an investigation of the significance of dogs disturbs theology as much as any other discipline. St. Francis preached to the birds, but rarely have theologians addressed animals with a combination of sympathy and understanding. In chapter 1, after I outline my own theological method, I survey the biblical record on the treatment of animals and show how there are surprising resources in Judaism and Christianity for an ethic of compassion toward animals. I then examine two theological approaches to animals, one based on the Bible and the other on an appropriation of philosophical rights language. I conclude that neither strategy is adequate to both the complexity of the issues involved and the particularity of our actual relationships with animals.

In chapter 2 I look at two other theological options, process thought and environmentalism, that connect our treatment of animals to the basic principles of ecological holism. While I learn something from each of these options, I also analyze their limitations, most notably, the way they encourage us to think about animals in terms of the economy of the whole rather than as individual gifts of intrinsic value. I end chapter 2 with a discussion of the ecofeminist movement, which retrieves the intuitive and emotional side of our relationship to animals and thus opens the way to a more visceral interpretation of the self's relationship with others. I compare the feminist ethic of care with the philosophy of animal rights, which can be so determined to protect the otherness of animals and so careful to avoid the charge of sentimentalism that it consequently misses a valuable dimension of our relationship to animals.

Those who think about pets inevitably have their favorite theory about what pets are and what they do, theories that are, perhaps, reflective of how the theorist actually relates to animals when not just thinking about them. In chapter 3 I investigate the way in which scholars too often treat the phenomenon of petkeeping as something functional or utilitarian, reducing a symbiotic relationship to a calculated exchange. The simplicity of using economics as a master method or ruling trope in the interpretation of all human behavior is too tempting for many who reflect on our relationship with animals. Indeed, the usual approaches to pets—scientific, economic, and psychological, as well as philosophical—tend to reduce the human-dog relationship to some function of human (social or personal) need, so that the other animal becomes an extension of the human self. In this hermeneutics of suspicion, pets give us only what we want, thus affirming who we already are. Pets are a psychological extension of the narcissistic ego or a way of exercising domination tinged with affection. All of the critical theories of pets no doubt have elements of truth, but I want to suggest another dimension to the pet relationship, one that is more congruent with my own personal practice.

Discussing otherness in the realm of the sentimental must seem an insuperable task. In chapter 3 I show how most accounts of otherness are suspicious of affection and touching as ways of bridging the gap between self and other. It is as if the other can only be other at a distance. Consequently, in both critical histories of pets and in the animal rights movement itself, the exuberance of the relationship, which all dog lovers know by experience, is minimized or completely lost. My intention is to support the animal rights movement by supplementing it with a reflection on something that movement too frequently flinches from, as if the silliness of pets could only pollute the seriousness of moral argument. My own theory of pets, which takes seriously the affective and dialogical aspects of petkeeping, might seem uncritical, yet it challenges the easygoing cynicism of our culture and encourages a transformation in our responsibilities for and our perceptions of other animals.

Actually, the very concept of otherness is problematic from the start. Linguistically considered, speaking about the other (*any* other), who lies outside of our understanding, is a contradiction; we can only put the other into words, words that are, of course, of our own making. Especially with wordless others, like dogs, we tend to supply what is missing, so that dogs are made to speak our own language. Thus, in so many animal stories the animals speak a human language so that we can imagine them only as fanciful fabrications of ourselves. All too often, we end up speaking instead of, and not on behalf of, the other animal. Not surprisingly, philosophers who emphasize language as a uniquely human trait frequently downplay the possibilities of understanding animal otherness. Wittgenstein once remarked, "If a lion could talk, we could not understand him" (1978: 223). The lion's form of life, presumably, would be so different from our own that there would be no shared context for communication to take place. Another philosopher, Robert Nozick, has suggested that even if a lion could talk, the most we could learn would be the confirmation of the longstanding prejudice of giving members of one's own species more moral weight than members of other species: "Lions, too, if they were moral agents, could not be criticized for putting other lions first" (1983: 29).[2] The only alternative to Wittgenstein's agnosticism about animal intelligence seems to be Nozick's confidence that animals illustrate that which we already know. Only by analogy can we incorporate the strange into the familiar by finding in the other the reflection of one's own self. Yet with analogy the animal becomes an idea, an instrument for making an extrinsic point, and not, to use Kant's terminology, an end in itself.

Is there a language we share with animals, especially domesticated animals, that enables us to hear what they have to say, even though they are speechless? We are commonly tempted to think that animals have inner processes that are obscured by their inability to speak, and thus we pretend that they could talk, if only they were physically able. Wittgenstein (1978), however, taught that there are no private languages, and that thinking or reasoning always takes place in the public medium of language, so that if animals cannot talk, then it is difficult, if not impossible, to say whether or not they think. Wittgenstein did not want us to try, like metaphysicians, to penetrate phenomena in order to locate some inner essence or hidden unity. Animals are not just like us, yet unable to speak, because our language is who we are.[3] But Wittgenstein also alerts us to the various kinds of language games that occur in diverse situations, and surely among these games are certain modes of communication that humans and some nonhuman animals share. Animals, after all, show us what they nevertheless cannot say. I argue in chapter 4 that the language of mutual giving is a form of communication we develop with some animals that allows both parties to maintain their own identities. This discourse lets us understand the other even when we must do all of the talking.

Of course, the difficulty is to articulate just how these giving relationships differ from economic transactions. Giving, I want to argue, is a kind of rhetoric, a mode of communication that can be practiced even between those who do not share the same language, or who do not speak at all. This "language" is best examined in the everyday practices of dog lovers, but it can also be investigated in the much-maligned and discounted genre of fiction pertaining to animals. Postmodern critics warn us that the imagination inevitably consumes what it identifies, creating the other in its own image. Some fiction, I argue in chapter 4, liberates an excess in the animal other that resists reduction, assimilation, and incorporation. Some fiction helps us to understand pets as conspicuous and extravagant, entities that cannot be ensnared by our imaginations or explanations, creatures, indeed, that really suffer, desire, ponder, and enjoy. This excess draws us out of ourselves, extending and amplifying our need for connection and belonging. The best animal stories do not speak in fables, reducing the animal to an analogy to the human. Instead, they speak in hyperbole, acknowledging the extravagance of our desire for palpable otherness and the graceful giving that satisfies that desire.

The best animal stories offer us not a cheap sentimentalism but a demanding and releasing hyperbole. Indeed, they show us that the dog—so plastic that the word summons no single form but rather the particularity of some dear friendship—is hyperbole incarnate, exaggeration in the flesh. What I call the rule of hyperbole takes us to the other while yet reminding us that the other is always rhetorically construed and never something identifiable beyond the boundaries of language. Likewise, such hyperbole magnifies our concern and care for the other while still reminding us that our interest in the other originates in our own desires, never in purely altruistic compassion. Dogs thus teach us about excess in itself, those thoughts and feelings and beings that have no place in the efficient weighing of competing alternatives for scarce valuable resources.

Christianity too values that which has no rightful place, and I argue in chapter 5 that Christianity provides a helpful bridge between the particularity of care and the demand for broad changes in individual attitudes and social structures. Theologians can take the excess of pets seriously because the gift relationship between the human and the dog is an important example of grace in action, of a relationship powered by a spontaneity and smoothness that belittles human efforts at control and manipulation. Moreover, theologians should confront the category of excess in terms of its ramifications of waste and surplus. Is there room in a universe created by a good God for relationships and creatures that do not serve a specific purpose, that do not conform to utilitarian constraints? How does God value that which does not serve God's purpose? Does the human-dog relationship say something not only about us but also about God? I argue in chapter 5 that the image of God as a dog lover is a wonderful way to express the dynamic of God's grace.

In chapter 6 I investigate the fundamental reasons for theology's historical lack of sensitivity toward the question of animals. A Christian theology that treats creation as a gift from God could celebrate the dog's ability to give himself or herself freely and fully to human service; yet, as my analysis of Karl Barth instantiates, theologians frequently focus on the relation between human reception and divine benevolence, leaving no room for gifts from and to animals. More tragically, Christian theology has frequently continued the language of sacrifice to justify animal suffering and killing. Of course, among many ancient peoples, including the Hebrews, animals functioned as a kind of discourse between humans and the divine in sacrificial rituals, but the Hebrew scriptures place such rituals in a broader narrative that assigns a value to animals greater than the exchange of sacrifice. The Hebrews combined a recognition of the covenant between humanity and domesticated animals with a limitation on meat production and eating through a very controlled and humane process of ritual slaughtering. The early church, however, in an attempt to establish its own identity, disregarded the Torah's rules regarding working animals and secularized the act of slaughter. One would think that Christian theology would replace sacrificial ritual with a different discourse or economy concerning animals, but theologians rarely reflect on the implications of sacrificial rhetoric for animals. I conclude chapter 6 with a discussion of the ways Christianity potentially and actually subverts the logic of sacrifice and how the life and death of Jesus Christ can be interpreted as liberating for animals as well as humans. In chapter 7 I expand on this portrait of Jesus Christ as the face of God that puts a stop to nonvoluntary sacrifices and holds out hope for the redemption of all who suffer, including those who are speechless. Central to my analysis is a defense of what I call the "vegetarian eucharist," a reinterpretation of the central ritual of Christianity.

Throughout this book, I am trying to catch the tone of the rhetoric of Christianity, the emphasis on the boundless and surprising nature of love as it is evidenced in relationships of graceful and mutual giving, even though I am aware that many traditional interpretations of the Bible and the Christian tradition cannot be said to support all that I work toward. To be a Christian today is to live in the midst of contradictions, and to be a theologian forces one to take risks, to speak where the Bible is silent, and to repent of much that has been said before. A healthy and vital theology must learn to speak more personally if it is to regain the wider audience it once enjoyed. Theology must risk the absurd in order to do justice to faith. System building, in the context of multiple commitments and the suspicion that even the best traditions have distorted their own moral messages, can be accomplished only on the basis of a willful innocence and a persistent blindness. Theology is, in the end, accountable to a peculiar combination of suffering and salvation, pain and liberation, not the demands of any single philosophical method or program. Much of the resistance to the animal rights movement, I suspect, stems from the fact that once animals are recognized as capable of suffering, it is overwhelming to contemplate the animal holocaust that is occurring daily in our midst. As a character in a story by Isaac Bashevis Singer sadly notes, "For the animals it is an eternal Treblinka" (1989: 335). I insist in the last three chapters that only a God who suffered like an animal, who faced cruelty without resistance or denial, can empower us in our own efforts to acknowledge and challenge that which is truly unspeakable, the suffering of countless victims who cannot themselves speak in their defense.

This is the sum of my book, which, as part of the second generation of works on ethics and animals, is not a comprehensive account of any of the issues I raise. I do not list all of the horrors that have been inflicted on animals nor do I rehearse all of the arguments in favor of treating animals more decently. I do not survey all of the prejudices that history records against animals, nor do I recount the very real progress of the recent past. Except as they pertain to my own thesis, I avoid summarizing and criticizing the various philosophical arguments, from Aquinas to Kant, that limit and constrict the justification of compassion for animals. All of this has been done in great detail in the first generation of writings about animals and ethics, and my notes will lead the curious reader to the bulk of this instructive and provocative literature.

For the most part (at least until the epilogue) I avoid many of the practical questions that vegetarians are often asked, opting instead to focus on a basic orientation and vision that would show many of these challenges to be misguided. What I am after are cultural configurations that transcend individual intentionality and awareness. As long as it is more acceptable to say that we love meat than it is to say that we love animals, our views on animals will continue to be deeply distorted. The philosophical tradition, at its best, has limited animal concern to indirect duty, arguing that our treatment of animals is dependent on our treatment of each other or the development of good character.[4] Obviously, I think something can be said about our very direct involvement with animals, a participatory relationship that entails its own commitments and encourages its own kind of philosophical elaboration.

The literature on companion animals is usually divided between scientific, explanatory accounts of our affection for pets and nostalgic celebrations of the wonder of animal friends. It seems impossible in one work to be both rigorous and sentimental about dogs, but that is what I intend to do. It is difficult to talk about dogs for long with an objective and scientific voice—at least, such is my experience. Yet any discussion of the importance of animals to theology and philosophy must take into account all of those methodologies and disciplines that try to locate and explain the human urge to domesticate and cohabit with animals. I have tried to blend together my passions with the rigor of logical argument and the background of historical research. Nevertheless, my views in the end will not be as systematic as some might want; that, in fact, is an aspect of my approach to these issues—the displacement of the usual valorizations in academic philosophy and theology of the head over the heart.

I want to add a note here about terminology, since my book deals with language and some may question my use of terms. It has become common among some animal rights activists to criticize the word "pet," replacing it with the phrase "companion animal," and I also use this substitute phrase in this work. Nonetheless, I have for the most part retained the word "pet" because it connotes something very personal, physical, and intimate that reflects well on my argument. "Pet" as a verb, adjective, and noun can be applied to people or animals, and in all of its meanings ("caress," "favorite," "domesticated animal") it implies something not necessary but nonetheless meaningful and pleasurable. While the word can imply condescension, it also encapsulates a tender gesture that embarrasses only those who insist beyond reason on rigid borders and limits. I also use the phrase "humans and animals" even though it would be more correct to say something like "human animals and nonhuman animals." Not only is the latter phrase more awkward, but also I want to maintain, contrary to some animal rights activists, a certain level of difference between humans and animals in order better to argue our responsibilities toward them. In any case, as this previous sentence demonstrates ("our" and "them"), I do not think that our language can be evacuated of the kinds of distinctions that so often become pernicious and malignant. The point is not to eliminate but to learn to live with and enjoy differences.

Indeed, I am not unaware that the very term "animal" refers to an enormous range of beings in a very sloppy and general way. When speaking of animals and what we can give to them, it is convenient to follow the advice of Tom Regan (1983: 243–48), who suggests that animals who are "subjects of a life," that is, who have beliefs and desires and some sense of their past and future, should be our primary concern. Regan minimally includes in this group all mammals over the age of one year. Although I realize that it is impossible to extend compassion to absolutely all animals, I do not want to limit compassion only to animals who are identical or similar in relevant respects to us. I am interested in the many ways we can empathize with animals and the many ways they can respond to our gestures of empathy, and I want to interpret such responsiveness broadly to include any relationship we can have with animals that is mutually enriching and transformative. Animals can surprise us with their difference, and that difference can be just as demanding and obliging as any similarity.

Finally, although I prefer the label "animal compassion," which conveys the feminist retrieval of the role of intimacy and connectedness in morality, I also use the more common banners of "animal rights" and "animal liberation." Though both rights and liberation replace the more traditional sounding "animal welfare," they are not synonymous. The former is the more popular term, and it can be used in a general sense to include all those who work for the decent treatment of animals and in the more technical sense of extending the privilege of legal rights to include animals. The latter can conjure the media image of fanatics and terrorists (or movie stars and musicians!), but it also helpfully puts the animal defense movement in the context of other liberatory revolutions. Since I am suspicious of the idea of rights altogether, and I do not think that animals need to be liberated from all human contact, the phrase "animal compassion" best suits my purposes, but my choice usually depends on the context. Even the word "compassion" falls short of my purposes. It conjures a gulf crossed only heroically, and it is inevitably tinged with condescension and pity rather than a shared intimacy, a mutual participation that is better called love. The love of animals means not only our love for animals but their love for us as well. Animals, after all, have their own passion, which includes not only horrific suffering but also unspeakable joys, and some of those joys include us.

PART I

Surveying the Options

CHAPTER ONE

God and the Giving of Animals

Theological Method

To be honest, writing about animals from a committed Christian viewpoint is a difficult task. Although Abraham Lincoln is said to have mused, "I would not give much for that man's religion whose cat and dog are not the better for it" (quoted in Stephens, 1992: 183), most people in the Christian West do not connect the love of animals with religious obligation and duty. Can theology speak about animals with both integrity, rooted in scripture and tradition, and creativity, in dialogue with a philosophical movement that often has been critical of Christianity? Two basic strategies are available to any theologian who wants to address the animal liberation movement. The first involves a rereading of the Bible rooted in traditional Christian dogma but from the perspective of compassion toward animals, which can result in a surprising and refreshing view of the Bible and animals. The second is a theological appropriation of the animal rights agenda, which can demonstrate congruencies between theology and animal rights that are too frequently ignored by both parties.

Both strategies, however, have their limitations. I will argue that the Bible does display surprising sympathies for animals, that, in fact, the biblical tradition includes a hidden history of vegetarianism. Nevertheless, any animal-friendly interpretation of the Bible must read it against the grain of traditional interpretations, so that the first strategy must be willing to challenge and transform traditional understandings of Christian faith. To do this, a biblical theology of animals will need to be in dialogue with and borrow from other voices

17

on the value of animals. Nonetheless, I will also argue that the biblical vision of animals has its own integrity and distinctiveness, so that what it has to say in those dialogues is different from what animal rightists are saying, a difference that makes real dialogue possible. The second strategy thus needs to resist making theology a mere supplement or support for purely philosophical considerations. It needs to be open to the possibility that Judaism and Christianity might provide a striking alternative to the language of animal rights.

To develop a theology of animals that has both integrity and openness, I will use a method that Paul Tillich called (and practiced to near perfection) correlational theology, theology that critically correlates contemporary concerns with theological convictions.[1] David Tracy (1987) has defined such theology in terms of a good conversation, with give and take and a large amount of indeterminacy in its outcome. I would add that correlational theology is hyphenated, that is, it takes place in the "theology and———" mode, so that it has no essential form or structure. Such theology, at least as I practice it here, is messier than dogmatic theology, not only because it challenges specific Christian doctrines and beliefs but also because it doubts the assumption that those doctrines and beliefs can be developed and interconnected in a systematic and abstract manner. Correlational theology is also less rigorous than the philosophical theologies that have long dominated the theological scene. It does not assume that the conversation between church and culture can be governed and controlled by a single philosophical method. Nor does correlational theology allow the category of the political to determine the consequences of that conversation. Indeed, correlational theology learns from the political but also subjects it to a theological critique and transformation.

Yet correlational theology is not as haphazard and indiscriminate as this description might suggest. In fact, it strategically combines all of the concerns of dogmatic, philosophical, and political theologies for a persuasive goal. Tillich, for example, used the correlational method as an apologetical tool in order to illuminate the religious dimension to existence, that is, to uncover the basic religious depth that secular culture tries to obscure but cannot destroy. He did so on the basis of an imaginative vision at once theological, philosophical, and political. While Tillich's correlations were guided by an abiding concern, even an obsession, with synthesis and completion, correlational theology today, in dialogue with the postmodern suspicion of all metaphysical systems, must be content with more humble and provisional goals.

Indeed, today there is less confidence that the religious constitutes a dimension that pervades all aspects of existence. With so many claims as to what is really real, no single claimant can monopolize the position of ultimacy. There is even less confidence in the very metaphor of depth; the surfaces of life seem all too complex and appealing to admit to a unitary and single depth yielding only to metaphysical explication. Language is the pervasive human reality, postmodernists argue, and the deeper one goes, the more language one finds. Consequently, the practice of correlational theology must become more rhetorical—chancy, occasional, passionate—than metaphysical. Yet correlational theology is still based on the assumption that something religious is missing in secular accounts of various activities. It is driven by and toward a religious horizon, and the task of theology is to make that horizon explicit. The correlational theologian seeks to follow outward and forward an impulse toward understanding initiated by the reception of some illuminating grace, some mystery that makes more sense the more it is solicited. The mystery I am following in this book is our graceful relationship with companion animals, a relationship that is, significantly, linguistically constructed, so that what we say about our pet animals shapes what we actually do with them.

Christianity is a religion that finds significance in details—salvation in the particular, essence in incarnation, meaning in narrative. It seems less helpful to try to make Christianity fit into a philosophical system than to try to find in our most intimate practices the echo or residue of Christian sentiment, the response to God's grace. My guiding insight throughout this book is that grace makes theology what it is, a certain openness to a vision of the world as given, splurged, and abundant, freeing us from the twin anxieties of possession and self-assertion. I want to create a conversation between the theological interpretation of grace and the phenomenon of human-animal compassion and concern. I do not want to suggest that all human-pet relationships are full of grace; where there is such passion and closeness, all sorts of distortions are possible, even inevitable. After all, people can commit sins against pets as well as against other people. Nevertheless, I do want to suggest that theology shares with petkeeping a common language, so that a conversation between the two should be beneficial.

This work thus constitutes a serious attempt to attend to and appropriate Christian tradition from the perspectives of both postmodern irony and playfulness and political passion and commitment. I cannot pretend to be able to sort out the different weights of theology, philosophy, and politics that are combined here. The Bible contains some provocative visions of human-animal peacefulness—especially in the Hebrew Bible, where there are progressive rules regarding the humane treatment of animals—but the Bible as a whole has not significantly contributed to the animal liberation movement that recently has become so contentious and influential. The lamb might lie down with the lion someday, according to prophetic foresight (Isaiah 11:6–9), but in the meantime will the lamb attain peace with humans? On this question, the Bible needs a strong reading to uncover its ultimate position on animals. What I offer is neither narrowly biblical nor generically philosophical. Rather, I intend to respond to the grace that I find present even in the world of animals and to reread both the Bible and theology on the basis of that grace. Along the way I hope to show that theological resources exist for the philosophy of animal liberation that have been ignored or minimized for far too long.

The Biblical Record

Before I examine representatives of the two primary theological options (one biblical and one philosophical) concerning the treatment of animals, I need to substantiate my point that the Bible alone is for Christians a necessary but not sufficient basis for developing an ethics of animal compassion. The unmistakable fact is that the Bible is more clear about the value of animals than many of its critics or sympathizers realize (see Rimbach, 1982), yet this material needs to be highlighted and emphasized in order to establish a difference between what the Bible says and how the Bible customarily has been used on this issue. What is distinctive about the Jewish tradition, and what might help explain why so many readers of the Bible think that animals are an insignificant part of it, is that it demythologizes animals by neither divinizing nor demonizing them. The Bible contains no animal magic, animals are rarely symbolic of a greater mystery, and animals do not influence human affairs.[2] In a word, the Bible is more realistic than romantic about the world of animals. Because much ecological literature romanticizes animals, the integrity and power of the biblical vision of animals are often lost or distorted. The Bible treats animals as others who are really different and yet similar enough to merit kindness and to be included in God's plan for the world. By treating animals as animals, the Jewish tradition has been able consistently to insist on fair play between humans and animals while acknowledging the special role humans have in that relationship, an outlook that has ample scriptural warrant.

For example, the Genesis account of creation provocatively portrays a vegetarian world ("God said, 'See, I have given you every plant yielding seed that is upon the face of all the earth, and every tree with seed in its fruit; you shall have them for food'" [Genesis 1:29])[3] in which the humans exercise authority over the animals but do not use or kill them. Indeed, land animals are made on the same day as humans, showing their similarity to humanity, but they are also made before humans and pronounced good independently of humans, showing that they too are created out of love. Likewise, the story of man naming (and thus knowing and enjoying fellowship with) all the animals before woman is created demonstrates both the importance and the limitations of animal companionship.[4] The use of the phrase "all flesh" *(kol basar)* in Genesis joins together the human and the animal in a basic kinship of creatureliness under the shared providence of a merciful God (Genesis 6:12, 13, 9:11, 17).

Only after the fall is this harmony dislocated, as symbolized by the enmity between the woman and the serpent. Historically, biblical commentators speculated that meat eating was permitted after the fall because humanity's physical constitution had deteriorated and thus required the denser food of meat, the work of cultivating the arid soil required a more robust diet, or the fruits and herbs of Eden lost their original goodness. Given what we know about diet today, these reasons sound a lot like rationalizations. In Deuteronomy 12:20, God seems to allow meat eating due to the uncontrollable cravings of the Israelites. Whatever the case, the ideal of Eden continued to play a regulative role in establishing Israel's identity. When Deuteronomy 8:7–10 describes the ideal land and diet for the Hebrews, for example, meat is excluded (also see similar descriptions in Jeremiah 29:5; Amos 9:14; and Hosea 2:22).

The covenant between God and the Hebrews tries to restore the world to God's inclusive intention by spelling out the obligations involved in the basic kinship of all creatures. The Sabbath as the day of rest, for example, was meant to apply to animals as well as humans, as seen in the Fourth Commandment, which forbids all to work on the Sabbath, including cattle (Exodus 20:10). Jewish law also clearly allows the Sabbath to be desecrated if a human or an animal life is at stake. Even an animal's discomfort was deemed a sufficient reason for violating Sabbath regulations. Exodus 23:10–11 tells the Hebrews to let the land lie fallow in the seventh year, so that the poor may use it, and what they leave behind is for the wild animals. The seventh day, the seventh year, and the Jubilee (the fiftieth year) allowed for a periodic righting of all relationships, and the New Testament uses this background to understand the climax of the Messianic future, in which creation itself will find fulfillment in the consummation of a peaceable kingdom.

To fulfill the covenant meant to care for nature; to violate it moved the Hebrews further away from the garden and closer to chaos. The land and its inhabitants could prosper only if order was maintained. The Prophet Hosea is clear that one of the dire consequences of immorality is the languishing of the land and the animals, the birds, and the fish (Hosea 4:1–3). God warns the Hebrews through Zephaniah that their actions can unmake creation, leading to the destruction of both humans and animals (1:2–3). When the Prophet Joel imagines the final days, he thinks of the suffering of animals: "How the animals groan! The herds of cattle wander about because there is not pasture for them; even the flocks of sheep are dazed" (1:18). The greatest symbol of the constructive role humans can play in assisting God's good intentions is, of course, Noah's ark, which provided a sanctuary from the flood for representatives of all the animals. God's anger toward the whole world shows just how far nature had fallen from its original state, just as Noah's rescue mission demonstrates how crucial human effort is on behalf of animals.

The Mosaic covenant is full of practical ordinances that embody a vision of the mutual dependence and common interests between humans and animals. An ox and an ass are not to be yoked together, presumably because the differences between the pair might cause difficulties for the weaker of the two (Deuteronomy 22:10). Mother cattle are not to be slaughtered with their young on the same day (Leviticus 22:28). The warning not to take a mother bird sitting on her eggs has a motive-formula ("that it may go well with you and you may live long" [Deuteronomy 22:6–7]), which "suggests that the concept of filial piety has analogies extending beyond the merely human sphere" (Murray, 1992: 115). Indeed, the law of helping another's donkey to stand when it has fallen under a heavy load (Exodus 23:4–5; Deuteronomy 22:1–4) is, through the rabbinic principle of analogy, the basis for the Talmudic duty to relieve the suffering of all living beings. (The principle of *tzaar baalei hayyin*, literally "pain of living beings," though not in the Bible, is accepted by the rabbinic tradition as a biblical ordinance. For a survey of this principle, see Cohen, 1976.) Many scholars, however, continue to argue that these laws were motivated by a desire to distance the Hebrews from "pagan" practices and not by a desire for animal compassion. Scholars also suggest that biblical legislation is concerned with domestic and useful animals because it is in owners' self-interest to treat their property well. Is such legislation nothing more than sound and practical advice that is ultimately for the benefit of the human master?

The Hebrews did use diet to distinguish themselves from their neighbors. The so-called Holiness Code symbolizes the separation of Israel as a holy people (Leviticus 20:24), and this separation is nowhere more concrete than in the dietary laws forbidding the eating of certain animals as impure (Leviticus 11–15). Philo speculated that pork and scaleless water creatures, being, he thought, the most delicious of meats, were forbidden by Moses in order to restrain gluttony. He also thought that wild beasts and carnivores were forbidden in order to keep humans themselves from turning into beasts. Maimonides wrote that "the object of these laws is to restrain the growth of desire" (quoted in Houston, 1993: 75). Some scholars today have returned to this ancient interpretation. Walter Houston argues that the restricted diet mediates the vegetarianism of the original creation and the unrestrained violence of the flood period, enabling God to be present among God's people (1993: 77). The dietary code puts into practice, in a limited but concrete way, the possibility of humans living in peace with God's creation. By vastly limiting the number of species allowed as food, reverence for life is thereby promoted.

Eating and animals are thus more than symbols; food becomes part of the daily struggle of obeying God. The Book of Daniel, for example, tells the story of how Daniel and his friends refused to eat the impure food of Nebuchadnezzer, the Babylonian king. Instead, they ate only vegetables, and "at the end of ten days it was observed that they appeared better and fatter than all the young men who had been eating the royal rations" (Daniel 1:15). It is tempting at this point to argue that even the Bible understands that eating less meat is better for one's physical as well as spiritual health.

Of course, the Israelites did practice animal sacrifice, and I will examine that topic more closely in chapter 6. Clearly, the biblical tradition balances two potentially opposed viewpoints; it allows for the use of animals even as it insists that they are worthy of God's justice and mercy.[5] The story of the ark is not an anomaly in the Hebrew scriptures. After the flood, God makes a covenant with all living creatures (which is emphasized by several repetitions in Genesis 9:8–17), and it is clear throughout the Bible that wild animals are included in God's blessings for all of nature. In general, however, it is important to emphasize that while God cares about all of life, the Hebrews were asked to worry most about the animals who were dependent on them and upon whom they were dependent. The Hebrews were commanded to treat their domesticated and working animals, in a way, as pets—that is, as individuals with whom the intimacy of a shared life creates responsibilities and obligations. Recall, for example, the wonderful story of Balaam's ass, who, after being beaten, pleaded for respect and fair treatment. Even the angel criticizes Balaam's harshness toward the innocent animal (Numbers 22:21–33). Also consider the story of how Eliezer chose a suitable wife for Isaac on the basis of whether she would offer water not only for himself but also for his camel (Genesis 24:14).

Actual pets are rare in the Bible. Dogs (*kelev* in Hebrew) were used as watchdogs (Isaiah 56:10) and for guarding sheep (Job 30:1), though there are no hunting dogs in the Hebrew scriptures. Even though dogs were not feared (Proverbs 26:17), most references to dogs are negative, and cats do not appear at all (see Toperoff, 1995). Dogs fed on blood (which was forbidden to the Hebrews), were greedy (Isaiah 56:11), and the term "dog" was used as an insult (2 Kings 8:13). Maybe some Hebrews disliked dogs because the Egyptians loved them, though tradition states that not a single cur barked the night the Exodus began (see Exodus 11:7).[6] Because they did not bark or howl to warn the Egyptians that the Israelites were leaving, God apparently told the Hebrews to give their unclean meat to the dogs as a reward (Exodus 22:31), but gradually this association came to mean that dogs, being scavengers and parasites, were themselves unclean. Dogs were sometimes given the dead to eat, which could not have added to their standing in the community (1 Kings 14:11, 16:4, 21:23). The one story about a faithful dog is in the Apocrypha, where a little dog follows Tobias throughout his long journey, setting out with him when he is a bachelor (Tobit 6:1) and returning with him when he has a wife (11:4). There is also the interesting rabbinic tradition that the sign of protection God gave Cain was a dog.

Sheep are another matter altogether. Nathan tells the story of the poor man's pet lamb ("It used to eat of his meager fare, and drink from his cup, and lie in his bosom, and it was like a daughter to him" [2 Samuel 12:3]), which was stolen and slaughtered by a rich man (prompting David to reply, "As the Lord lives, the man who has done this deserves to die; he shall restore [that is, pay

for] the lamb fourfold, because he did this thing, and because he had no pity"
[12:5–6]). Genesis 33:13–14 contains a moving description of Jacob's tender
concern for his flock. The weak and defenseless sheep is an appropriate symbol
for the weak and defenseless human being, and God is often portrayed as a
shepherd who loves his flock dearly (Psalms 23; Isaiah 40:11). Indeed, God's
care for animals inspired many of the prayers and hymns of Psalms, some of
the admonitions and warnings of Proverbs ("The righteous know the needs of
their animals, but the mercy of the wicked is cruel" Proverbs 12:10), and some
of the most pointed visions of the prophets. The Talmudic rabbis strengthened
this tradition. The rabbis tell the story that it was only after Moses tracked a
runaway lamb and, finding it exhausted, carried it back to the flock, that God
said, "You who have compassion for a lamb shall now be the shepherd of my
people" (Kalechofsky, 1992: 26).[7]

The New Testament continues this theme of animal compassion by favoring
not the lion but the lamb, not the eagle but the dove, animals (like the lowly
ass) that do not prey but instead are defenseless and in need of human protection and care. Yet Christianity also changed the Hebrew context for animal
compassion. While the relationship between the Hebrews and animals was mediated by a multitude of rituals and laws, Christians celebrated their freedom
from the law, neglecting the ethical problems involved in dealing with animals.
The Hebrew tribes were commanded by the Laws of Moses not to defile their
bodies with unclean foods, but Christians argued that it is not what goes into
the mouth but what comes out of it that is morally significant. In a dream
while hungry, Peter saw "all kinds of four-footed creatures and reptiles and
birds of the air," and God's voice said to him, "Get up, Peter; kill and eat" (Acts
10:12–13). While the point of this vision is to annul the Jewish dietary laws for
those who wanted to be Christians, the story is used today, along with Matthew
15:11, to justify the eating of animals.[8]

Christianity intensified the Hebraic secularization of the animal world to the
extent that Christianity largely lost the connection between justice and nature.
The New Testament was written over a shorter period of time than the Hebrew
scriptures, for an urban rather than an agricultural audience, and with the
expectation of the coming end of all things, so that much of the Jewish tradition of wisdom about nature is deleted. Moreover, the polemic in the New
Testament against Jewish legalism has the unfortunate consequence of putting
many areas of life outside of the religious realm and thus demoting animals as
objects of moral deliberation. The focus in much early Christian theology is on
the individual soul, imperiled in a chaotic world, not on the preservation and
enhancement of all life. The promised land becomes the heaven above or the
whole cosmos, not a particular place where all creatures live to their fullest.

Sometimes animals are present in the New Testament in more symbolic ways
than in the Hebrew scriptures. In the New Testament God descends twice as a

dove (once to Mary and again at Jesus' baptism), and Jesus is portrayed as the lamb of God (a vision that dominates the Book of Revelation).[9] In general, however, Christian scripture follows the Jewish precedent in its realism toward nature: animals are not totemic codes for divine messages or tropes for the unknown. As in the creation account, where animals are created first, Jesus was born in a place that first sheltered and nurtured animals (Luke 2:6–7), and upon birth he was placed in a manger (a feeding trough for animals). Animals gather to witness and rejoice in the birth of Jesus, and shepherds "keeping watch over their flocks at night" were the first to hear of his birth.

Because Jesus declares his Father's love for the sparrows (Luke 12:6; Matthew 10:29), portrays God as a feeder of birds (Luke 12:24; Matthew 6:26), and compares himself to a hen gathering together her brood under her wings (Matthew 23:37), he is often described as a lover of animals.[10] According to Mark, Jesus spent forty days in the wilderness among the wild beasts, perhaps signifying his ability to restore nature to creation's original harmony (Mark 1:12–13).[11] Jesus also states that you can pull an animal out of a pit even on the Sabbath (Luke 14:5), implying that the law should not come in the way of compassion, but most interpreters think that the main concern of this teaching is not the animal but the appropriate range of legal requirements. His references to dogs, following the usage of his day, are not generally positive. "Do not give what is holy to dogs," he says (Matthew 7:6; also see Philippians 3:2; 2 Peter 2:22; and Revelation 22:15). In one story, however, he imagines dogs tenderly attending an otherwise abandoned poor man by licking his sores (Luke 16:21). He also states that it is not right to give the children's bread to dogs, although he agrees with a non-Jewish woman who tells him that even the dogs (which symbolize, in this saying, the Gentiles) eat the scraps that fall from their masters' table (Mark 7:26–28; the Greek in this passage, *kunarion* instead of *kuon*, refers to little dogs, indicating pets).

Most Christians follow Paul in showing little concern for the world of animals, although with Paul, too, the evidence is ambiguous. Paul can speak about the whole universe as frustrated and awaiting God's liberation (Romans 8:19–22), yet his need to distance himself from the legalism of his youth makes him overlook the ethical care for animals in the Hebrew scriptures. About the Law of Moses, which states, "You shall not muzzle an ox while it is treading out the grain" (Deuteronomy 25:4), Paul asks, "Is it for oxen that God is concerned? Or does he not speak entirely for our sake?" (1 Corinthians 9:9–10). Paul's question is purely rhetorical; he already knows the answer. In Paul's anthropocentric and allegorizing hermeneutics, this humane law from Moses really applies to Christian missionaries who should be rewarded for their evangelism, not animals who should be fed when they work the fields. Paul does not even consider the alternative of a literal reading of the text.

All of Paul's arguments ignore the ethical reality of animals. He does not think that eating meat sacrificed to idols is wrong because the idols do not exist (1 Corinthians 8). (Note, however, other scripture, Acts 15:20 and Revelation 2:20, that rejects the eating of pagan sacrificed meat.) He totally disregards Hebrew animal sacrifices as a way of placing meat eating in the context of repentance and thanksgiving. Paul persistently sought the essentials of faith in Jesus Christ, and one of the main consequences of Christian freedom for Paul is that it no longer matters how or why animals are slaughtered. Paul is much more concerned about sexuality than food, and he nowhere makes use of the ancient connection between gluttony and fornication. When Paul criticizes Jewish law, he is more concerned about circumcision than the rules of eating *(kashrut)*, taking a very practical, not ritualistic, approach to food. "Outside of mild warnings against drunkenness and greed, Paul perceived no great danger in eating. In this he is unusual among the moral preachers of his age" (Grimm, 1996: 71). He does not want dietary restrictions to function as a distinctive sign of the new Christian movement, but he also does not condemn Christians who want to keep the Jewish food scruples. Beyond the question of survival, food is a matter of indifference to Paul. Given his eschatological expectations and his need to keep peace and order in his missionary activities, he had more important things on his mind.

Because early Christians met in private homes and spread their faith through social gatherings, hospitality and conviviality were necessary prerequisites for the proclamation of the Gospel. The weekly agape or communal meal was a crucial expression of Christian solidarity and spirituality, so Paul was quick to criticize any behavior that might cause disharmony or friction in these intimate settings. In Corinth, the rich stuffed themselves with food they brought with them to the community meals, while the poor went hungry. The problem in the Roman church was a bit different. Here, in the words of Ernst Käsemann, "it is not a matter of meat offered to idols, as in 1 Corinthians 8–10. It is a matter of fundamental vegetarianism" (1980: 367). Perhaps this group abstained from meat eating because they were Jewish Christians who felt that animals not properly sacrificed to the one God should not be eaten, or perhaps they were also influenced by philosophical vegetarianism from Greek and Roman sources. Unfortunately, the self-understanding of this group is lost in the midst of Paul's rhetoric, which establishes the precedent for all subsequent theological reflection on food.

The controversial actions of the Roman vegetarians were extremely important because at issue was "virtually all meat offered for sale in the public meat markets or served by a pagan host at a dinner" (Meeks, 1986: 132). The predominance of pagan sacrificial meat meant that vegetarianism could be interpreted as a form of religious protest against the ruling pagan culture. Wealthy Christians, however, would have found it awkward to abstain from eating meat sacrificed to idols in social and business situations, while the poor, who could rarely afford meat anyway, would eat meat mainly on cultic occasions, therefore associating it with pagan worship.

Paul turns the conflict into a meditation on two kinds of faith. "Some believe in eating anything," he argues, "while the weak eat only vegetables" (Romans 14:2). He thinks both are right, as long as they do not judge each other. True, he does say that "if your brother or sister is being injured by what you eat, you are no longer walking in love. Do not let what you eat cause the ruin of one for whom Christ died" (Romans 14:15). At the very least, these words should lead carnivores to pause and reflect. The strong should not choose to exercise their liberty (just as Jesus gave up his divine privileges and Paul declined the right of payment for his missionary labors). Nevertheless, Paul hastens to add that the Kingdom of God is found in justice, peace, and joy, not in eating and drinking. In the end, he tends to favor protecting the troublesome and tender scruples of the vegetarian. "It is good not to eat meat or drink wine or do anything that makes your brother or sister stumble" (Romans 14:21).[12] Yet he is clear that Christians with a robust conscience can eat whatever they want, even as they should tolerate those with a more narrow viewpoint.

Paul's advice "nicely serves the interests of a few socially elevated members of the group by permitting them to ignore the religious dimension of civic life" (Meeks, 1986: 136).[13] Although his main concern was church unity, Paul established the very influential idea for Christianity that vegetarianism must be a form of superstition and that Christian freedom must mean the complete secularization (and thus indifference) of food preparation and consumption (see, for examples from the Pauline tradition, 1 Timothy 4:4 and Colossians 2:16–17). The true Christian is free from the law, and so all things are permitted, as long as they are pursued in the spirit of love. Meat is one of God's many gifts, and it can be enjoyed in a spirit of gratitude for the bounty that God provides. Paul's influence continues today, when many North Americans look at the mass production of animal flesh in factory farms as one of the chief signs of our country's freedom, prosperity, and equality.

Clearly, it is possible to interpret the Bible (especially the Hebrew scriptures) favorably on the issue of animals but not without a struggle with the dominant theological tradition. After all, animals are used, eaten, and traded in the Bible, and humans are clearly the main focus of the biblical narratives. The task is to see a pattern even where others find conflicting signals. Gary Comstock has stated: "I have come to interpret the Bible's views on the killing of animals in the way I interpret its views on the owning of slaves. Even though each practice is implicitly, if not explicitly, condoned, the practice is still shown to be wrong by the larger story of salvation in Jesus Christ" (1993: 114). Yet if the Bible is wrong on the occasional detail, even if not on moral principles and themes, it remains to be shown how many Christians could have missed for so long these broad themes in their interpretation of particular facts. In this regard, Jonah

4:11 is a most revealing scripture. Here God reprimands the recalcitrant Jonah, saying, "Should I not be concerned about Ninevah," a great city with thousands of people and "also many animals?" The animals seem to be themselves added like an afterthought, hardly central to God's defense of the divine compassion, and yet they are there, not overlooked by God even though Jonah surely did not give them any thought.

Indeed, the Bible often seems to be telling two stories about animals simultaneously—God's divine plan and human use and abuse (or, as in Jonah's case, indifference). If the first story is not always kept in mind, the second story can seem to legitimate all sorts of practices that animal rightists would find abhorrent. The Bible, then, must be read with the aid of extrabiblical arguments and sources in order to find in it a consistent vision of animal concern. The challenge is twofold. I want to show, contrary to the religious assumptions of most Christians, how the use of animals that the Bible legitimates is at odds with the many abuses of animals that occur in the modern world; yet I also want to show, contrary to the basic assumptions of the animal rights movement, that the Bible articulates a distinctive and subtle vision of how humans can have authority over animals within the context of mutuality and interdependence.

The Christian Tradition

Is the Bible's influence on Christian tradition completely negative regarding animals? In many works on animal rights, the Christian tradition is dismissed as totally irrelevant for the movement, but this is a shortsighted and incomplete judgment at best. Eating a lot of meat is a sign of abundance and prosperity in our culture, but that does not mean it is a sign of grace. As St. Ambrose wrote in his homilies on Genesis, "We ought to be content to live on simple herbs, on cheap vegetables and fruits such as nature has presented to us and the generosity of God has offered us" (1961: 88). True, the early Christian tradition was not always as sensitive about animals as some aspects of the Greek tradition were. Celsus, the second-century critic of Christianity, wondered why the Christians, who got their antipathy to eating meat sacrificed to pagan gods from the Jews, did not go further and simply "abstain from the flesh of all animals" like Pythagoras (Hoffmann, 1987: 117). Origin, in his response to Celsus, was quick to argue that Christianity respects only rational souls and upholds the superiority of humans over animals.

Other church fathers were quick to draw from ancient and contemporary pagan attitudes toward diet and animals in formulating their own opinions,[14] so it is important to understand what those attitudes were. A healthy diet, for Greek and Roman medical philosphers, consisted of balancing hot and cold foods as well as wet and dry. Strong foods like meat were believed to be the most nourishing but also the hardest to digest. Strong foods also heat the body and function like an aphrodisiac. Blood was thought to be distilled from wet food, and semen was the most highly distilled form of blood. Meat, then, as both a hot (cooked) and moist food was connected with an increase in sexual activity and desire (see Grimm, 1996: chap. 2). Most ancient philosophers argued that a good and wise person exercised self-control and moderation in eating. Gluttony thus could serve as a metaphor for all kinds of social immorality. Christian theologians were heavily influenced by these assumptions and took them even further by arguing that frugality and fasting were effective means of mortifying the body and controlling lust.

Tertullian is a good example of Christian criticism of meat eating. His treatise *De Ieiunio* (On fasting), written during his involvement with Montanism, defends fasting from meat as a way of growing closer to God. He was worried about the declining standards of Christian morality and equated gluttony and flesh eating: "For to you your belly is god, and your lungs a temple, and your paunch a sacrificial altar, and your cook the priest, and your fragrant smell the Holy Spirit, and your condiments spiritual gifts, and your belching prophecy" (Roberts, 1956: 113). He especially advocates the dietary practice of xerophagy, the eating of dry food only, with no meat, sauces, moist vegetables, or wine. The aim of the diet was to dry out the body, but Tertullian does not emphasize this connection to the ancient idea that wet and hot foods incite one's sexual urges. He thought that originally humans were vegetarians and assumed that meat eating was practiced only after the flood. He thought that God let people eat meat after the flood because humans had demonstrated that they were not capable of following God's orders (104), and he used the story of Daniel as an example of the healthiness of a vegetarian diet (107). He insists that Christians do not eat meat with the blood still in it, and for following such Jewish customs, his opponents accused him of being a Judaizer.

Tertullian's ingenious essay is full of arguments that theologians are only now beginning to take seriously, yet the defensive tone of the treatise shows that he is fighting a losing battle. Christians by and large did not want to eat any differently from their pagan neighbors. His contemporaries thought that meat eating was so natural and habitual that they looked at his ideas as novel and thus heretical attempts to restrict their Christian freedom. Christianity had so lost its connection to Judaism that dietary restrictions were regarded as radical innovations rather than as a continuation of God's covenant with Israel. If fasting in Christianity were to have a positive meaning, it had to be a reflection of the self-denial that Jesus practiced to perfection on the cross. If it were given any other grounds or purpose, it was in danger of being seen as a sign of heresy. Tertullian and his Montanist friends were fated to be dismissed in Christian history as spiritualists, enthusiasts, and extremists. By challenging something as basic as diet, they were criticized for setting themselves up as a new authority that usurped the role of traditional church teachings, even though they appealed to the Bible for most of their arguments.

Clement of Alexandria also sought to regulate the body in order to better serve God. The purpose of the *Paidagogos* (the tutor or instructor) is to pinpoint precisely what kind of conduct in all aspects of daily life is most acceptable to Jesus Christ. For his critique of gluttony, he relies on ancient sources. He was influenced, for example, by Philo, who in turn knew Plato's *Timaeus*, which calls gluttony (excessive eating of meat and drinking of wine) the enemy of philosophy and an obstacle to holiness. As Clement advises, "We must guard against those articles of food which persuade us to eat when we are not hungry, bewitching the appetite. For is there not, within a temperate simplicity, a wholesome variety of eatables? Bulbs, olives, certain herbs, milk, cheese, fruits, all kinds of cooked food without sauces" (Roberts, 1962: 241). Clement seems not to have insisted on strict vegetarianism, but he did favor the meatless diet, and he thought that "the apostle Matthew partook of seeds, and nuts, and vegetables, without flesh" (241). Clement greatly admired Pythagoras, the father of vegetarianism (which was, until the 1840s, called the Pythagorian diet). Indeed, he thought that Pythagoras derived his ideas about diet from Moses. He (mistakenly) claims that in Romans 14:21 Paul is in agreement with Pythagoras (Roberts, 1962: 240) and says about the Mosaic food laws that "altogether but a few [animals] were left appropriate for their food" (242), suggesting that God wanted to limit the meat eating of the Israelites.

Although scholars rarely make the connection, historically asceticism meant, in practice, vegetarianism. St. Benedict forbade the eating of meat for all except the sick in his religious community (see chap. 39 of his Rule for monasteries). In order to control one's own flesh, it seems, one must not eat animal flesh. This opinion was so widespread that Eusebius, the first church historian, reports that James, the brother of Jesus, "drank no wine or intoxicating liquor and ate no animal food" (1965: 100).[15] Athanasius writes about St. Antony, the founder of Christian monasticism: "His food was bread and salt, and for drinking he took only water. There is no reason even to speak of meat and wine, when indeed such a thing was not found among the other zealous men" (1980: 36). St. Antony, it should be noted (like Pythagoras!), lived a long and vigorous life.

Early Christian saints, however, did not merely avoid meat in their diets; they also actively sought out contact with animals in an effort to restore nature to its original harmony. Just as Jesus spent forty days in the wilderness, so did many early ascetics journey into the wild, not only to battle Satan but also to establish a peaceful world, in contrast to the chaotic urban environment they had fled. Some hermits, so the stories say, were fed by wild birds and animals, which has a biblical precedent in the story about God ordering Elijah to flee into the wilderness but also ordering the ravens to feed him (1 Kings 17:2–6).

Many of the stories about the Desert Fathers might have their origin in the Fathers' ability to tame and coexist with wild animals. Like Daniel in the lion's pit (Daniel 6), the Desert Fathers demonstrate that friendship with animals is a special sign of holiness.

According to one story about the desert monks, a hyena once brought Macarius of Alexandria a blind pup. Following the example of Jesus, Macarius put spittle in the pup's eyes, and the pup was healed. The mother returned the next day with the hide of a large sheep as a gift. Macarius was upset and made the hyena promise never again to kill sheep or any other creatures but only to eat animals already dead. He offered to feed her if she did not find enough carrion. The hyena took the old man's advice and continued to return to him for food. The story ilustrates that the desert ascetics were concerned not only with befriending the wild animals but also with reducing the amount of suffering among them (Bratton, 1988: 38–40). Indeed, the saints are often defined by their special relationship with animals. St. Columban would take walks in the woods and call the wild creatures to him, "and the wild things and the birds would leap and frisk about him for sheer happiness, jumping up on him as young dogs jump on their masters" (Waddell, 1996: 48). The saints even tried to change the diet of the wild animals. There is the story of the Irish St. Ciaran who had his shoes eaten by a fox. He chastises the fox, saying, "If thou hadst a longing, as is thy nature, to eat flesh, Almighty God would have made it for thee from the roots of these trees, if we had asked Him" (Waddell, 1996: 95). The saints are forerunners of the eschaton, drawing all creatures toward a peaceable diet and harmonious relations.

Vegetarianism was thus taken for granted as the appropriate diet for the holy. However, the hermits not only declined to eat meat but also often ate alone, ashamed of their bodily needs and functions. Indeed, the connection of a meatless diet with extreme bodily self-denial proved to be unfortunate. Asceticism grounded vegetarianism in self-denial (implying that meat was a luxury, something good but not necessary), which overshadowed the message of compassion for animals. By making abstention from meat rare and heroic, asceticism thereby confirmed the value of what it avoided and denied. Asceticism allowed the great majority of people to think that vegetarianism was a supererogatory act too difficult and costly to be widely practiced.

Asceticism also connected vegetarianism to zealous and sectarian religious groups, to those who wanted to overcome the world on their own terms, without reliance on the mediation of Jesus Christ and the church. Indeed, many gnostics were vegetarians. The Manicheans, for example, were members of a popular religious movement that embraced a dualistic cosmology that expressly forbid meat eating for the elect, those who could keep their souls pure by avoiding decayed substances, which they thought were void of divinity. St. Augustine drew on the Bible to contest the Manichean idea that what we eat determines who we are: "Christ himself shows that to refrain from the killing of animals and the destroying of plants is the height of superstition, for, judging that there are no common rights between us and the beasts and trees, he sent the devils into a herd of swine and with a curse withered the tree on which he found no fruit" (1986: 102).[16] After the Manicheans were banned in 381, vegetarianism was inextricably linked with dualism, heresy, and superstition. "Timothy, Patriarch of Alexandria, was so alarmed by the spread of Manicheanism that he instituted food tests among his clergy and monks; those who refused to eat meat would then be interrogated" (Spencer, 1995: 142). Vegetarianism became a creed and lifestyle for outsiders, extremists, and separatists—both radical pessimists and utopian visionaries.

The voice of church leaders like St. Basil the Great, who spoke eloquently about the value of animals, became lost in the midst of debates about orthodoxy and the need to use religion to solidify and justify social order. The Bogomils, Cathars, and Albigensians, popular medieval heretics, all rejected meat eating, but their metaphysical dualism, which denied the value of the material world, put them at odds with the theological consensus of Christian Europe. Their vegetarianism, which was consistent with their distrust of authority and their emphasis on peace and compassion, only exacerbated their social isolation and the suspicion that they were a threat to the common good. However, while we can admire their courage and radicality today, it is difficult to sympathize with their motivations for abstaining from meat, which seem based more on hate (for bodily needs and pleasures) than on love. In any case, it was probably not very difficult for many of the peasant followers of these movements to restrain their diets, because, in the premodern world, the poor often did not eat much meat anyway.

In the Middle Ages, portraits of a virgin with a unicorn on her lap represented Mary and Jesus, and many Christians were increasingly drawn to the myths and fables of popular bestiaries. Even so, the medieval world made room for some compassion toward real animals, as evidenced by the practice of not eating meat on Fridays (in remembrance of the death of Jesus), which was one of the most visible signs of being a Christian. Indeed, scholars are only beginning to examine medieval attitudes toward meat (see Bazell, 1997). The Protestant Reformation, however, in its zeal to obliterate special pious practices and any differences between the monastic orders and the laity, rejected the idea that giving up meat could be a form of fasting pleasing to God. The historian Steve Ozment quotes a Roman Catholic pamphlet that criticizes the Protestants because they do "not go to confession, fast, pray, attend church, give alms, or make pilgrimages. You also eat meat [whenever you wish]" (1992: 84). For Protestants, giving up meat was just another effort to earn salvation and another superstitious belief in need of reform.

Even before the Protestant Reformation, however, Aquinas set the stage for much later Christian thought by arguing that we have no direct duties to animals. For Aquinas, only intellectual nature is free; humans cause their own behavior, while animals, representing pure passion, lack self-control. Animals, then, are naturally instruments of human welfare. Following this tradition, Pope Pius IX in the mid-nineteenth century refused permission for the establishment of a Society for the Prevention of Cruelty to Animals in Rome on the grounds that it would mistakenly suggest that humans have duties to animals. The exuberant love for creation preached by St. Francis of Assisi provides a marginal counterbalance to the Thomistic tradition, but it should be noted that he was not a vegetarian, so that his love for nature ("Brother Sun, Sister Moon") did not translate into the rights of individual creatures.[17]

Vegetarianism, then, continued to be a suspicious and idiosyncratic lifestyle. John Wesley, for example, was a vegetarian, but few Methodists today know this biographical detail. Wesley might have stood out for practicing what he preached, but what he preached about animals was in the mainstream of Protestant belief. In his sermon, "The General Deliverance," Wesley argues that in the Garden of Eden animals lived in harmony with humans. He cautions, however, that this does not mean that God regards humans and animals equally. Indeed, "man was the great channel of communication between the Creator and the whole brute creation" (Outler, 1985: 442). The fall alienated people from animals, so that animals also lost the blessings that flow from God. "A few only, those we commonly term domestic animals, retain more or less of their original disposition, and (through the mercy of God) love him [man] still and pay obedience to him" (443). Domesticated animals look both backward to Eden and forward to heaven, but meanwhile their obedience to humanity is abused and manipulated. Wesley argues that animals will be not only restored to their original perfection in the next life but also granted the additional benefit of human intelligence so that they can partake of the glories of God. "Whatever affections they had in the garden of God will be restored with vast increase, being exalted and refined in a manner which we ourselves are not now able to comprehend" (446). If God can make us equal to the angels, Wesley wondered, why cannot God to something equally miraculous for the animals?

The potential for the widespread acceptance of vegetarianism emerged only in the nineteenth century, and Christians played a significant role in the burgeoning movement. The Bible-Christian Church, founded in England by William Cowherd in 1809, was the first Christian church to defend and require vegetarianism on orthodox theological grounds, and the members of this church had a great impact on their contemporaries. Cowherd himself was influenced by Emanuel Swedenborg, who thought meat eating was a symbol of the fall. The Bible-Christians attracted a large following of the working class, perhaps because the church offered food that was both nutritious and cheap. A follower of Cowherd, William Metcalfe, emigrated and founded a Bible-

Christian church in Philadelphia in 1817. It was the first church in North American to develop and preach a systematic theology of vegetarianism.[18] This church produced a remarkable number of publications, sermons, organizations, and other efforts on behalf of vegetarianism. Metcalfe influenced many early advocates of health and diet reforms (see, for example, Alcott, 1838), and members of this church were instrumental in the organization of the American Vegetarian Society in 1859.

In an age of "hog and hominy" when gluttony was the rule and dyspepsia was the national complaint, America was ready for a religious message about diet. One of those influenced by the Philadelphia Bible-Christians was Sylvester Graham (1794–1851), an ordained Presbyterian minister and immensely popular speaker who advocated the curative powers of brown bread and based his teachings on the Bible. He developed his spartan diet to control the craving for alcohol and to discipline sexual urges (see Money, 1985), and he ranted against the refinement of flour by arguing that what God had joined together should not be put asunder. Indeed, during most of the nineteenth century vegetarianism was connected to the temperance movement, and many vegetarians were against all stimulants, including salt and spices, the absence of which surely must have hurt their cause by making their dishes less savory.

The rejection of stimulants (which were often blamed for causing excessive sexual desire and activity), not animal compassion, is the main motivation behind the vegetarianism of Seventh-Day Adventism, a unique Christian health movement which rejects coffee, tea, tobacco, and alcohol as well, all in order to purify the believer's body and thus hasten the second coming of Jesus Christ (see Bull and Lockhart, 1989). In Otsego, Michigan, in 1863, Ellen White, whose revelations guided the Adventists, had an inspired vision of the need for vegetarianism that was surely influenced by her reading of Graham, and the Adventists founded a sanatorium in Battle Creek, Michigan, to promote their views on healthy and clean living. John Harvey Kellogg, the inventor of the breakfast cereal, was chosen to run the sanatorium, where he invented dozens of vegetarian dishes to make nuts and whole grains more popular and palatable (see Carson, 1957).

Such fervor did not die away completely in the twentieth century, although it did become increasingly rare. An exception is Rev. J. Todd Ferrier, founder of the Order of the Cross in 1907, a vegetarian Christian society. He wrote many books aimed at recovering the theme of animal compassion in Christianity. He also argued, less convincingly, that Jesus was a member of the Essenes, an ascetic and celibate group that did not eat meat, and that his vegetarianism was omitted or misrepresented in the Gospels and distorted by Paul. He interprets Jesus' response to Martha's anxious dinner preparations—"only one thing is necessary" (Luke 10:42)—as a recommendation of vegetarianism.

With the rise of modern agricultural technology in the twentieth century, meat became cheap and plentiful, and the Christian vegetarian movement was soon forgotten. By the end of the nineteenth century, the voice of biblically based vegetarianism had lost its power, and vegetarianism increasingly was seen as just one of the many crazy health and diet fads that proliferated during that time. In the twentieth century, people were more likely to connect vegetarianism with the theosophy of Annie Besant than with the Bible or traditional Christian beliefs. Some conservative Christians continue to preach abstention from alcohol, but they pass over in silence the gluttonous consumption of meat that is so much a part of our culture.

Only recently have theologians once again begun to reflect on the religious significance of diet. The garden, the ark, and stories about saints provide the background for a distinctly Jewish and Christian emphasis on the potential harmony between humans and animals and the importance of kindness in bringing about that harmony (see Shepherd, 1996: chap. 17), but these basic features of biblical faith are rarely integrated into a broader theological program. The best that one can say about the Christian tradition is that the pieces are there to reconstruct a biblical vision of animal care, but those pieces remain fragmented and even contradicted by other pieces, so that their interpretation will depend upon one's vision of the Christian narrative as a whole, which in turn will be informed by one's vision of the normative heart of the Jewish and Christian stories.

Hauerwas and Berkman on a Biblical Foundation for Animal Welfare

Even given these problems with the historical record, the desire to say something distinctively Christian on these issues leads some theologians to seek within the biblical narrative a foundation for animal welfare. Stanley Hauerwas and John Berkman represent both the strength and the weakness of trying to ground animal welfare in a biblically based theology alone. Their chief concern is not an agenda for social change but the definition of a disciplinary matrix; they want to protect the vulnerable integrity of theology from the intermingling of other disciplines. They do not want to be theological mercenaries who use theology to support a cause that can be defended on other grounds. They believe praxis shapes theory, and thus they want the theory of theology shaped by specifically Christian practices rather than some secular political goal. "Just as we believe that Christians are not called to be nonviolent because nonviolence is a strategy to free the world from war, but because as Christians we cannot conceive of living other than nonviolently in a world of war, so it may also be true that Christians in a world of meat eaters are called to live nonviolently" (1993: 72). Of course, the problem is that most Christians practice a diet based on dead animals, so that a Christian theory true to Christian practice will find it as difficult to change the church as it is to challenge the world. Someone eating a hamburger is not and cannot be objective about the issues of vegetarianism and animal liberation. Indeed, there is no neutral ground on this issue, with conversations swinging back and forth between judgmental nagging and self-interested defense, so that theologians are inevitably influenced by a dietary practice that, since the beginning of Christianity, has been accepted and sanctified.[19] How, then, can a Christian theology be true to itself and yet still call into question the dominant cultural assumptions and activities of meat eating?

Hauerwas and Berkman begin their theological reconstruction by reinterpreting the traditional account of the creation of humans in the image of God. The doctrine of creation, for these theologians, does not sanction an anthropocentric worldview of hierarchy and authority, as it has throughout much of Western history. Neither does it classify humanity as the only rational animal and thus categorically different from all other species. Instead, creation should be read in trinitarian terms as an expression of Christological and eschatological convictions. The peaceful kingdom of the new creation that Jesus taught is the meaning of the nature that God pronounced good. In the beginning we should find the end, that is, the purpose and goal of humanity's relationship to the world and all that is in it. Eden lies at the end of history as the divine goal toward which God draws all of creation.

The location of Eden in a future that even now is breaking in upon us does not mean, though, that we can adopt a radical egalitarianism or anarchy in our relationship to animals. Rather than arguing that humans are not unique and thus leveling the differences between humans and nonhuman animals, Hauerwas and Berkman argue that the only significant difference between humans and animals is the unique purpose given to humans by God. Furthermore, "this *unique purpose* which God gives humans with regard to animals lies in our job of telling animals who they are" (64). Our capacity for understanding bears the great responsibility that we are necessary for the self-understanding of animals. The authors make the analogy that animals need humans just as Gentiles need Jews to tell them their story. The model for our treatment of animals is one of mediation, not domination (or the opposite, detachment). "In the same way that animals are privileged through One who became human, so we Gentiles are privileged through One who became a Jew" (65). We are to be Christ figures to animals, enabling them to become what they otherwise could not achieve.

The chief end of humanity, for Hauerwas and Berkman, is not survival. They realize that nature is not synonymous with creation, that, in other words, nature is fallen. The fall precipitates a struggle in which we are tempted to convert the inevitability of sin into a necessity. Nevertheless, we cannot point to carnivorous animals or to the weight of custom and habit as justifications for meat eating. The chief end of humans is to serve one another as signs of the coming Kingdom of God. Such service means that we cannot sacrifice others' lives for our own. Neither can we sacrifice animals for our own desires. Animals exist to serve God's pleasure; they manifest God's glory on their own terms. Humans are to rule over animals not because of any special capacity or trait they possess but merely because of God's appointment, and how we rule is to be modeled on God's own progressive reign in the cosmos. Christians are to be a witness to the world as God meant it to be. "Such a witness does not entail romantic conceptions of nature or our fallen creation, but rather is an eschatological act, signifying that our lives are not captured by the old order" (72). God governs through the service of Jesus Christ, so Christians too are to shape their leadership according to Christlike love. The ultimate end of such governance is a community of all flesh.

In the course of pursuing the peaceable kingdom, Hauerwas and Berkman note, there might be exceptions, cases when animals will be killed due to a direct conflict between animal and human life, like protecting one's neighbor or self-defense. As in the just-war tradition, we should presume nonviolence but be prepared to specify the exceptions to pacifism. The burden of proof is clearly on those who choose to take animal life. When we do kill animals, the theological idea of sacrifice will be relevant. "If any form of meat eating can be justified, we believe this must be understood as animals making a sacrifice for us that we might live, analogously to the way soldiers are seen to be making a sacrifice of their lives for their nation-state, empire or tribe" (72). The authors hasten to add that they do not intend to underwrite the language of sacrifice to justify all meat eating. That language is certainly used too casually and thoughtlessly by many Christians today.

Their introduction of sacrifice, however, raises the very problem that they are trying to overcome. What value do animals have that they can be killed when their interests compete with our own? When are such sacrifices appropriate? Although I have learned much from these authors about the importance in Christian tradition of recognizing the responsibility that comes with human authority over animals as well as the need to confront the single and unitary origin, plight, and destiny of humanity and animals, somehow the radical relationality that they find in a trinitarian doctrine of God is not translated into human-animal interactions. By placing the value of animals solely on the central role humans play in God's creation, they bypass not only any investigation of animal reality as a value in itself but, even more important, the ways in which humans and animals can create value by affecting each other. Humans are to protect and cherish animals just as God loves us, but this implies that animals cannot challenge us with their own interests and needs, just as we cannot change or challenge God. Hauerwas and Berkman thus risk continuing the old hierarchical version of the doctrine of creation. Moreover, their very general reading of Christian theology, interpreting the major doctrines as animal friendly, betrays their initial goal of fidelity to the biblical tradition. Many Christians simply do not find an overwhelming message of animal compassion in the Bible, and so they are quick to apply the language of sacrifice to animal death. By insisting that theologians should develop an animal ethic without a serious dialogue with philosophy and the social sciences, Hauerwas and Berkman open themselves to attacks from those who, with some good reason, will argue that they have imported the ideas of animal liberation into their theological reconstructions. Christianity does have a distinctive message to proclaim about animals, but at the same time, theologians also need to admit that, at least on this issue, they need all the help they can get.

Andrew Linzey and the Theology of Animal Rights

Just as a purely theological position is an inadequate foundation for animal care, so is the opposite tactic, a systematic appropriation of philosophical rights language for the theological agenda. Andrew Linzey, more than any other theologian, has tried to attend to both the biblical tradition and the claims and arguments of the animal rights movement, so his balancing act should be instructive of the promise and risk involved in this approach. His first book, *Animal Rights: A Christian Assessment,* published in 1976, earned him the title of "the unofficial chaplain to the animal welfare movement." His second book, *Christianity and the Rights of Animals* (1987), was less polemical and more careful in its treatment of the theological tradition. Here Linzey does not use theology as a prop for animal rights; rather, he tries to derive animal rights from theology while still acknowledging their relative independence. He begins his work with reflection on the generosity of God, adopting the traditional argument that God did not need to create the world, so all that exists is a gift from God's abundant grace. He then quickly moves from the creation ex nihilo to the claim that everything in creation has independent worth. Everything has value, he asserts, because God values it. According to God's intentions, then, everything is free, or authorized, to pursue its own course. The divine generosity—the origin of all things in God's transcendence—has come to sanction the relative independence and autonomy of all beings, from each other as well as from God.

As with Hauerwas and Berkman, Linzey draws from the story of the fall to explain the present situation of animal suffering and human cruelty. He quotes Luther that Adam "would not have used the creatures as we do today," that originally animals were used "for the admiration of God and a holy joy" (1987: 13). Today we see such harmony as incurably romantic precisely because we have lost our innocent relationship with animals. Now nature strikes us as both blessing and curse. The point is not to ignore the negative side of nature but to avoid turning a blessing into a curse. Unfortunately, much of the Western theological tradition has argued that nature is a blessing to humanity precisely because animals can be bent to the will of human benefit. It is a circular argument: humans must be the focal point of God's activities because animals seem delivered into our hands by divine providence.

To combat this vicious logic, Linzey draws not only on the original vegetarianism of Genesis but also on covenantal theology. He wagers that only a theocentric, as opposed to anthropocentric, theology can give animals their rightful place in the world. All life is a gift from God, just as all life is united in the ark, which in 1 Peter is used as a symbol for the church. Violence and disorder are secondary and ultimately transient phenomena, which means that animal suffering should not be casually accepted as an unchangeable feature of God's plan. Christology gives the original covenant of the Hebrew scriptures even more relevance for animals. The incarnation is not just a yes to human beings but an affirmation of all sentient longing and a redemption of all suffering and pain. God's embodiment in the world means God's compassion for all materiality, regardless of intellectual development or communicative skills. God does not waste anything; on the contrary, God values and saves even that which has no discernible purpose or function, that which seems superfluous and redundant.

I will continue to develop many of these theological themes in chapters 5, 6, and 7, where my debt to Linzey will be great. Linzey's work is problematic when he translates the intrinsic value of God-given creation into the idea of rights. Linzey begins his argument by claiming that only God has absolute rights because only God "owns" the world. Nature is not "unclaimed property" (Moltmann, 1991: 3) there for the taking because it is owned by God and only borrowed by us. What rights we have, then, are the byproduct of God's gifts to us and not something based on our own self-interests. All creatures, as gifts of God, are inherently valuable to God, and thus the rights of all living things are based on God's giving and valuing.[20] Linzey calls such rights "theos-rights." What God has given should be respected and honored. Linzey realizes that rights language is usually employed apart from theological reflection, but he suggests that it is appropriate for Christians to utilize the strongest moral language available in order to further God's plan.[21] Theos-rights are not based on a form of contractualism, the reciprocity of duties, so they avoid the problem that, strictly speaking, animals have no moral responsibilities to humans. Theos-rights also are not based on a theory of animal intelligence or consciousness, so they avoid those problems as well. Humans are not unique when it comes to God's benevolence; God elects all creatures into a covenant of mercy, and thus we should acknowledge the moral standing of all creatures.

Linzey's adoption of rights language is not without problems. His main contention is that creatures have the right to be valued as God values them. This immediately raises the question of whether God values all creatures equally. If God does so, then we should too, which seems an impossible task. But if we cannot treat all creatures equally, does this mean that God loves creatures differently as well? We are forced either to say that God has preferences or to admit that we cannot live up to the scope and range of God's love. If we cannot love as God loves, then perhaps the language of rights is not the best way to model our treatment of animals. Linzey realizes that his critics who propose an alternative to theos-rights draw on the biblical language of stewardship, not on the philosophy of rights. Stewardship implies particular responsibilities and difficult choices, not uniform and comprehensive rules. Stewardship also implies our cooperation with, not imitation of, God's rule over the world. Linzey recognizes that the idea of stewardship is essential for any Christian response to animal suffering. Nevertheless, he is quick to point out that this language is often distorted into the utilitarian discourse of speciesist greed and self-interest. Moreover, he insists that the language of stewardship, properly interpreted, does not entail an easier set of tasks than the language of rights. The two languages can complement and support each other.

Are these two languages so easily translated into each other? Is the language of rights appropriate to a world born from and sustained by God's gratuitous beneficence? Linzey admits that rights theory does not avoid conflict.[22] Arguably, in fact, the very formulation of this theory presupposes conflict. The discourse of rights traditionally focuses on free, autonomous individuals who are eligible to make certain claims based on what they inherently are. We can recognize each other's rights because we understand what others possess on the basis of what we know ourselves to own and have. In theory, rights demand respect and acknowledgment. In practice, rights more often are ways of asking others to leave us alone rather than obligating others to aid and assist. As Hauerwas and Berkman argue, the language of rights is appealing only "in a society where individuals can no longer sustain their civic order on the basis of shared ends and purposes" (1993: 65–66). Rights presuppose a society at war with itself, wherein individuals need protection from each other. Rights arise when trust breaks down, which means that rights will quickly be overridden when interests intervene and the occasion permits. To redefine rights by extending them to the animal domain seems a precarious procedure at best.

At the very least, the idea of rights cannot do justice to our relationships with pets, which are governed by acts of love and not the protection of mutually recognized self-interests. In fact, Linzey is ambivalent about companion animals. On the one hand, his emphasis on covenant should make pets crucial: "If we are to include animals within a covenant relationship with man, then it may be argued that some form of companion relationship with them is only right and inevitable" (1987: 133). Pets can symbolize the concrete aspect of covenant, the fact that responsibility is always mediated through particular relationships and specific connections. On the other hand, Linzey's focus on the intrinsic value of creation makes him suspicious of a relationship that necessarily involves some form of intervention and interdependence: "I am not at all sure that allowing animals to become emotional supports for human beings sufficiently allows for their dignity" (1987: 137). Linzey has trouble reconciling emotional attachments with the rights agenda.[23] This trouble is understandable. As Hauerwas and Berkman note, "Any appeal to rights pales in relation to the peace and love of Christ to which the Christian is called" (1993: 67). Rights provide minimal warrants for protection from each other; they do not encourage attentive gestures of affection and attachment.[24]

Linzey admits that rights language is not the only moral theory Christians should use, nor does it replace or condense all Christian moral values. He is also clear that theos-rights are absolute only in the sense that their infringement must be justified. Our morality, he argues, is ultimately tied to the will of God, which is gracious, expansive, and inclusive. Christians should not just prevent the worst but promote the good, "for generosity is surely an important notion and rights language must be careful not to limit it even if we cannot persuade ourselves that it has the status of a declared 'ought' " (1987: 95). In his most recent book, *Animal Theology,* he calls the specifically Christian approach to animals the "generosity paradigm," and he argues that this approach means that we owe animals more than equal consideration: "Whenever we find ourselves in a position of power over those who are relatively powerless our moral obligation of generosity increases in proportion. If our power over animals confers upon us any right, there is only one: the right to serve" (1994: 38). For the Christian, costly action that exceeds the duty to minimize animal suffering is required. We are "the world's high priest," and the offering we present to the world must be one of self-sacrificial (not other-sacrificial) love. As Linzey stresses, we have the capability of becoming the servant species; anything short of that is faithless ingratitude.[25] Linzey realizes that the generosity paradigm runs the risk of paternalism and philanthropy, a noblesse oblige that acts out of condescension and not care. The generosity paradigm also runs the risk of undermining the presuppositions of the rights agenda. Indeed, the coexistence of this theological ethics with rights language is uneasy and problematical, even though Linzey tries to bridge the gap by talking about the animal's right to generous treatment. If generosity is a right that can be demanded, then how can generosity be freely given?

I want to argue that the notion that grace is sufficient for all challenges the assumptions and the mechanics of rights discourse. God's giving suggests that what we have is not ours to keep and that who we are is dependent on where we have come from and to whom we give ourselves in turn.[26] Rights can only be given to animals by humans; animals do not have a sense of their own moral claims on each other or us. Therefore, no matter how strategically important rights language is for the animal liberation movement, it is still preceded by and grounded in acts of charity. Giving is the more fundamental gesture, the personal act of compassion that rights language tries to codify and promulgate through clarification and systematization but cannot initiate or replace. Even if the rights of animals are inscribed in law and enforced by the state, animals will still be dependent on us to voluntarily limit and alter our power over them and to go out of our way to protect and nurture them.

Linzey himself, when he is most passionate, relies more on the language of giving than on rights: "Every act of making animals suffer harm, pain or deprivation for our pleasure or entertainment is a practical sign of our ungenerosity to God. It shows that we have not begun even in a minimal way to grasp divine benevolence" (1987: 105). Grace has as much to do with how we give to others as with what we receive from God. Grace is uplifting, and it has a horizontal as well as a vertical dimension. Through grace, the physical can be made to bear the spiritual. Too frequently we resist finding in relationships with those who are "beneath" us the same grace that is given to us from "above." In the interpersonal realm, grace is a surplus that enables us to acknowledge our dependence without resentment and empowers us to give to others without regret. Surely theological reflection on grace should lead to a transformation of the ways in which we separate ourselves from each other, including the ways in which we flaunt our superiority over animals, instead of just extending to animals the same independence and autonomy we possess and that grace itself calls into question.

Hauerwas and Berkman and Linzey all try to be systematic in their theological approaches to animals, Hauerwas and Berkman focusing on a trinitarian reading of the Bible and Linzey on adopting the philosophical analysis of rights. It is possible that they fall short of their goals because, on this issue, a systematic approach, whether from the perspective of scripture or philosophy, is neither possible nor helpful. In fact, contrary to Hauerwas and Berkman, the theologian needs to admit honestly that there are too many loose ends, too many contradictory signals in the Bible and church history, and too many unanswered questions in past theologies to pretend that dogmatics can give us a completely satisfactory account of animals while maintaining theological integrity and autonomy. The theologian also needs to resist, contrary to Linzey, the temptation to adopt the philosophical language of rights, thus rendering religion a marginal supplement to concerns that can be given less particular and more rigorous expression by others. What theology needs is the confidence to speak of issues that once resided outside of its domain without the restriction of sticking to traditional interpretations of Christian dogma and without the attraction of privileging secular accounts of animal worth. A theology of animals must be dialogical, both committed and open, and eager to translate provocative philosophical insights into novel readings of the Bible and Christian tradition. A theology of animals, like all theologies, must also be rooted in an experience of grace and be willing to follow that experience to its furthest limits. If I am right that the phenomenon of our relationship with animals has a religious component, then theology has much to contribute to what is one of the most urgent issues of our time.

CHAPTER TWO

Ecology versus the Peaceable Kingdom

Process Thought and the Luring of Animals

In their attempts to make theology more systematic and relevant by connecting it to, respectively, metaphysics and ecology, process thought and environmental theology are closely related. They share a recognition of the integrity of animals within a vision of a context of relationships that transcends all individuality. God gives and sustains life through the provision of our environment, and we should be grateful to and respectful of this powerful source of existence. Both of these positions have revolutionary consequences because they begin to apply the language of grace to the realm of animals, yet they also tend to subordinate the worth of individual animals to the value of the ecological whole, so that we need to look elsewhere for a God who empowers us to love animals immoderately, as individuals who are, in the traditional language of morality, ends in themselves. After discussing process thought and environmental theology, I will conclude this chapter with a survey of ecofeminist theology and a critique of the philosophy of rights from the perspective of a feminist ethic of care. The ethic of care allows for a revaluation of the emotional aspects of our relationship to animals and thus points toward a theology of pets and grace—a theology with roots in the Hebraic covenant of responsibility between God and humans and animals alike.

Theology traditionally portrays God as transcendent and yet in control of the world, distant but loving, not needing us yet involved with us anyway.

Bridging the gap between this unchanging and eternal power and the expression of human-animal love is a heroic task. Is God's love for us really so different from our own love, including our love for animals? Process theologians make the radical claim that God is dependent on the world just as the world is dependent on God. In fact, God develops through experiencing the world, sharing in our achievements as well as our sufferings. God is the structural principle of all reality primarily because God is internally, not just externally, related to the world. Process thought accentuates the becoming rather than the being of God: God becomes God by experiencing what we experience. The process God is, in concrete terms, relative, contingent, and vulnerable, even as God's consistent involvement in the world is unchanging and absolute. God persuades and lures all creatures toward the good. Like the relationship between a human and a companion animal, God's power is rhetorical and aesthetic, not coercive. God intervenes invitationally, not unilaterally. God tries to maximize the creativity of all creatures by promoting novel, complex, and harmonious experiences.

Daniel Dombrowski draws on the process philosophy of Alfred North Whitehead and Charles Hartshorne to challenge not only the traditional portrait of God but also the traditional ways of thinking about animals.[1] Dombrowski thus uses metaphysics to mediate animal rights and theology. He suggests that process metaphysics is strongly similar to, and can be interpreted as an explication of, certain presuppositions of environmentalism. Indeed, "metaphysics is already implicit in ecology: a *logos* (rational understanding) of the *oikos* (the cosmos viewed as one household) presupposes, to say the least, a wide-angle view of reality" (1988: 3). The connected character of reality that process metaphysics seeks to illuminate is identical to the interrelatedness of ecology.

Just as God helps to explain natural reality, the structures of the world also help to explain God. Indeed, metaphysical claims about becoming and relativity apply to all entities, including God, so that process thought has radical consequences for animals. Hartshorne's panpsychism (the idea that sentience is continuous throughout nature) permits differences only of degree between the mental and the material. Feeling is the key category that illuminates the ways in which individuals experience each other. "Compassion is a metaphysical truth, not merely a psychological achievement" (Neville, (1984: 131). Animals cannot think about God, but they can feel God. Being related—not intelligence—is the stuff of value. The point of ethics is to understand and promote the intimate relations that connect us with others and God. "Ethics can in a certain light be seen as nothing other than the heightening of importance of internal relations" (Dombrowski, 1988: 46). We need to bring our intuitions and our practices into an explicit, and even theoretical, unity in order to reform our lifestyles in accordance with the interconnections of which we consist.

Vegetarianism, Dombrowski suggests, allows us to experience and contribute to the richness of animal life with the most intensity and diversity.

Dombrowski's vegetarian ethic is, however, the exception, not the rule, among many process thinkers. After all, the very image of the term "process" conveys the stubborn fact that we are all processed (or consumed) by somebody else eventually. It is no entity's fate to stand alone for long. Many process thinkers follow Charles Birch and John Cobb in inferring from the premise of the absolute interdependence of all life the denial that any finite thing has infinite value. They argue that treating all things as equally valuable necessarily and unfortunately renders our moral judgments ad hoc, random, and spontaneous. Giving animals rights thus does not take into account the specific situations we find ourselves in, where attachments of love and need direct our moral deliberations. Birch and Cobb exercise a moral realism that is skeptical about the rigorous consistency required by the idea of rights. "As long as the rights of animals are viewed as demands upon human beings which are costly to us, they are almost certainly to give way in practice" (1981: 144). Their rejection of animal rights does not mean that they accept the traditional distinction of humans as ends and animals as means. Instead, they want to recognize that all creatures are both ends and means. It is not wrong, then, to treat animals as a means, as long as they are not treated only as a means. Animals do have intrinsic value in terms of the richness of their experience, but we must balance that value with their instrumental worth. Such balancing, which resembles the utilitarian calculus, is more an art than a science and is increasingly difficult, the authors admit, the more complex an entity becomes.

Birch and Cobb privilege complex relationships as intrinsically valuable, but they certainly do not want to say that we have a responsibility for helping all other animals realize their potential richness of experience. Instead, they defend an ethics of disengagement, not involvement. "For the most part, there is little humans can do positively to enrich the experiences of animals. The focus of concern is much more on avoiding those actions that prevent rich experience" (155). Domestic animals are more means than ends, while wild animals more closely approach being ends in themselves. As Cobb states, "The domestic animal is inferior to its wild counterpart in the range of capabilities and sensitivities" (Cobb, 1993: 185). Somehow, animals that live in the wild are thought to have more complex relations than animals that live with humans, so that the first priority of environmental theology is to protect natural habitats rather than worry about animals that are already a part of the human domain. Even so, they admit that the world is getting so crowded that not every individual can claim the inherent right to exist.[2]

When direct contact with animals is unavoidable, in situations where animal life conflicts with human interests, Birch and Cobb are eager to justify animal killing. Indeed, Birch and Cobb do not hesitate to acknowledge the asymmetry of most of our relationships with animals. They want to hold together our ability simultaneously to use and value animals, and farm animals seem to be their model of how we can do this. Although human value is also both intrinsic and instrumental, humans are able to increase their own value by using nonhuman animals. This is permissible because humans, with richer experiences, have a greater knowledge of death, so their death is more important; human death also has a greater impact for others than does animal death. Domestic animals, by contrast, can be traded for even trivial human desires because, with their more limited self-awareness, they are all (within a given species) alike. The species, seemingly, feels and experiences, not the individual. Farm animals are therefore replaceable. "If the death of one chicken makes room for the raising of another, the values lost are largely replaced by the values gained. The quality and amount of chicken experience remain largely unchanged" (1981: 159). Nature counts by species, not individuals, and so should we. Ironically, this process-oriented environmental philosophy, which begins with the significance of particular relationships, ends by reducing animal individuals to their species groupings. By romanticizing the freedom and individuality of wild animals, Birch and Cobb downplay the mutuality and thus the value that domesticated animals can have for humans, relations that enable us to see them as more than mere representatives of species groupings.

Do animals that have relations with us lead less complex lives than wild animals, and do we have fewer responsibilities toward them? The lessons of evolution should teach us, I want to argue, that domestication is a natural process, that cooperation among species promotes survival, and that species who choose domestication are strong opportunists, not weak conservatives.[3] Indeed, all species are successful, in that every species survives only because it adapts to its own ecological niche. Species who survive through domestication are able to adapt to richer and more complex situations requiring skills of negotiation and reflection. Defense mechanisms are traded for tangible benefits. Of course, breeders do look for those traits in a species that can make it more amenable to human control and profit. Nonetheless, domestication is not solely a human invention, imposed on innocent others; farm animals acquire their traits due at least as much to their own adaptiveness and flexibility as to our manipulation and control. Nature is interconnected from the very beginning, and mutual dependence is written into the very fabric of reality, as both evolutionary theory and process philosophy demonstrate. Domesticated animals are evidence of the fact that relations are both inevitable and valuable and that responsibility increases along with increases in relations. For many people, domestication is an indication of humanity's power over animals or of our right to eat them. Speaking strictly theologically, however, domestication is a sign (no matter how distant or distorted) of the original harmony of humanity with animals, a reminder of the way things were meant to be and an anticipation of what is yet to become.

More than any other process theologian, Jay McDaniel emphasizes the importance of our particular relations to animals. In *Of God and Pelicans,* he argues that we need to reconceptualize God's relationship to us in order to change our relationship to animals. Process thinkers make the radical claim that God is all-loving but not all-powerful. God cannot prevent, even though God can identify with, all suffering. Indeed, process thought emphasizes God's incredibly specific involvement in worldly affairs. God is both an agent and a patient, reciprocally affected by all that occurs in the world. The "inexhaustibly large-hearted" (McDaniel, 1989: 24) love of God is limited by creaturely freedom and natural laws and structures, so that God can feel the suffering of creatures even though God cannot always act to change that suffering. McDaniel argues that wherever God feels pain, there is the cross through which God experiences and redeems suffering: "A God who suffers only with humans is too small. Our task is to recognize that there are countless crosses in the world, nonhuman as well as human, to which countless victims are involuntarily nailed, often by powers that have nothing to do with human agency" (29). God's perfection is constituted by a complete immanence in which God is totally empathic with all feeling and experience.

The relational model allows for both chance and intentionality in natural processes. Because God does not control the course of events, the connections of individuals and the environment are unpredictable. This gap between natural occurrence and divine plan allows McDaniel to argue, contrary to many environmental theologians, that the creativity of nature should not be identified with the creativity of God. Rather, "God is found in the anticipatory—or goal directed dimension—of creaturely existence" (38). God is ahead of the world, ushering in the immediate future, providing opportunities for growth and maximal self-realization. God lures and inspires all entities toward the most satisfaction possible relative to their situation. God, in fact, distinguishes, evaluates, and ranks the various kinds of experience, which can help us to discern and judge interests as we recognize that life inevitably lives off of life. Our moral decisions should follow God's lead in maximizing the range and depth of relationships. "The greater the intensity of a creature's interests, the greater our obligation to respect them" (69). Every entity who experiences anything should be respected, according to McDaniel, but when it comes to practical decisions, creatures have more relative (or relational) than intrinsic value, and thus the egalitarian monism of rights language does not do justice to the complex comparison of experiential needs and desires that comprises the moral life.

What makes the question of theodicy—the justification of God in the context of the problem of evil—in process thought so pressing is that the pursuit of increasingly intense experience entails risk to oneself as well as limits to others. Animal life represents both a fall and an advance in nature. Greater opportunities exist for frustration and pain as well as for complex and rich experiences. God's management of the whole network of relationships ensures that the net benefit of this upward fall outweighs the particular costs, but the idea that God economizes pain so that short-term losses lead to long-term gains is no comfort to individuals who suffer for the sake of others. God lures us forward, even when it hurts, but does God lure us against each other, so that an experiential advance for one entity constitutes a loss for another?

God's luring, according to process theology, hurts God as well, which is some consolation. The very logic of luring means that God must relinquish much of the divine power and prerogative. The sacrifice God makes is that God's own suffering is amplified by the fact that competing strategies of survival are not easily harmonized with God's own ultimate purposes and goals. Perhaps one of the reasons that Christians resist dwelling on animal suffering is that it frustrates one's ability to imagine God's capacity to comprehend such suffering. As McDaniel observes, "If one considers the countless billions of painful experiences suffered by creatures since animal life began, and imagine in each instance that suffering was shared by an all-empathic God, the suffering of God staggers the imagination" (41). How can God love the violent world of nature, and what difference does that love make? The point is that God could not love creation into pain-free forms of life; pain is God's reality as well as our own.

What about the victims of evolution, though, those who experience no satisfaction, those sacrificed to the proliferation and fecundity of life? Does God lure animals against each other? Victims certainly contribute to other animals, as food, for example, but does such wanton and wasted suffering also contribute to God? If so, does process thought risk reducing victims to instruments of God's expansive memory and experience? At this point, McDaniel is forced to imagine creaturely fulfillment beyond this life. After all, if humans can be thought to survive death, it is no more difficult to think of animals as doing so. The hope, McDaniel is quick to note, is not that all creatures have the same kind of afterlife but that all creatures share in a fulfillment appropriate to their own constitution. Moreover, he adds, the hope is not for eternal life for all creatures but "that they live until they enjoy a fulfillment of their needs as creatures" (45–46).

Such speculations—and I will return to this topic in the last chapter—raise many unanswerable questions, of course. What about, for example, animals whose sense of satisfaction involves eating other animals? Can animals change their nature and still be themselves? McDaniel is right to suggest that it is not too difficult to imagine carnivorous animals finding ultimate completion in less violent ways of life, even though their immediate satisfaction entails harm to others. Arguably, animal nature is in bondage to violence just as human nature is, so animals too need liberation, and such liberation will not destroy violent animals any more than it will destroy us. In any case, McDaniel also suggests that we should not be too quick to generalize about the suffering of animal experience. "Because our nonhuman friends cannot speak in languages we understand, we should be wary of concluding that things would have been better had they never existed at all, and thus that, if their lives are to have any meaning at all, they must survive death in order to find satisfaction" (48). Animals too can accomplish a joy in living even in the midst of fear and pain.

The crucial insight of process thought is that our fulfillment lies in our contribution to the divine life. Life has a purpose, a final cause that drives it forward. God exists in the future, and the future is, in a way, God. Although some nonprocess environmental theologians tend to collapse the futural dimension of God into the interconnections of the present, the theocentric and the biocentric overlap when the telos of individual life is conceived of in terms of relations that transcend contemporary considerations. Environmentalists have long determined the value of forms of life as a function of their contribution to a biotic community. As Aldo Leopold, who developed the idea of a "land ethic," states, "A thing is right when it tends to preserve the integrity, stability, and beauty of the biotic community. It is wrong when it tends otherwise" (1949: 224–25).[4] The holism of "deep ecology" is an appealing position to those who worry about the Western emphasis on individualism and autonomy. Feminists like Catherine Keller (1986) and Rita Nakashima Brock (1988) have argued that the atomistic self, isolated and set apart, reflects masculine values, while a feminist transformation of selfhood would envision the self as essentially embodied, material, and connected. Process metaphysics sees relations even where we want to deny them, and God becomes the name for the web of all relations, a whole that is greater than the sum of the parts.

Process theology's emphasis on the specific value of every relationship could begin animal liberation by focusing on the particular obligations we owe to domesticated animals and push us to see that individual animals count, but instead relationality often means that no animal is of ultimate significance.[5] Indeed, holism, with its interest in systems and structures, has trouble acknowledging the concept of intrinsic value. Because feeling is continuous throughout all of nature, animals are only a specific instance of a general rule and thus do not merit special care. Trees and plants also feel and have their place in the biotic community, so that they too have interests that contribute to the maintenance of the whole. When the holistic perspective is applied to animals, it leads one to be more worried about members of endangered species than about individuals of other species. Predators too are prized as a natural way of restoring harmony and balance. The land, which is a synecdoche for the sum of all of the relations of an ecological system, counts for more than any part.

The problem is that relationality is an ambiguous term, connoting a mutual dependence but also a violent usurpation. All entities feel each other, but they also take advantage of each other, so that the economy of nature is not only relational but also parasitical. Strictly interpreted, holism finds animal suffering to be beautiful if it contributes to an interlocking system of symmetry and equilibrium (see Webb, 1996a). As Dombrowski explains, "The world itself is beautiful when the happiness of creatures harmonizes under divine influence, although not even God determines such harmony in its concrete particularity. This is a beauty of which every creature catches glimpses, and to which it makes contributions, but only God enjoys it as a whole once it comes into being" (1988: 125). Theologically speaking, it is as if God is unable to care intensely for each individual, since individual interests conflict, so God instead cares for the community as a whole. What is troubling is that God seems to value, remember, and cherish even those experiences that cause suffering in others, as long as they advance the individual toward a wider richness and complexity. The divine matrix compensates individual loss by guaranteeing the profit of the whole. God is that whole, the ultimate environment within which all creatures have their being, and the sacrifice of individuals seems to be necessary for the maintenance and growth of this theocentric ecology.

Environmental Theology and the Reclamation of Nature

In theological circles nowadays it is popular to reconnect Christianity and nature by reinterpreting the doctrine of creation (see, for example, Moltmann, 1991; Primavesi, 1991). That God said the world is good means that it is good enough for us, if only we would treat it properly. Theology thus joins ecology in envisioning the world as one interrelated whole; by implication, human destiny cannot be separated from the future of the earth. Furthermore, the interlocking connections of the earth are said to be paradigmatic for human behavior. The model of environmental interdependence suggests that we should work against dualistic hierarchies in order to democratize social organizations by redistributing power on a more equitable basis. We need to revise our attitude toward nature from something to be used to something to be revered because we are a part of "it." Gaia, the name given to the earth as an organism with its own integrity and individuality, is capable of healing itself, but it is also vulnerable to human manipulation and abuse. We need to begin giving back to the earth what we have long been taking from it in order to ensure the whole world's survival.

Along these lines, many theologians have been arguing that the notion of a transcendent God, who crafts the world and then stands back from it in order to use it as the background for redemptive action, does not provide a sufficient foundation for the necessary partnership between God, world, and humanity.

As Sallie McFague has argued in *Models of God* (1987), this God is both too removed from the world and too capable of intervening to destroy or save the planet at a whim. A God who controls the world from above does not encourage human worry over or need cooperation in the destiny of the earth. What is needed, McFague argues, is a retrieval of God's immanence, a doctrine of God working through and with nature, redeeming the world in and not from its materiality and concreteness. Thus, McFague suggests that we think of God as mother, lover, and friend rather than as father, king, and lord.

In a subsequent work, McFague (1993) pursues the image of the world as God's body by arguing that the entire cosmos is the sacred expression of God's agency.[6] God feels the world directly, and all parts of the world have equal value for God. God works through all of matter, so that the bodies of humans, let alone animals, are only parts of a greater body that comprises the whole. Indeed, God's immanence can be emphasized only if nature is understood in positive terms, so that it makes sense to see God working through and in nature rather than redeeming nature from above. For animal liberation, one consequence of the insight that nature is not inherently violent is that the extension of human care into the natural world seems less foolish and irresponsible. The exile from Eden into nature can be seen as a step upward into increasing complexity, which expands the opportunities for a connected and caring self. When we experience the environment, the source of all that sustains us, we experience God.

Given the immanence of God within the world, theological environmentalists argue that we can model our care for animals on the operations of nature itself. Rosemary Radford Ruether, for example, in *Gaia and God* (1992), urges a retrieval of the connection between the Hebraic covenant with God and the gift of land. What God promises in the Hebrew scriptures is not a heaven above but a specific place that flourishes only if humans act responsibly. She infers from this connection that a land ethic should mediate our relationship with animals, just as it mediates our relationship with God. Ruether acknowledges that the animal rights movement originates in particular relationships with pets: "The horror that is felt at the abuse of such animals on farms or in laboratories draws on this emotive bonding to the pet" (219). Yet the land teaches us to justify the killing of animals on the basis of nature's own violence. "Not only do carnivorous animals depend for their existence on eating other animals, but all life forms exist through an interdependence of consuming and being consumed" (223). In fact, Ruether does not think that a harmless diet is possible because plants also deserve our care and consideration. "Nor is it sufficient to claim that one does not eat beings with whom one can have an interpersonal relation. As a vegetable gardener, I expend great loving care over each plant for months of every year and feel great pain when I see one that is ill, but I still intend to eat them" (223–24). Here she misses the point of vegetarianism—that it tries to minimize pain to others, not to oneself. Finally, she criticizes vegetarianism as the diet of the affluent since it is not always possible for those with fewer luxuries to obtain sufficient protein without eating meat. She does not seem to be aware that this is an issue many defenders of vegetarianism attend to, usually arguing that vegetarianism is only morally required for those who have access to protein sources other than animal flesh. In the end, Ruether relies on the ancient idea that giving thanks for dead animals justifies such consumption: "It is not idle sentiment to thank the animals and plants that provide the sources of our life before we make use of any material thing" (228). She overlooks the fact that gratitude is appropriate only for voluntary, not involuntary, sacrifices.

The root problem of environmental theology for animal liberation is that reconnecting humanity to nature does not guarantee the protection of animals from human use and abuse. Such reconnection places human ambitions and desires in a humbling context, but by doing so they tend to mitigate the power of love to redeem lives regardless of such limitations. The same can be said for reconnecting God and nature: an immanent God makes sense only if nature does not need restoration and animals do not need liberation. Seen from the viewpoint of evolution, not theology, interconnection is another word for violence, since the web of life that environmentalists celebrate makes pain and death an inherent part of growth and propagation. An ecological theology of nature is thus faced with an alternative: either minimize (and idealize) nature's destructiveness or reinterpret God's plan for peace and harmony as promoting lifesystems that benefit from suffering and loss of life.

James Gustafson (1981) provides an interesting case for bringing humans and nature more closely together by emphasizing, in a distinctive move, God's transcendence, not immanence. He wants to enlarge our moral perspective by demonstrating how God's focus is on the whole of things, not just human beings. Gustafson offers a sober assessment of God's love as concerned with more than individual human value. Although Gustafson criticizes anthropomorphic views of God's benevolence, he does not thereby move animals into the scope of God's infinite concern. Instead, God is the term that refers to the interdependence of the ecological whole, where no creature is favored or privileged. Gustafson is able to rethink the value of animals only because he sees God as not ultimately valuing any individual—human or animal. Animals are promoted because humans are demoted, but both must not rebel against their place in the whole. Gustafson does not idealize nature, but he does portray God as quite willing to overlook individual welfare for a collective good that hardly redeems or compensates particular suffering.

I would argue that we can love animals as individuals even as we recognize the inevitable harshness of nature, but I realize that it is difficult to do both of those things at the same time. Sometimes environmental theologians talk as if we need to think that nature is good, in the sense of being harmless, in order to encourage a better treatment of natural resources. Caring for individual animals, however, does not mean that nature as a whole must be idealized. Nature is a blessing, but to make nature naturally good is to render redemption redundant. In spite of all of our manipulations and interventions, nature represents a power, both on the outskirts of human existence and at our very centers, that signifies something utterly other. Nature's drama unfolds with minimal regard for the human actor. Animals too are victims of the proliferation of life. Nature both affirms and denies the mystery of God's love, so theologians should not appeal directly to the evidence of nature for theological constructions.

Caring for animals also does not mean that humans should be responsible for eradicating all violence in nature. Nature does live off of itself in creative and resourceful ways, chaining all of life together in a circular fashion. Death leads to life, and we cannot change that. It is easy to admire the wild in nature—innocent animals that express themselves so effortlessly—and our inability to make moral judgments about them tempts us to romanticize them instead. We somehow lose the idea that God sides with the victims when we think about nature because we are not sure what it would mean for us to side with animal victims. Moralizing human institutions is hard enough, so that trying to transform nature as a whole is a Promethean conceit. Arguably, we need a way of understanding the religious significance of the environment that is appropriate both to the immanence of God and to nature's fearsome interplay of sustenance and scarcity, growth and decay, and life and death. We need a way of loving what is other in full recognition of our inability to control nature or to escape its limitations and conflicts.

The point is not to totally divest ourselves of power in relation to animals, as if power ever could be so easily minimized or extinguished. Humans are, after all, the distinctively moral animal, as well as the animal who speaks for all other animals. To put it in blunt terms: omnivorous humans are the only animal that can eat all other animals, and do.[7] Humans are also, then, the only animal that can identify with and protect all other animals. Denying this power only means that it will be replaced by some other form of power; no relation takes place in a power-vacuum. There is, no doubt, a value in powerlessness to which religions attest, but powerlessness is best thought of not as an abstract ideal. It is an act that takes place in a lived relationship, a context of give and take that is very different from the hands-off powerlessness that some environmentalists imagine. Christian powerlessness, or weakness, puts power into a surprising and unpredictable circulation, where power increases as it is given away, returning like something lost but not forgotten. Powerlessness—charity, giving, generosity—finds the self by attending to the other, in a kind of game of mutuality in which excitement stems from what one discovers by letting oneself go. In these relationships, which include our relationships with animals, power flows to the weak, while the strong feel the power of a new kind of weakness, called love.

Ecofeminism and Animal Compassion

Does environmental theology necessarily lead to a utilitarian comparison of animal interests with human wishes or the needs of an ecological whole? One promising venture of thought is what has become known as ecofeminism, a combination of ecological and feminist concerns. Feminists have long been suspicious of both utilitarian and rights moral theories, instead wanting to emphasize the role of compassion and connection in moral decision making. Feminist environmentalism, then, should avoid some of the ways in which ordinary environmentalism is quick to sacrifice individual animals to some pressing need. The basic argument of ecofeminism is that all oppressions are interconnected, products of self-other dualities, reductive hierarchies, and brutal stereotypes, so that combating one prejudice should contribute to overturning them all. The logic of the various forms of interlocking domination is single and unitary. This assumption allows some ecofeminists to trace the ideology of oppression to the masculine will to dominate nature. A common way of diminishing the status of minority human groups, after all, is to compare them to animals—dehumanizing often involves animalizing—so that an investigation of the systems of representation that inculcate cruelty to animals should also uncover and indict racism and sexism.

Indeed, theories of human nature, propounded by men, are anxious to distinguish and separate the human from the animal. These very qualities also have been used by men to separate men from women. Like animals, women have been deprived of basic rights because of supposed biological differences from the ideal animal, the male human being. The connections between women and animals are more than symbolic. Women are thought to be closer to animals, in part because they maintain animal functions (reproduction and child rearing). Female skills are assigned to the instinctual and thus do not deserve proportionate rewards. Women are frequently allocated jobs that are dehumanizing in their routine and status. For example, most of the approximately 54,000 nonunionized North American meatpacking workers are Hispanic or African American women with a high school education or less. This job is considered one of the most dangerous in the United States. The most oppressed segment of the population is chosen to carry out the destruction that consumers do not want to face. Our domination of animals is mediated so that we can obtain immediate gratification without any hesitation or guilt.

If women are not quite men but not really animals, what are they? As Carol J. Adams writes, tradition holds that women are neither men nor beasts: "The human/animal boundary is left secure, while women are moved from one side of it to the other" (1994: 11). Feminists differ on how to respond to this situation. Liberal feminists want to move women permanently from the animal side to the human side. Women should have all the freedom and rights that men have; they too should benefit from the domination of nature. Eating meat is thus privatized as a domestic, personal-choice issue (or, when such issues are made public, they are subjected to the economics of the market).[8] Adams argues instead for a complete revaluation of the human/animal divide in the first place. Rather than lifting women out of the realm of nature and into the reign of culture, feminism should interrogate the very dualism of culture and nature and the subsequent equation of animals with instinct, passivity, and corporeality. Radical feminism does this by challenging the portrait of humans as rational, autonomous, and independent. To retrieve the material, bodily aspects of human nature is to reform our prejudices about animals as well. Animals, after all, represent the purely material, and thus they do not matter. Making animals count challenges the patriarchal prerogative of devaluing those beings who are not like men themselves.

Of course, to argue with rigor and logic against the definition of human nature as rational and autonomous risks reaffirming what is negated by the critique itself. Consequently, feminism should make a difference in terms of not only what is counted as a relevant object of moral concern but also how moral theorizing is actually practiced. Feminism, then, should challenge the style of moral philosophy that usually dominates animal issues. The contractarian ethical theories of male philosophers make morality a matter of mutual agreement but only among those who qualify to enter into the negotiations of balancing conflicting interests. These theories, exemplified by John Rawls (1971), leave out those—not only animals but all moral patients—who do not or cannot make the complicated calculations that lead to measured agreements.[9] Full membership in the moral club is limited to those who can make decisions and appreciate their obligations and duties. Others are granted only indirect value. Feminists, by contrast, base moral reasoning on the multiple ways we actually value others, regardless of their ability to weigh self-interests and sign contracts. One way to see this difference is to say that feminists find more value in inconsistency—the particularities of moral obligations and passions—than consistency. When the standard of consistent behavior toward animals is thought to be impossible, many male moral theorists become frustrated and dismiss the importance of animals altogether, while an openness to the inconsistency of our moral lives allows some feminists to take animals seriously, even when they cannot act out of an absolute equal regard to all.[10]

Not all ecofeminists agree about what to do with animals. Some link domestication to sexism and thus argue for the complete independence of animals from human control.[11] For them, adopting a pet is a presumptuous exercise in unwarranted authority. Others see the links between animals and women differently. Women (and children) have long been grouped with animals in terms of their alleged emotionalism and their closeness to biological processes. This kinship has powerful consequences. Not only do women resemble animals in the sexist representations and prejudices of a patriarchal culture; they also, more constructively, have developed a greater capacity for sympathy for animals.[12] This makes sense, according to ecofeminists, because women generally give more moral weight to the concrete as opposed to the generalized other (see Benhabib, 1987: 77–95). As Beverly Harrison writes, "We know and value the world, *if* we know and value it, through our ability to touch, to hear, to see" (1985: 13).

The traditional philosophical emphasis on autonomy envisions the self as ultimately separated from rather than connected to and participating in each other's realities. To many men, sentimentalism is a pathology, tolerable in small children but dysfunctional in adults. They consider intense identification with the suffering of animals as a soft, feminine trait that needs to be masculinized through an education in the acceptance of hard, real world-reality. Men do not flinch when they witness animal pain; they do not allow emotion to distract them from the duty at hand. That is what it means to be a man. (This cultural definition of masculinity also means that many men are especially attached to their pets as a way of expressing what is otherwise not encouraged for them.) The question remains: Can empathy provide a powerful perspective for the critique and transformation of all that is taken for granted concerning animals? Can the weakness of vulnerable love become the strength of social reform and individual dignity?

The Rhetoric of Rights and the Demands of Care

How does the language of care compare to the usual and more rigorous philosophical approaches to the question of the ethical treatment of animals? Does caring say something that philosophical arguments frequently omit? The most respected of the recent philosophical attempts to address our responsibility to animals are constructive developments of the two traditional languages of morality: utilitarianism, as represented by Peter Singer, and rights theory, as represented by Tom Regan. Both systems begin with and defend the premise that animals (some, at least) can feel pain and suffer, and that some animals are self-conscious to some degree. Then, utilitarians like Peter Singer argue that this suffering must be taken into account when making decisions to maximize happiness or pleasure and minimize pain, and rights theorists like Regan argue (against Kant) that this characterization of animals should force us to extend to them the notion of rights that is usually understood as a property of the human species alone.[13]

Both Singer and Regan adopt a tone of seriousness, of moral earnestness, that is quick to preempt charges (charges against "animal lovers" that go back at least to Spinoza)[14] of sentimentalism, anthropomorphism, and naiveté. Regan has emphatically written that "it is not human kindness, not human generosity, not a tender human heart, not any human interest that is the basis of respectful treatment. It is justice, understood as treating others as they are due" (1993: 216). Singer agrees. His influential *Animal Liberation* (1990) begins with a recollection of a visit with, significantly, a woman who is a pet lover and who mistakenly thinks that Singer will share her passion. His reaction to her admittedly superficial expressions of affection for dogs and cats, spoken as she eats a ham sandwich, is only somewhat short of brutal, and he proudly proclaims that he has never been "inordinately" fond of pets, that he does not even "love" them.[15] He is more serious than that.

Singer re-creates this little melodrama in order to proclaim a turning point in the animal rights movement, a deep division between the traditional humane-society approach to animals (historically and stereotypically dominated by women and mostly concerned with companion animals) and the radicalization of the movement (dominated by white, male philosophers and mostly concerned with the scientific, industrial, and agricultural exploitation of animals). For Singer, it is clear that animals are not to be approached under the auspices of aesthetics or emotion; instead, animals challenge us to rise to a new level of objectivity and consistency in our moral outlook. Animals serve as an index to our own moral respectability, letting us measure our capacity for impartiality. Animals are not something to pet or talk to but something to think or talk about.

Theorists like Regan and Singer are caught in the irony that the most distinctive features of our relationship to animals must be suppressed in order to defend the very integrity of that relationship. Consequently, the dismissal of pets as a philosophically serious problem and as a potentially profound starting point for reflecting on the nature of our relationship with animals merely reflects and reinforces those prejudices that attempt to privatize and sentimentalize our relationship with animals in the first place. The discourse about domesticated animals not only has the potential to interrupt more ordinary and acceptable modes of serious discourse but also, by that very disruptive power, can show us something about the limits within which we ordinarily speak and the styles of which we are frequently unaware.

What is missing in both of these positions, commendable as they may be, is a more phenomenological grounding of our relationship with animals. "Animals," after all, is only a word, and a clumsy one at that; there is no such thing as an animal, but only individuals; even the propagandists for animal rights organizations realize that people react to animals best not as an abstract category but as individual beings with their own needs, interests, and desires. Most philosophers, however, are overly cautious about relying on personal and particular experience or emotion in discussing animal rights.[16] Animal rights activists are often accused, ignorantly, of operating from a sentimental mode, and so (male) philosophers go overboard in proving their uninformed critics wrong. The result is a level of discourse that is academically proper but emotionally dry. The calculative morality of utilitarianism and the rigid universalism of rights theory privilege the masculine virtues of analysis, detachment, and consistency over a feminist ethic of care, intimacy, and compassion.[17] The ethics of animal rights tries to achieve a universal point of view, which keeps animals at an abstract and therefore safe distance. Nearness and immediacy are beside the point.

Regan suspects that care alone is not enough to motivate the fundamental changes that are needed when somebody becomes sensitive to the value of animal life. Regan has even argued that for the ethic of care to work, it must adopt some features of those ethics it rejects. He sharpens this objection into the form of a dilemma: "*Either* their [the feminist's] theory lacks the theoretical wherewithal to mount the desired attack on human chauvinism, *or* it contains the means to mount this attack. If the former, then the theory is deficient because of the barrenness of claims to human superiority. If the latter, then the theory is still deficient, judged by its own standards, since in this case it must incorporate elements of the very conception (the patriarchal conception) of the human person that it seeks to replace" (1991: 98–99). In other words, how can feminist theory dismantle the bulk of patriarchy (the claim of man's rational superiority over animals and man's right to dominate and control nature) without relying on some part or aspect of that patriarchy? Regan thinks that humans have to assume responsibility for their rational superiority over animals, and it is that superiority that can lead to clearer thinking about animal worth.

Regan does not want humans to abdicate their uniqueness because he is convinced that the uniquely human rigor of logic and argumentation can convince anyone and everyone that animals deserve better treatment. Even his definition of animals worth protecting—those with complex self-consciousness—privileges rationalism. What most characterizes rational thought, for Regan, is reason's capacity to compel us toward outcomes we might want to avoid. Ethical reflection does this by relying on what can be called the rule of consistency. In its simplest form, the rule states: isolate those features that are the basis of the scope and range of your ethical activity, and then apply that activity to all creatures who exhibit those features, regardless of their species. So, if you act to alleviate or minimize pain, then act to alleviate all pain, regardless of whether that pain belongs to an animal or a human being. Likewise, if you assign rights to humans who are capable of a minimal degree of self-awareness and consciousness, assign those same rights to all creatures who are similarly self-aware and conscious.

The consistency argument is designed to defeat moral positions that assume what has come to be called speciesism—the unfounded limitation of moral concern to the human species alone on the assumption that other species do not deserve or warrant such attention merely because they belong to another species. As Regan comments, "The point of such arguments is to highlight the moral arbitrariness of excluding some individuals from the circle of one's moral concern" (1991: 96). The intended impact of consistency arguments is to coerce us to bring our caring in line with our reasoning on the assumption that the scope of reasoning, unencumbered by the limitations of physical contact and personal acquaintanceship, is greater than personal caring permits. Reasoning, with its overtones of universality and compulsion, is a better basis for morality than intuition or feeling, with its handicaps of particularity and idiosyncracy. Reason judges, convicts, and demands, while the emotions only try to persuade. From the perspective of consistency, moral actions should be rule governed. Indeed, consistency, though not a sufficient condition (one can be consistently immoral), is a necessary condition of moral agency. To be moral is to seek the maximal establishment of some good (whether a positive good, like happiness, or a negative good, like avoiding the affliction of pain and suffering) for all relevant entities, so that acting morally is not conceivable except on the basis of a consistent pattern of activity. To be inconsistent is to be immoral.

Can a morality of animal compassion emerge from the inconsistent ways in which we actually care for animals? Does the love of pets have any philosophical meaning? Both Singer and Regan focus on a single capacity (the capacity to suffer or to have interests) that serves as a necessary and sufficient condition for being treated morally. This approach renders relationships irrelevant, just as it strips individuals of their particular histories. It also treats animals as valuable only to the extent that they are the same as us. As Deborah Slicer argues, "In effect, animals are represented as beings with the *kind of capacity* that human beings most fully possess and deem valuable for living a fully *human* life" (1991: 111). The ethic of caring, by contrast, does not presuppose a common definition of those objects that are worthy of care. Indeed, while caring can be defended as a universal moral norm, every act of caring is also different because caring attends to the particularities of the cared-for object and the distinctive features of the caring situation.

Nonetheless, caring can be characterized in such a way that it runs into the same difficulties as consistency does in rights theory and utilitarianism. Some feminists, for example, see caring as a way of leveling all differences, so that there is no single factor that makes one thing count more than another. Slicer approvingly quotes Marti Kheel's complaint that "many writers on the subject of animal liberation may raise the status of animals to a level that warrants our moral concern only to exclude other parts of nature, such as plants and trees" (Slicer, 1991: 112). Those interested in environmentalism frequently suspect the animal rights movement of privileging distinctions that caring is meant to overcome. Caring can be for anything, some environmentalists argue, and at its best it should be for everything, disregarding the question of human-animal similarities. Caring is thus more consistent than animal rights because caring is totally inclusive and resists value judgments of any kind. After all, one can care as much for a tree as for a dog.

A caring that does not make distinctions, however, is just as bad as a caring based on human value alone. Environmentalists too often ground their concern for nature in "the completion of a process of (masculine) universalization, moral abstraction, and disconnection, discarding the self, emotions, and special ties" (Plumwood, 1991: 7). For environmentalists, in other words, concern has to be generalized in order for it to be valid. A caring that is for everything, however, risks overlooking those who need our caring most. A care ethic is powerful precisely because it values the particular for its own sake, not as an illustration of a broader principle. Indeed, the act of caring does not necessarily mean that everything has equal value. Hierarchies and dualisms are challenged and inverted, but real commitments, priorities, and differences remain. When we care, we are attracted to things because of the difference they make for us, and our caring makes those differences the basis for an intimacy that transgresses ordinary categories and boundaries. As Deane Curtin notes, "A feminist ethic tends to be pluralistic in its intention to recognize heterogeneous moral interests" (1991: 64). An ethic of care is thus able to correlate moral concern with substantial differences as well as similarities. The care ethic does not have to deny what humans and animals share and thus deny the special place animals should have in our ethical deliberations, but it also does not have to use a human characteristic as the standard for all moral value.

The ethic of caring draws from any and every relationship that is based on responsibility and mutuality. The presupposition of rights moral theory is that interests are always competing, which makes relationships based on mutuality the exception, not the rule. The goal is to find principles for when one desire can and cannot override another. This agonistic vision of life assumes that somebody's interests must always be sacrificed for somebody else's. Rights are thus based on the adversarial idea of exchange. We give others rights when we can benefit, in the long run, from this gift, and we give others rights when we need them ourselves. Rights are a product of negotiation, a process that accepts trade-offs only so that all can profit. Regan appropriately asks why the interests of animals are *always* sacrificed for human interests. Most people will respond with another question: What do humans have to gain by extending rights to animals? As long as the value of rights is connected to an exchange model of relationships, granting rights to animals will be seen as too costly and inconvenient.

The real question is whether all relationships are really reducible to the principle of economic exchange (see Webb, 1996b). The theory of care suggests that interests can coincide and support each other. Ethics is not only about protecting each individual from all others but also about promoting a mutuality of interests, the sharing of affection and love. Responsibility arises from relationships, and relationships are structures of emotion more than reason. Caring places the moral life in particular contexts that make all abstractions suspect. There is no single reason for why we care or why we should care more. To talk about an ethical commitment, then, is to tell the story of a particular relationship, a complex narrative (not an abstract principle) of the diverse ways in which interests can be mutually supportive and enriching.

Of course, we have the strongest emotional bonds with members of our own species, and ethical principles (like Singer's and Regan's) that cut too cleanly through those ties will strike us as heartless and unrealistic. Ethics should not be about our willingness to turn our backs on those we love. Reason is always contextualized, and we cannot think outside of the community to which we belong. Nevertheless, we also have emotional ties to members of other species, and every day many of us balance the needs of family and friends with the needs of the animals we also love. An ethic of care finds in our ties with animals the same richness and responsibility that we have in our ties with human loved ones. The point is not to overcome relationships but to broaden them, to extrapolate what we know and feel to include ever larger circles of compassion and concern.

How does caring about a particular other become caring for all such others? Caring is a context-dependent activity, but does this mean it must be limited to local rather than global acts of compassion? Conceptually, it is difficult to hold together the particular and the general, but in practice morality usually begins with specific commitments that only later become more inclusive. Being moral is telling the story of how our desires have been educated, so that compassionate gestures become more lasting and range more broadly. Nevertheless, formulating an ethic of caring that is rooted in but not restricted to the particular is a complex task. Nel Noddings, for example, defines caring as an act that finds completion in the response of the one cared for. To care for (rather than just care about) is thus to enter a reciprocal relationship. A specific other initiates our caring, but caring also has a momentum of its own.

When we take a creature into our home, name it, feed it, lay affectionate hands upon it, we establish a relation that induces expectations. We will be addressed, and not only by this particular creature but also by others of its kind. It seems obvious that we might live ethically in the world without ever establishing a relation with any animal, but once we have done so, our population of cared-fors is extended. Our ethical domain is complicated and enriched, and to behave uncaringly toward one of its members diminishes it and diminishes us. (1984: 157)

We do not, then, have a general ethical obligation toward animals, but when we do love a cat, for example, we should love all cats. But what about all animals? Must we be careful to not let our care go too far?

For Noddings, caring occurs after a relationship is formed, and relationships are contingent and accidental. I think this is an accurate portrait of how caring develops. She also insists, however, that authentic relationships are reciprocal, so that compassion is most powerful in relationships that are bounded by direct contact. If caring best occurs in close encounters that involve physical proximity, then people who care about the whales or seals they see in magazines or on television are not really caring. In many of these cases, she suggests, "the effort seems very like campaigns to save valuable objects and works of art" (158). Caring for creatures with whom one is not in a relationship runs the danger of a "nearly pure sentiment and I risk talking nonsense as I act upon it" (159). She is not even certain that animals we live with are responsive to us. "We can see clearly that animals are not capable of entering a mutually or doubly caring relation with human beings, but as their responsiveness or perceived responsiveness increases, our natural caring increases also" (159). Finally, she almost suggests that in caring for animals we are only responding to ourselves: "Whether or not the creature is responsive, I am responsive to the possibility of its responsiveness" (159). For Noddings, relationships with animals are an attractive addition to our moral lives, but their omission is not morally blameworthy. Moreover, Noddings urges us to be prudent in the way we care for animals; to love beyond a particular relationship is to risk the sentimental and the ridiculous.

Noddings raises the question of whether caring must be limited in order to be legitimate. She suggests that a consistent program of caring would not venture into acts of compassion that are not realistically rooted in close and immediate relationships. She shows how those who emphasize consistency can end up not in defending with Regan a rights-based approach to animals but in constraining the range of our concern for animals. However, if she is right that inconsistency risks looking foolish, then her kind of consistency risks not being moral at all. Who can condone the way people who love dogs eat equally intelligent and personable pigs? I do not want to perversely advocate inconsistency for its own sake, but I do want to insist that the risk and trust involved in caring can never be reduced to a formal ethical system. If caring is to have value, then a certain kind of inconsistency—a love that begins in personal attachment but also dares to reach beyond the personal—must be taken as a virtue.

How, then, does caring lead to social changes beyond the specific relationships in which it is practiced? Some feminists have argued that caring needs to be politicized in order to channel its energy into social change. Joan Tronto characterizes caring as an act that transgresses the boundaries between morality and politics, the private and the public, and the subjective and the objective. Because we all care (about something) and we are all dependent on care, caring has the power to make us rethink social priorities, prejudices, and policies. Yet Tronto also warns against a too quick universalization of care: "Care is distorted if we separate the principles of care—that care is necessary—from the particular practices of care in a given situation" (1993: 153). She suggests that caring is a necessary but not sufficient condition for public morality; caring needs to be supplemented by a political vision that integrates it into social structures. In other words, caring needs political and social support; otherwise, it will remain marginalized and undervalued.

I agree that caring should challenge our political and social priorities, but the transition from specific acts of care to a politics of care must be mediated by a reflection on the ultimate truth and value of caring that does justice to the haphazard ways in which we actually care. No political system can make caring completely just and fair by distributing the responsibilities of caring to all classes of people and rewarding caring with its actual worth. By its very nature, caring is a vocation that transgresses the corrective decisions of the courts and the calculations of the market. An alternative exists to saying that all animals have the right to be cared for and all humans have the duty to care for all animals. In chapters 5, 6, and 7 I will develop a theology of caring that can bridge private acts and social transformation by giving cosmic significance to the particular entanglements of affection and love. My claim is that something powerful resides in the very inconsistencies of our attachments, which enables caring to overflow the particular and thus challenge general customs and habits. One must be called to care, so that we need to learn again to listen to those traditions that give us special obligations by demanding our rebirth in acts of compassion.

What is needed is an investigation of the potential power of compassion in full conversation with the ways in which a patriarchal culture has marginalized and feminized animal love. What is at stake is root paradigms of relating to animals. As Carol J. Adams notes, "An ideology that ontologizes animals as usable precedes the issues associated with animal rights discourse and feminist theory" (1994: 15). A theology for the dogs would ontologize them as animals capable of receiving and returning affection, not as objects governed by the demands of the market. This theology would learn to listen to what animals can tell us of their own hopes and concerns. Listening to some voices means learning not to listen to the clamor of other sounds. As Emily Dickinson wrote, "They talk of Hallowed things, aloud—and embarrass my Dog" (1958: 178).

Dogs are moved more by a few firm and affectionate words and even shared silence than by philosophical disputations. Ecofeminists can teach us how to value what has long been devalued, those moments of sharing that defy economic analysis and philosophical gravity but move us to respond to otherness with a gentle and uplifting grace sufficient for moral and social change.

PART II

Thinking about Pets

CHAPTER THREE

What Are Dogs For?

The Other as More of the Same?

Are other animals more of the same, or can they be truly different, a "more than" that makes us change who we are? Ecofeminism emphasizes our particular and emotional relationships with others, including animal others, yet the literature on animals is often reluctant to examine the power they hold over us. Academics are in a hurry to affirm every variety of otherness, every group that has been marginalized or silenced, but animal others are usually treated as mere appendages to the human project, fantasy versions of ourselves. We live in a world that tries to retrieve the lost and the forgotten, but it is also a world that is becoming increasingly suspicious and skeptical of our ability to understand what is different and other. If we are not sure that we can understand each other any longer—if anthropologists warn us that we can never truly know another culture and if Republicans and Democrats no longer speak the same political language—it seems an impossible task to ask people to take seriously what we share with the animal world and to wonder about that seemingly speechless and most vulnerable group in our society called animals.

Their speechlessness is precisely the problem. What we see in them, many argue, is what we ourselves say. In a word, language gets in the way of otherness. Metaphysics, as well as religion, makes *man* the measure of all things, and to the extent that *man* is defined by his use of language, then it seems problematical to inscribe within language the arguments for treating animals as ends in themselves, that is, as beings who exist with value outside of the domain of human making, doing, and speaking. Precisely because animals are (allegedly) speechless, the words we speak for them, the words we put into their mouths, are our own and cannot do them justice.

Can we see in animals something that sees us rather than a mirror reflection of ourselves? John Berger has argued that animals first entered the human world as magical and sacred beings; they came from over the horizon of our own origin, making them mysterious but invaluable. They offer a companionship that extends beyond our individual loneliness to our isolation as an entire species. It is their looking at us that sets us to reflection. "Man becomes aware of himself returning the look" (1980: 2–3). Today, Berger laments, animals have disappeared because they can no longer hold us with their gaze. The animal as a machine is emptied of mystery. In zoos—animal museums—animals look about nervously, but they do not look at us; zoos are a "monument to the impossibility of such encounter" (19). Animals, Berger claims, now exist more in our mind than in reality. Wild animals are idealized, but the fact that we observe them so closely shows that they are objects of an asymmetrical examination that leaves us unchallenged and unchanged. Berger asserts that the animal as a pet is part of a general withdrawal into the realm of the private and insignificant where humans are not questioned. The pet is too dependent on us to look at us from afar. The look of the pet allows us to see whatever we want to see.

Berger's pessimism is not, however, complete; he idealizes the peasant-class, small-time farmers who economically depend on animals in very practical ways and thus still have the wisdom that comes from direct participation and involvement. He longs for a looking that is mutual, but he suggests that domestication places the animal at a disadvantage. He disparages modern petkeeping practices, yet he ends his essay nostalgically hoping that those who live off the labor of animals can still see them in ways the rest of us cannot. Ironically, he implies that only by using animals can we really know them, so that only those who profit from the labor and death of animals can really experience their otherness and mystery. Is it possible to know animals in ways other than as products of our own consumption?

Perhaps the most common way to talk about animals is to use the language of analogy, that is, to say that something unknown is similar to something that is already known. The use of analogy, however, risks reducing animals to instruments of human cognition. Animals are "good to think," as Claude Lévi-Strauss writes, suggesting that we can think about them but we cannot think how they think (1973: 161–62).[1] Animals are a language (that we speak), not an object (in and for themselves).

One of the most helpful guides to sorting out the philosophical problems of talking about animal otherness in analogical terms is Mary Midgley's *Beast and Man* (1978). Drawing on Edward O. Wilson and Konrad Lorenz, Midgley addresses the conundrum of understanding the animal aspects of our human nature and how that project affects the way we understand animals. Midgley shows that the animality of human nature is a largely mythical beast. Animals symbolize whatever it is that a given philosopher or theologian thinks is the negative side of or limit to human nature, and this negativity is then projected onto real animals. Vice, for example, becomes equated with acting in an inhuman or animal manner (note Augustine's remark that the vice of humans is the nature of beasts), and animals thus come to symbolize immorality. Humanity's most ancient relationship with animals, then, is built on the shaky foundation of an irreparable division internal to human nature, and animals are a necessary means for the articulation of this process of self-definition as self-differentiation. Animal nature is a pure materiality against which humans can measure the meaning of their lives. For most of Western history, animals have not been the other of humanity; they are inside us, and only incidentally other than what we most fear ourselves to really (almost) be.

Part of the problem here is that we have no real way, or language, for understanding the nature within ourselves, so we cannot understand the nature that is outside of us, let alone the nature that is in those others who are so strangely proximate and yet so far removed. Is it possible to think about animals in a nonmetaphysical way, that is, to think about animals as others who are truly other and yet really matter, others who are more than just meat? Midgley's solution to this set of problems is to try to envision nature as totally independent of human needs or desires. In other words, she conceptualizes nature as something ultimately inassimilable into the categories of labor and conceptuality. Nature is the anti-instrumental realm of free spirit, play, and art: "The world in which the kestrel moves, the world that it sees, is, and will always be, entirely beyond us. That there are such worlds all around us is an essential feature of our world. Calling the bird's existence 'pointless' means only that it is not a device for any human end. It does not need that external point. It is in some sense . . . an end in itself" (1978: 359). To substantiate this point, she draws on Kant's notion of the sublime,[2] which demarcates that which is so overwhelmingly impressive (like the mountains or the ocean) that it frustrates our need for understanding and our desire for control, forcing us into a state of amazed admiration. "We need the vast world, and it must be a world that does not need us; a world constantly capable of surprising us, a world we did not program, since only such a world is the proper object of wonder" (362). Midgley concludes her book *Animals and Why They Matter* (1983) with a helpful contrast between a minimalist ethic, based on the principle of parsimony and ruled by prudence, and an expansive ethics of imagination, based on curiosity and sympathy.

Although Midgley's call for an anti-instrumental view of nature is certainly one step toward a constructive position on animal meaning, it is important to note that she does not analyze the ideas of uselessness, excess, and luxury through which she understands the animal world. Indeed, the structure of her argument for the sublime, her assertion that we *need* a world that does not need us, is a bit puzzling: it announces the otherness of the world on the basis of human needs—the world must be other because that would be nice for us; it would fit in well with our needs. Midgley's pointless world secretly serves a fairly specific pedagogical purpose. Excess teaches us humility and perspective. Has her own discourse once again reduced the other to the same, that is, reduced the animal world to an extension of our own needs, wants, and desires? Has she subjected the (il)logic of excess to the logic of analogy? If so, the question remains: What would it mean to get the point of a totally pointless object? What would it mean to know animals as others who are both distant and familiar, both unknowable and intimate?

Clearly, the analogical use of animals threatens to reduce the other to the same, appropriating new knowledge only on the basis of what we already know. Is there a different kind of discourse that is more appropriate to the way animals can transform human knowledge, giving us something we do not already have? Philosophers, historians, social scientists, and psychologists frequently have treated animals in terms that downplay their capacity to challenge us with their integrity and demands. In this chapter I will investigate two strategies, sociological and psychological, that reduce animals to extensions of the human realm. In these strategies, animals are a mere exaggeration of human reality; they are not excessive in the sense of making claims on us that we cannot avoid or deny. Throughout this chapter I will suggest ways in which animals resist reduction and explanation, and in the next chapter I will more fully explore the dynamic of excess in our relationship with animals.

The Other as Social Self

Do animals tell us not only what we already are but also the more that we can become? The socio-historical aspect of the question of animals is aggressively pursued by Keith Tester in *Animals and Society: The Humanity of Animal Rights* (1991), in which he argues that the discourse on animal rights is actually nothing more than a discourse on social morality.[3] Animals, he insists, are blank paper upon which we inscribe classificatory schemes that reflect our own social organizations, our own attempts at self knowledge, and not any concern for animals as such. By combining the perspectives of Durkheim and Marx and drawing on the examples of Medieval bestiaries and animal trials,[4] Tester is able to argue that all cultural activities and representations ultimately refer to social processes. Animals are crucial because through them societies as a whole are able to delimit themselves. This becomes most evident, Tester argues, in the emergence of the animal welfare movement in nineteenth-century England, where animal compassion is permitted only in proportion to the growing distance between humans and real animals. As regular contact with animals declines, their symbolic importance grows, so that the animal welfare movement is able to argue against any and all contact with animals based on their purely symbolic (as opposed to economic) value.

Tester uses the example of vegetarianism to bolster his argument. Tester interprets vegetarianism, with its classical antecedents in Pythagoras, Plutarch, and the Neoplatonists, as an alienated rejection of the social order by, primarily, intellectuals.[5] Meat, after all, is the ultimate symbol of socialization. Cooking, along with language, is the universal symbol of humanity's differentiation from and triumph over nature (see Lévi-Strauss, 1969, and Detienne and Vernant, 1989). It takes group effort to raise, slaughter, and cook animals, and eating meat has always functioned as a metaphor for social processes, whether subservience to the gods or declaration of social status. Meat eating, for carnivores, is a sign of eating life, a symbol (tempered in the ancient world by animal sacrifices) of strength, privilege, and power. For vegetarians, of course, eating meat is eating death, not life. If the cooked is the social, then the raw is the natural, which allows vegetarians to argue that socialization is a process that ultimately has done more harm than good for humans and animals alike. One way to make a statement against the homogeneity of modernization is to refrain from eating meat. Paradoxically, becoming more civilized, for vegetarians, means returning to a more natural way of life.

Tester, like a good Marxist, traces this romantic ideology of naturalism to its historical preconditions, in this case, urbanization. A vegetarian diet could only become popular, Tester argues, as "a city-based attempt to turn away from the looseness of urban and social existence" (1991: 145). Eating animals becomes a taboo for those who, caught in the massive urbanization beginning in the nineteenth century, assuage their alienation by nostalgically longing for a naturalness and harmony that never actually existed. Vegetarians legislate a victimless diet because they live in an urban setting without animals, and thus they can afford the luxury of idealizing a humanity independent of animal labor. The symbolic knowledge of urban culture replaces the real and direct knowledge of rural life, so that city dwellers are able to be vegetarians because animals exist only in their imaginations and thus can be thought of without being eaten.

Vegetarianism, for Tester, is the dessert to a frugal meal of self-centered moralism. By seeking purity through declining all contact with the animal world, vegetarians reward themselves with a satisfying sense of moral superiority. The structure of Tester's argument against vegetarianism is odd. Although he assumes that animals always represent the human, he is especially critical of vegetarians for using animals to establish their own self-identity. He suggests that the condemnation of meat eating is really a repression of the animal nature within humanity. Vegetarians try to "expunge or exteriorize their own animality, which they see as contaminating, an abomination, lurking at the heart of their identity and constantly compromising that identity" (Baker, 1993: 213). Vegetarianism is an ideology that cannot countenance the violence and aggression of animal behavior. As a result, it uses animals as part of a moral project that wants to dissociate humans completely from the animal world. The animal rights movement is thus not about animals at all. This movement can acknowledge animals only by acts of self-denial that have nothing to do with compassion or affection toward animals. The vegetarian, then, is a human being who does not want to be an animal, and not eating meat is a way of purifying oneself of all that is not uniquely human. Much of what Tester says rings true, but must vegetarianism be based on the separation of humans and animals, or is there an interchange of humans and animals that is not based on self-alienation and self-righteousness?

Tester's argument about urbanization is certainly important. Historians like Harriet Ritvo and James Turner have connected the beginnings of the animal rights movement to the rise in industrialization and increasing class conflict.[6] The first bill introduced into the British Parliament on animals, a bill abolishing bullbaiting, was as concerned about social order as about bulls and dogs. Bullbaiting was a popular sport for the lower classes, an opportunity for a festive and illicit break from the workday. Foxhunting, by contrast, the proper sport of the upper classes, was not equally protested and prosecuted until recent times. Indeed, much of the nineteenth-century language about cruelty to animals reflects a bias against the lower classes. The Royal Society for the Prevention of Cruelty to Animals, for example, organized a private police force to enforce the standards of decency that were violated most often by cab drivers and others who had to labor with animals. Controlling the use of animals could serve as a means to disciplining people as well as redefining the social boundaries of acceptable and civil behavior.

Significantly, the antivivisection movement, which confronted the power and wealth of the scientific establishment, was never enthusiastically supported by humanitarian groups, and after achieving a peak of sorts by the 1870s, it was destined, by the beginning of this century, to be seen as a fringe movement of cranks and eccentrics. It is not too difficult to read its failure as a triumph of middle- and upper-class stability over revolutionary currents. The socially accepted anticruelty groups believed in human progress and fought cruelty as a particularly stubborn sign of antiprogressive forces. The radical antivivisectionist groups were more suspicious of human progress and saw science as representing the elitism and cunning that was increasingly dominating both nature in general and animals in particular. Due to the increasing recognition of the ambiguity of the notion of progress and the limits to the reliance on technol-

ogy, the more radical antivivisection wing of animal protection groups is growing rapidly in power and influence today.

Contrary to Tester's single-minded thesis, the example of the antivivisection
movement demonstrates that animals are not only a means by which societies
establish limits but also a way in which groups and individuals can test social
limits and constraints. Take Coral Lansbury's account, in *The Old Brown Dog*
(1985), of a series of antivivisection riots that took place in Battersea, England,
in 1907. She tells how women and the working class identified with the dogs
killed by scientists and how all three groups—women, the poor, and dogs—
were dominated and controlled by the same logic and language that fueled the
vivisectors' practices.[7] Vegetarianism, which traditionally has been a marginalized and unorganized movement of protest submerged within dominant social systems, also deserves closer scrutiny. Not only (male) intellectuals but also
women (intellectuals and otherwise) have challenged the power of the meat
culture. Indeed, Carol J. Adams (1990) has argued that the connection between
meat eating and sexism gives diet a revolutionary potential. Historically, she
points out, meat eating has been a male prerogative, but even more fundamen-
tally, the language about meat has structural parallels with the language men
use about women.[8] Pornography, for example, is filled with associations between women and animals, and meat is a metaphor for men's sexual pursuit of
women. Meat eating is also similar to animal experimentation in that both are
products of what Adams calls the "arrogant eye," the practice of looking at
animals as objects to be used, while not seeing that animals can look back at
us as beings that experience and feel.[9]

As Tester's own analysis demonstrates, complex historical factors are involved
in what must be considered a massive paradigm shift in Western sensibilities:
throughout the nineteenth century the Victorians were becoming increasingly
sentimental people, sensitive to pain and suffering as they began idealizing the
animal world, especially dogs and horses. Although pets were not uncommon
in the Middle Ages, they were for the most part the playthings of courtiers and
members of the privileged religious orders. In 1387 William of Wykeham criticized the nuns of Romsey Abbey for spending alms on pets that could have
been given to the poor, a charge still aimed at animal lovers today. Working
dogs were ubiquitous in the Renaissance, but pet dogs remained an upper-class
phenomenon, especially connected to women. A contemporary describes the
lapdogs of noble ladies as "little and prettie, proper and fine, and sought out
far and neere to satisfie the nice delicacie of daintie dames, and wonton wom-
en's willes; instruments of follie to plaie and dallie withall, in trifling away the
treasure of time."[10] Even today, pampering is seen as a stereotypical female
vice.

In early modern England, the distinction between work dogs and pet dogs became well established and took on a new significance. Keith Thomas in *Man and the Natural World* (1983) argues that all the features of present day pet-keeping were in place by 1700, although the Victorians took this art to its most melodramatic heights.[11] Ritvo suggests that the technological mediation of our relationship with nature made petkeeping possible on a wide scale. Once nature was subjected to widespread domination and control, it could be approached with sensitivity and affection. Animals could be interpreted "as reassuring evidence of human power, rather than as a troublesome reminder of human vulnerability" (1988: 20). Domination thus serves as a precondition for compassion. The pet symbolizes nature that is not just conquered but also submissive, nature gratefully surrendered to human superiority. Early dog breeding especially demonstrates this combination of care and control. The Victorians invented many dog breeds, and the standards they enforced were frequently arbitrary, signs of human imagination rather than animal function or skill.[12] The practical difficulties of breeding helped to define pets as a luxury, something the lower classes could not afford.

Thomas offers a similar reading of pets, mapping the shift from domination to kindness and compassion as a result of decreasing contact with work and farm animals. Simply put, as our dependence on animals decreased, the moral treatment of animals increased. Animals as toys replaced animals as tools. "It was not these necessary animals," Thomas explains, "but the unnecessary ones, hounds and lapdogs, which received the real affection and the highest status" (1983: 102). Unlike Tester, however, Thomas finds in these "instruments of follie" a new kind of morality that would have enormous consequences: "There is no doubt that it was the observation of household pets which buttressed the claims for animal intelligence and character" (121). Ritvo concurs. The practice of valuing what was previously without value, she argues, helped to tip the balance of humanity's relationship with nature from fear to friendliness. "Pet owners probably saw the nonhuman world as a less threatening and more comfortable place than did most of their contemporaries, who understood their relationship with the forces of nature primarily as a struggle for survival" (1988: 20). Ritvo suggests that the increasing practice of keeping pets is connected to a revaluation of the softer, so-called feminine emotions, what an earlier age would call, and perhaps we still call, emotional indulgences. Following these suggestions from both Thomas and Ritvo, I want to argue that in the closeness that petkeeping establishes between humans and animals lies not only the temptation of projection, born of narcissism and manipulation, but also the magnification of an excess that can be liberating, for people and animals alike.

To make this argument is to move away from the confident generalizations of functionalist explanations, which try to establish a general law to cover all social interactions. Certainly, pets can be connected to human desires rather than animal needs. Because pets conjure devotion regardless of the cost, they will always represent a potential misguiding of emotions and priorities. As James Serpell notes, this connection is ancient: "The early Greek inhabitants of Sybaris in Southern Italy, whose name has since become a byword for luxury and opulence, were also besotted with lapdogs, taking them to bed with them and carrying them about wherever they went, even to public baths" (1988: 35). For those interested solely in the equal or most equal distribution of resources, then, pets are a pernicious stumbling block on the road to justice.[13] Indeed, there is a tendency among English historians to treat petkeeping as a purely Western tradition. This plays into the hands of the Marxists and functionalists, who connect pets to the rising—affluent and separated from the harsh realities of nature—middle class. Nevertheless, the story that pets are a buffer to alienation and an amenity of rising income is only one among many possible stories about the ways in which humans share their world with animals. There are also stories about those who have been victims of a culture that cannot understand animal love. "At the time of the English witch trials (1570–1700), for example, the possession of an animal pet or 'familiar' was frequently used as evidence for accusations of necromancy, and most of the victims of this persecution were elderly and financially impoverished" (Serpell, 1988: 40). Somehow, men can find it threatening when women become too close to their pets, as demonstrated by the ancient myth of Circe, who was both a mistress of animals and a witch. The culturally marginalized often have been identified with animals, treated like animals, or separated from their animals in order to maintain social divisions between the properly human and that which is subhuman and thus animal-like.

Pets cannot be reduced to characters in the simplistic story of Western progress, characters who demonstrate our anxiety over the potential purposelessness of modernization and secularization. There is a lot of evidence, in fact, that petkeeping is close to a universal phenomenon. Serpell (1986) has shown, for example, that for Native South Americans pets were extremely popular until the intrusion of Western culture brought about a decline in petkeeping practices. Indeed, he amply documents the case that petkeeping, like singing, dancing, art, and friendship, is a constant in most societies, something people prefer not to live without. The evidence is plain in the sacred stories ancient peoples liked to tell. An amazing number of creation myths from primordial peoples portray God with a dog, not explaining the creation of the dog but merely assuming that God had a dog. Ancient peoples obviously loved their dogs and could not imagine going about the work of creation without this paradigmatic companion.[14] Pets are not a modern, Western invention, as much as we would like to think so. Moreover, no single factor can explain such complex relationships.

In fact, reductive interpretations of any phenomenon are dependent on wider sets of issues that are not amenable to conceptual control. "Functional explanation, which appears to provide new explanations, is really a mode of narrative redescription" (Milbank, 1990: 111). To say that one thing really always implies something else is to substitute one story for another. What is substituted is often what is ready at hand, convenient, and already well understood. Indeed, the suspicions of functionalism are reassuring: functionalism finds in other peoples' experiences a basic level of reality, what is most true, that is what the functionalist believes to be most true of his or her own experience. It is thus comforting to think that economics drives the history of pets when it is economics with which modern Westerners are most concerned and most familiar. Suspicion turns out to be presupposition, and critique is redescription guided as much by a new mythology as analysis and investigation. Functionalist critiques of pets, then, generalize a metaphysical rule (say: all animal otherness is really human sameness) rather than relying on particular and thus personal accounts of the actual role of animals in our social lives. The passion for pets is often the object of reductive explanation because historians and theorists do not want to risk identifying with the seemingly trivial and personal. Once the particular experience of pets is taken seriously, however, general rules about what pets are and do become increasingly difficult to defend.

The personal attachment that pets create is difficult to speak about in generic terms. Scholarly discourse hardly knows what to do with such intense and apparently timeless affection. Personal devotion of this magnitude seems best left to the privacy of those who experience it. Even among friends, it can be embarrassing to talk about one's pet relationship in any detail. It seems easier to dismiss such excess than to find the appropriate words. Nonetheless, in examining the dominant discourses on animal otherness we must be sensitive not only to what is said but more importantly to what is not talked about, *how* we go about this not talking, and what that not talking might mean. As Alasdair MacIntyre has observed, "Every culture is characterized in part by what it conceals and obscures from view, by what its habits of mind prevent it from acknowledging and appropriating" (1990: 169). If our attempt to understand otherness is not merely self-referential masquerade, then we must listen to what is not said in order to understand possibilities that hitherto seemed impossible.

The Other as Personal Self

It is impossible to look at the personal ways in which pets interact with humans without relying on the methodologies of psychology. In our culture, the personal is the psychological, and psychology, like sociology, tries to give a comprehensive reading of behavior in its own specialized terms (for an overview, see Heiman, 1956). Such general readings are difficult. Surely the reasons people adopt animals are as numerous as the reasons people get married or play golf (see Garber, 1996). To one person, a pet symbolizes the spirit of freedom and independence, while to another the pet is a child substitute. Pets can be a hobby, a passion, a burden, or an afterthought to an impulsive purchase. They can represent the mysterious and the sacred or the quotidian and the everyday. For some, pets provide a way to be quiet without being lonely, while for others pets are facilitators of communication, someone to talk to and talk about as well as a way to meet other people. For children, pets can be very serious indeed. A pet's death is often the first time a child deals with the end of life. For adults, pets can give a permission to play that is often not otherwise encouraged. It is impossible to enumerate all of the binds that tie humans to animals or to reduce these binds to one master concept or motivation. Perhaps all that we can say at the most general level is that pets are about excessive emotions, and excess cannot be easily analyzed or articulated.

Although much talk about pets is informal and inexact, ethologists now study the interspecific communications between humans and pets with great subtlety and sympathy (see Beck and Katcher, 1983b). Psychologists, however, often still take Sartre's generalization as their motto in writing about pets: "When one loves children and animals *too much*, one loves them against human beings" (1981: 30).[15] Sartre assumes that excessive love in one place must betray an insufficient regard in another, as if all signs of exuberance were a diversion rather than a production of energy. However, he is not clear about the causal sequence: Does one love pets because one does not love humans, or does one's love of pets cause a lack of intraspecific love? Do pets fulfill a basic need (that could be filled in other, more healthy ways), or do they create new desires (that compete with old ones)? Psychologists frequently portray human nature in quantifiable terms, so that the love given to a dog must be taken from somebody else. After all, everybody knows people who have put their animals before their children, aging parents, or friends, to their own detriment and to the disadvantage of those they otherwise would have better loved and assisted.

Pets can be a fetish, or a petish (Szasz, 1968)—the object of all sorts of unresolved and therefore projected feelings. Like many long-term, complex, and committed relationships, the pet relationship can have elements of sexual transgression, enabling a comprehensive and relatively unconstrained display of human emotion. One can read from this relationship indications of the human's current psychological state, past repressions, or continuing unmet needs. Some psychologists have compared pets to dreams: because pets are what we make of them, they can be literally anything, and thus they usually are what we are unable consciously to desire or fear.[16]

Other psychologists emphasize the unstable combination of affection and domination in the human-pet relationship. A dog literally is the dog's love for the master, so the dog's devotion must be disciplined to create distance for both the dog and the human. Though such excess definitely cries out for organization and control, some see in domination itself the point or purpose of affection. Yi-Fu Tuan, for example, has argued that "affection is not the opposite of dominance; rather it is dominance's anodyne—it is dominance with a human face. Dominance may be cruel and exploitative, with no hint of affection in it. What it produces is the victim. On the other hand, dominance may be combined with affection, and what it produces is the pet" (1984: 1–2). Tuan insists not only that affection softens domination but also that affection is only possible in relationships of inequality. One must feel superior in order to reach out and pet. All touching is patronizing and condescending. The pet allows us to feel expansive and powerful without dealing with any resistance or unpleasant consequences to our power.

For Tuan, pets are a surplus part of the household economy, like gardens, fountains, facades, artwork, decorations, games, and toys. They are a "playful use of surplus power" (19). Like a fountain that makes water shoot upward, pets serve no useful purpose and thus circumvent the utility and efficiency of nature. Indeed, dogs bring us back to Eden, to an unspoiled garden full of the exotic that is transparent to the benign authority of human order and control. Pets thus should not be too vigorous. "The pet, if it is to find acceptance in a well-run household, must learn to be immobile—to be as unobtrusive as a piece of furniture. The single most important trick taught a dog is instant obedience to the order 'sit' or 'lie down' " (117). Pets, like meat, are a sign of the naturalness of submission. The dog exercises our need to make domination pleasurable.

In a fascinating and mischievous book about pets and sexuality, Midas Dekkers (1994) interprets every gesture of affection for an animal as a partial realization of the sexual act itself.[17] He pays the dubious compliment to the human-pet relationship of denying any difference between it and the human-human relationship. Humans are attracted to animals and love to touch them; the only difference is that the pet has all of the allure and excitement of transgression, and most people do not consummate with pets what they secretly intend. Dekkers does not allow for the possibility that human-pet relationships have their own structure and dynamic, that the affection of a human for a pet is not a stifled and limited version of human sexual intercourse. One's pet is not a substitute for human sexual partners just as one's child is not, although certainly abuses do occur. Pets arouse a different kind of affection, simultaneously very physical and very idealized. Such affection is mediated by the countless acts of responsibility petkeeping involves. Indeed, that is what attracts us to them, the possibility of a love that is incredibly intense and yet full of distance as well. In this way, pets are as much like friends, or children, as lovers, but Dekkers is right to see in pets an act of transgression with troubling social consequences. Loving an animal does violate species barriers, and it does provide an alternative expression to human relationships. It disturbs the speciesist assumption that only humans are worth loving.

The connection between pets and children deserves further exploration. Many ethologists argue that humanizing animals is a basic urge because it makes the world more familiar. In many cases, dogs have been bred in order to retain their juvenile or fetal features, such as large eyes, short legs, soft fur, large brain case, and small facial region on the skull. Neoteny (see Lawrence, 1989), the retention of the appearance and behavior of infancy or adolescence in adult animals, is the guiding force of domestication. The extreme submissiveness and excessive demands for attention of the dog are a continuation of puppy characteristics. Some people argue that we select for neotenic traits out of a dark urge to trivialize animals or to satisfy some sentimental human need, while Konrad Lorenz (1981) has argued that we have an innate preference for juvenile-looking animals, but actually these traits—lack of aggressiveness, fear, and territoriality, and the need for touching and protection—are the exact characteristics animals need in order to succeed in the human world. Domesticated animals are not debilitated and degenerative but well adapted to their environment. Mutual dependence and cooperation are the keys to survival as the nature of nature continues to change under the pressure of population growth.

Under such conditions, domesticated animals can teach us important lessons. Caring for a dog is, in a way, an extension (or substitute) for the nurturing given to human infants. Although some psychologists see animal nurturing as a retreat from human contact, it is now common knowledge that petkeeping is a biologically healthy activity (which makes it particularly tragic that elderly people are often forcibly separated from their pets when they enter nursing homes or federally subsidized housing). In medical terms, pets lower blood pressure, reduce some mental disorders, and protect from heart diseases like hypertension. Indeed, if the language of contemporary society is thoroughly psychological, then it makes sense that people now try to justify their enormous expenditures of resources and affection on pets in terms of the mental health they provide.[18] Alan Beck and Aaron Katcher refer to studies that show that pets make beneficial contributions to married people as much as they do to single people, which suggests that "pets do not just substitute for human relationships, they complement and add to them, giving a special and unique dimension to human life" (1983a: 22–23).[19] Animals are beneficial to us in part, Beck and Katcher argue, because they are indifferent to our social status, age, health, beauty, and other variables. Pets are a source of constant affection in lives that can change quickly and without warning. When a dog greets us at the door, the welcome signals that everything is as it was, safe and comforting.

The pet tells us that we have not changed, no matter how many changes we go through.

Pets also draw us out of ourselves. They are innocent, and thus they do not need to be perfected; they can be accepted as they are, with few expectations or demands. They also offer us an opportunity to play that is often denied after childhood. In playing with pets, we must keep their attention, but we are not involved in serious competition. Most significantly, feeding and loving animals holds us to the external world in habitual and pleasurable ways. We put up with the excrement of cats and dogs just as we handle the excrement of infants. Pets provide a step toward nurturing the entire planet, encouraging us to acknowledge the intermingling of hopes and destinies in a world growing ever smaller. Such love is not something we can enact in very many spheres of our existence. "Loving animals," Beck and Katcher write, "is thought to be a little bit childish, like crying at the movies. It feels good as long as no one brings up the house lights too quickly" (1983a: 39–40). We can keep alive certain elements of our childhood by loving pets. What we love in our pets is, in a sense, love itself, which we too frequently experience in indirect and nameless ways.

Pets play changing roles based not only on what we need but also on their own personalities and preferences. Because they represent a superabundance of love, pets can be parental figures as well as children figures. "The truth is that with our pets we are both mother and child, simultaneously and alternatively, with the pet playing the opposite part" (Beck and Katcher, 1983a: 86). Pets are not only family relations but also teachers. Much of the Pet Facilitated Therapy movement is predicated on the possibility of pets teaching us what we do not already know. Older cultures understood that there was much to learn from animals. As Beck and Katcher recall, "Chiron, the half-man half-horse centaur of Greek mythology, was the first physician and teacher of Aesculapius and could be considered the first pet therapist, or perhaps the prototype, teaching and curing" (164). Beck and Katcher suggest that today the pet can be considered a therapeutic clown, a kind of Id on four legs. Dogs, for example, represent to us the urges and habits that civilization makes impossible. They settle disputes with their teeth, eat garbage, break sexual taboos, defecate and lick themselves in public, think through smelling, eat in a gluttonous manner, and sleep in our beds, something we deny our children. "Dog feces become, for us, the only acceptable way to represent shit" (210). They are loved and cursed for essentially the same traits. Above all, they love unconditionally, which is something we praise but also suspect. Such unbounded devotion is often considered foolish and cowardly. It is easy to take advantage of this submission, and dogs are extremely vulnerable because they often love even those who abuse them.

Beck and Katcher end their book with a chapter on "being a pet." "The gifts that pets give us are too important to be exchanged only between animals and people. People can learn how to substitute for pets in certain emergency situations and take over their functions in others, as pets sometimes substitute for people" (288). In other words, the category "pet" does not apply to animals alone. Being a pet involves listening without speaking, talking through touching, finding joy in ceremonial greetings and submissive behavior, as well as allowing oneself to be touched. It consists of a certain kind of giving as well as receiving, an economy of generosity that transgresses the usual and expected. It also provides an opportunity for feelings of devotion that border on the sacred. "A loving worship of God should be fulfilling for people who want to have comfort from submissive, obedient love. Perhaps the dog is fulfilling a religious vacuum" (291). In the dog not only do we experience the obedience that we ourselves can know before God on occasion, but also we give to dogs as we want God to give to us. We enter into a relationship that is unbounded, intense, and all-encompassing. It is also a relationship that changes us, and we can imagine moving outward into other relationships with the same dynamic of giving and taking.

Dogs belong to the imaginary, the symbolic, the realm of fantasy. They give us a theater of emotions in which great melodramas of loyalty and devotion can be enacted with little or no actual consequences or complications. We can give so much to our animal companions because our motives are never doubted and reciprocity is insured. "These pets give their owners access to a sensual dialogue combining touch, talk, and mutual attention with a superabundance usually not available from other human beings" (Beck and Katcher, 1988: 55). Is this giving pure make-believe? Does it really create no obligations, leaving our daily lives the same, not altering our schedules let alone our basic attitudes and long-term memories? Much of the psychological literature that is positive about pets lapses into anthropomorphism by treating pets as an easy means of strengthening the fragile ego; psychologists thus inadvertently continue the tradition of valuing animals only as instruments for human benefit. I think pets challenge as well as console. Petting can overcome the arrogant eye— the white male gaze—that Carol Adams connects to vivisection. Animals help to decenter the human subject by changing the subject from human preoccupations to the concerns of others. As Gertrude Stein famously wrote in *The Geographical History of America* (1936), in opposition to the Cartesian cogito ergo sum, which equates individuality with rationality and autonomy, "I am I because my little dog knows me" (71). Human identity is radically relational, and we are constituted by the animals as well as the humans who know us. Pets know us in ways that differ from the ways we know ourselves. What we need is a further investigation of the twin themes of otherness and excess to see how they intersect and to measure the value of that which is more than we need but all that we desire.

By talking about the personal dimension of companion animals, then, I do not mean to suggest that pets represent some innocent field of experience, unpolluted by conceptual, social, or historical difficulties. Indeed, the personal is as much a construction as the social is. I do, however, want to listen to what pets do for individuals not by ignoring the social but by analyzing the language that governs this particular relationship, the stories people tell about pets, and the ways in which people who spend a lot of time with pets talk about their relationships. In the next chapter I will argue that when we listen closely to this language, we can hear something excessive that resists functionalism in all of its forms and promotes an expenditure of energy, attention, and care—mixed with and mediated through, no doubt, manipulation, domination, and cruelty—that nonetheless can guide our thinking about animals in ways that are liberating and transformative.

CHAPTER FOUR

The Difference That Dogs Make

Pets, Women, Meat, and Rhetoric

Perhaps something about theology makes it inimical to dogtalk. After all, theology is a serious thing, and the nature of seriousness is gravity, sobriety, and productivity. All scholarship approaches objects only under the cover, or category, of labor, working with material to get results, breaking things apart and seeing how they can be put back together, dissecting discourses as well as living beings. Dogtalk, by contrast, is a kind of luxury, something personal and private, an aspect of leisure. It inevitably appears, in the context of scholarly analysis, as amusing but wasteful, extravagant and conspicuous, an indiscretion broached only under the sign of excess, of hyperbole. This is, in fact, how we often treat our dogs, as extraeconomical objects, nonuseful splurges, recipients of surplus, frivolous affection, things to be given as gifts and given to with abandon, things to be treated, in a word, as toys.

A series of questions immediately arises: If conceptual and scholarly language fails to locate dogs as we experience them, is there a discourse that is more appropriate to dogs? If every subject matter has its own most appropriate rhetoric, what is the rhetoric of pets? Moreover, can this discourse teach us something about both the value of other animals and the limits to our search for understanding? Does the rhetoric that is peculiar to dogs entail an ethical dimension?

There is a rhetoric of dogtalk that is well known to dog lovers, even though it is not studied much by scholars. I am referring to the genre called animal literature, which can include sophisticated works of art, even though most dog stories tend to be informal. Indeed, what seems to keep such stories from being taken seriously by academicians is the fact that they appeal to such a wide audience and can be told by just about anybody. Dog stories are democratic; expertise is irrelevant to their telling or their interpretation. They are, supposedly, insufficiently complex to generate the kinds of multiple readings that keep scholarly analyses feeding on each other. They tend more toward intimacy and passion than ambiguity and irony. They often do not have a point beyond the particularity of this person and this animal and the amazing ways in which this person cares for this animal and this animal returns that care. Because animal care is privatized in our culture, such stories are treated as mere rhetoric, words without substance, stories told just for the fun of it. In fact, the discourse about pets resembles the discourse about rhetoric. An analogy exists between the two, in that both pets and rhetoric are embellishments that are enjoyable but not very serious or useful.

Rhetoric, of course, is a human art. By definition, rhetoric is employed when persuasion must rely on personal experience rather than the facts. In contrast to scientific documents, rhetorical texts are saturated rather than vacated by the author's style and presence. Another distinction between rhetorical and literal discourse is that rhetoric is self-referential in a way that scientific discourse is not. As with poetry, rhetorical language often seems to be about language itself: the sound of the words is as important as their meaning. Words become excessive, in the precise sense that they do not have a particular function. More words are used than is efficiently necessary to make a point. In a culture dedicated to precision and control, rhetorical language is troubling and frustrating. It should not be surprising that philosophers have connected rhetoric with femininity. "Eloquence," writes John Locke, "like the fair sex, has too prevailing beauties in it to suffer itself ever to be spoken against. And it is in vain to find fault with those arts of deceiving, wherein men find pleasure to be deceived" (1984: 147). Women epitomize rhetoric because their marginalization makes them useful (to men) only as diversions and distractions. In a patriarchal culture, women are perceived to be more related to style than to substance.

Carol J. Adams, in *The Sexual Politics of Meat,* (1990), argues that animals are as much the victims of the language we use as women are. Both are paradigms of what she calls the absent referent. In other words, our use of language incorporates animals as symbols and metaphors, the stuff of style, while real animals disappear. It is difficult to find any logic in the ways we make animals meaningful because in practice they always signify something specific but in theory they can represent literally anything. The world of animals thus can serve to symbolize, mirror, or echo the human world, allowing us to say things about ourselves in creative and oblique ways. For example, in most literature where they appear at all, animals are nothing but figures, rhetorical embellishments or marginal tropes; they are not to be taken literally, on their own terms.

The metaphorical nature of animal language means that the actual use of animals is affected by the way we talk. It is acceptable to abuse animals because they represent, in discourse, that which stands for something else. Animals as metaphors have no integrity of their own, and thus they are naturally inferior. Perhaps this is why women are often animalized in order to express male desires for domination. In male sexual fantasies, women are edible, to be hunted or farmed in meat markets, their body parts weighed and analyzed. Of course, animals are metaphors for positive values as well, as when we talk about someone being as loyal as a dog or having the courage of a lion. Whatever they stand for, however, animals are rarely allowed to stand for themselves.

The linguistic eclipse of animals is correlated to (both preparing and made possible by) their annihilation in the meals we serve, so that practice and discourse shape each other. Indeed, it seems that we are not able to take animals seriously precisely because we eat them. When we eat, we do not even think about where our food comes from and how it was prepared, so our talk about animals is a way of expressing and justifying this shallow thoughtlessness and callous disregard. As Steve Baker observes, "Contemptuous rhetoric is quite openly employed by the public, while at the same time much care is taken to conceal the contemptible practices from the view of that same public" (1993: 90). We say what we cannot think in order to keep from thinking what we cannot say. Whether through rhetorical embellishment or processing and packaging, animals exist in order to cease existing. How could we talk otherwise about animals when they exist only in our mouths, whether as words or food?

The connection between how we talk about animals and what we do with them—that is, how we eat them—is worth exploring in more detail. If metaphysics is the search for ultimate certainty, order, and stability, a search that, at least since Descartes, has focused on the human as the source and criterion of all value, then the culinary expression of metaphysics is the carnivorous diet, the way in which meat must be at the center of every meal, representing the substance or essence of eating.[1] The very word "meat," after all, is synonymous with essence. Borrowing a term from Willard Quine, Carol J. Adams calls meat a "mass term," a concept that denies individuality. "Mass terms refer to things like water or colors; no matter how much you have of it, or what type of container it is in, water is still water" (1994: 27). Meat is meat, whether living or dead, raised, slaughtered, processed, or packaged. "Meat" is a noun that needs no modification because it does not admit to specification; it is simply there, to be eaten. Consuming animals (the oldest violence) quite literally reduces the other to the same, with meat serving as the first principle, the condition for the possibility of, the subject whose appropriation of otherness obliterates all differences.

What began as a religious ritual and was then connected to luxury and surplus has now become a habit, something expected, demanded, but not thought. When we drink cow's milk, for example, an incredibly intimate act of dependence, few people think about the cows that are utilized for our benefit (see Shwabe,1984: 50–57). The cow, unthought, disappears. For most people in the modern West today, a meal without meat simply is not a meal; a meatless meal is thus unthinkable. Meat literally lies at the center of our plates, while supplemental vegetables are mere embellishment, rhetorical complements to a central and necessary core. When we ask what's for dinner, we mean what kind of meat. In this context, a vegetarian diet would be the willingness to eat without order or structure, a nonsquare meal freed from the desire to center the meal on the appropriation (ingestion, introjection, incorporation) of otherness.

While we cannot say what meat does not permit us to think (the dignity of animals), meat does enable us to express, according to Nick Fiddes, our superiority over nature: "Consuming the muscle flesh of other highly evolved animals is a potent statement of our supreme power" (1991: 2).[2] The supporting beliefs associated with meat are illuminating. Many histories of human evolution assert that hunting, not gathering and foraging, first separated us from the other animals, while prehuman "noble savages" are still frequently described as vegetarians. According to these speculations, meat eating literally created man, including the gender differentiation we still grapple with. Today we eat meat only from animals that we have domesticated; we are not, after all, scavengers. To eat meat is to be civilized, even though it was once a widespread belief that animals tasted better if they suffered a cruel death. Magically, to eat meat is to gain the strength and aggression of the animal eaten. Meat is heavy and substantial, and although it is commonly known that taste is a social construct, for most people only meat satisfies a certain voracious hunger. Beef is so connected to aggression and vigor that it is as much a verb (usually used with "up") as a noun, meaning both to reinforce and to complain. The redder the meat is, the more it is real meat; "bloodless" meat, like chicken and fish, is not considered meat at all by some people, and eggs and cheese are called "animal products" because they are the furthest removed from the essence of blood.

Of course, meat is also the most common food for avoidance, taboo, and regulation. Eating needs regulation because it is an intimate act that breaches bodily boundaries. Such intimacy cries out for social and moral comment. However, such rules usually have little to do with the animals themselves. Christian fasting from meat, for example, such as during Lent, is more about the surrendering of luxuries than about the anticipation of a vegetarian world. Such restrictions continue today, at a time when meat consumption is in decline, even as supermarkets replace local butchers and meat is packaged in ways that obscure its origins. Meat is a target of avoidance precisely because it is thought to be something special. Drawing on the fact that many ancient societies expend more energy hunting animals for meat than they gain by consuming them, Fiddes argues that meat is valuable not because it is cheap and efficiently produced; on the contrary, meat is valued because of its inefficiency and waste. Meat is always an extravagance, a sign of surplus, the triumph of strenuous human effort rather than the product of the careful stewardship of resources. It is a status item because it does not make good economic sense. It is more than we need for food, signifying our transcendence of depending on food merely for the sake of nourishment. In an era that turns every luxury into a necessity, meat is what we need in order to demonstrate the unlimited quality of our appetites.

Must the rhetoric we use to discuss animals always assimilate, like the meals we eat, animal otherness to human expectations? Does animal literature, for example, necessarily serve up animals, whether talking or not, on the plate of human interests and desires? Is there a kind of vegetarian discourse that permits the animal other to be really other, while originating from the mouths of carnivorous, meaning greedy, humans? Is reading an act of voracious consumption, or can it be something else—giving, feeding, petting—as well? These questions are not merely rhetorical, although they are about rhetoric.

Received wisdom delegates to childhood the ability to like or befriend animals. Some, like Bruno Bettelheim, have argued that this ability is connected to a natural state of animism in childhood, where children, like primitive peoples, are not able to utilize categories to differentiate between humans and nonhumans.[3] Everything is alive for children, and animals are just like us. Animal stories are thus an important access to the original imagination of humankind, but they also serve as a disenchanting rite of passage. In Bettelheim's psychoanalytic perspective, fairy-tale animals are not at all real. They merely facilitate the negotiation of the various conflicts of growing up. Indeed, a surprising number of children's books portray the "sacrifice" of a loved animal as a necessary step toward maturity. The death of an animal marks the transition from an imagination that is unbounded and inclusive to a conceptual awareness of absolute differences and rigid hierarchies. Animal stories teach children that they must learn to let go of animals as they grow older, and as children withdraw from animals they also turn away from the animal stories themselves. Animal stories are thus stigmatized as being for children alone, often read to them by women. Talking animals do appear in more sophisticated works of literature, but their very talking makes them transparent symbols of human reality.[4] Adults are supposed to be able to recognize that animals do not matter unless they say something about us.

As a general rule, then, animals vanish in the signs that represent them. Steve Baker explains: "The animal is the sign of all that is taken not-very-seriously in contemporary culture; the sign of that which doesn't really matter" (1993: 174). We see animals only as something else. They are a product of our own investments, and they contribute to our profit as passive and silent partners. Baker is pessimistic about the possibilities of representing animals in a more positive light. Animal art, for Baker, is irredeemably kitsch. "The reason is clear: the animal artist is too often concerned with the subject, the animal itself, and not with the proper and serious exercising of aesthetic discrimination. There appears to be an inverse relationship between the aesthetic seriousness of the image and the viewer's interest in the animal" (193). True, when people think of animal paintings, they often think of Edwin Landseer's early nineteenth-century dog paintings, which are saturated with human emotion and morality.[5] Baker puts the animal artist in a difficult bind: the more she emphasizes the actual animal, the less aesthetically successful her art will be. Baker's pessimism is thorough. All representations are cultural constructions, not natural depictions, so that the disappearance of animals for Baker is, in the end, inevitable, even natural. He does hold out some hope for images of animal abuse that are too difficult to look at, images that are awkward, upsetting, and provocative but nonetheless show the animal as an animal. The problem is to get people to see what they do not want to see, indeed, what they have not seen before, which is a difficult task.

Shocking images of animal abuse are not the only way to urge animal care. Stories that show the particularity of animal passion can affect readers as well. Martha Nussbaum (1990: 36–42) has argued that novels are crucial for philosophical and ethical reflection because they portray a world with qualitative differences not easily reconciled and because they sharpen our perception of these differences. At the same time, novels show us that there is an emotional quality to our discriminating responses to the world and, furthermore, that our emotions are tied to chance events that are out of our control. The crucial question is whether, in our various languages about animals, the possibility exists for animal otherness to appear not as something pure and unspoiled by human intervention but rather as a remainder, a surplus or waste that resists human digestion. Like Argos recognizing Odysseus upon his return home, can animals be portrayed as just themselves yet also that to which we turn to find ourselves? Are animals excessive to the point of forcing their otherness on us in ways that we cannot explain or deny?

Probably the most important feature of petkeeping is that pets are not overtly functional: they require financial sacrifices even for those with much disposable income. Although pets are bought and sold, in an important sense they reside outside of the economic order. Pets are excessive, both in terms of the unreasonable demands they make upon us and the attention we so readily give to them. They are emblematic of what Thorstein Veblen calls conspicuous consumption,[6] a commodity with no social utility or public purpose. They do not, in other words, add to the gross national product or increase anyone's efficiency. Such objects have, as the contemporary French philosopher Jean Baudrillard puts it, purely symbolic value because they are disconnected from the calculations of exchange, but they are not thereby emptied of any referential content.[7] Keith Thomas argues that it is precisely their uselessness that made petkeeping morally significant. Petkeeping

> encouraged the middle class to form optimistic conclusions about animal intelligence; it gave rise to innumerable anecdotes about animal sagacity; it stimulated the notion that animals could have character and individual personality; and it created the psychological foundation for the view that some animals at least were entitled to moral consideration. It is no coincidence that many, if not indeed the majority, of those who wrote on behalf of animals in the eighteenth century were, like Pope or Cowper or Bentham, persons who had themselves formed close relationships with cats, dogs or other pets. (1983: 119)

Pets, like any good gift, are demanding, and gratitude is a kind of labor. They force, by their very excess, a recognition of an animal reality independent of the human world. However, it remains contradictory to claim that something useless can be so useful, that something excessive can serve such definite ends. What is needed is a double investigation of excess and otherness in order to show how something so extravagant can also be so transformative.

Vicki Hearne on the Language of Training

No one has more thoughtfully meditated on the ethical significance of animals, dogs in particular, than Vicki Hearne. In *Adam's Task: Calling Animals by Name*, (1986), she pushes for a return to more traditional ways of looking at animals, and in fact, her own work is in continuity with classic stories like Rin Tin Tin, Lassie, and Black Beauty, the stories by which children were once taught the virtues of loyalty, trust, and bravery. Her basic argument concerns the defense of anthropomorphic language: the dignity of the discourse of animal trainers over against behaviorists and philosophers. Animals generate "skeptical terror" in us (a phrase she adopts from Stanley Cavell), testing the limits of our knowledge and our capacity to imagine real otherness. Animal trainers use morally loaded language, telling stories about heroism, courage, and grace, values that now seem to be archaic and antiquated. Animal stories seem to belong to a distant past, to childhoods that are now impossible to re-create, to a naive valorization of virtues that today seem irredeemably suspect and innocent. Yet these are the stories that trainers use to make sense of their animals, and, speaking strictly pragmatically, they work. Indeed, you can change an animal's behavior not just by using modification techniques but also by changing the story you tell about the animal.

Animals, Hearne suggests, seem to be aware of the stories we tell about them, want us to tell the right stories, and help us to tell those stories, if we let them.

If we treat them like Cartesian machines, then perhaps that is how they will appear to us, fulfilling our narrow projections, but even then individuality, alertness, and intelligence remain as a residue after we have reached the limits of behaviorism. In training animals we teach ourselves to respond to and learn from individuals who share enough of our world that they are able to stretch it further than the bonds of our language ordinarily allow. Training demands that we listen to the language of animals, a language that is unspoken, extralinguistic, but communicative nonetheless. Although many animal lovers today look at training as a restrictive and imperial (hierarchical) intervention into the carefree and wild life of the animal, training is actually a kind of language that requests the obedience of the animal only in order to expand the animal's capacities for responsibility, to enhance the animal's awareness of the human environment in which the animal lives, and to encourage the animal's desires for disciplined and thoughtful activity.

The main lesson the language of animal training teaches is the need to be responsive to otherness. Understanding is the prerequisite for Adam's task of naming. Naming a dog is not a poetic act of using language without reference; instead, the name invokes a relationship, thus making a difference in the world. For dogs, Hearne argues, loyalty and meaning are interdependent. Dogs are very attentive to surface grammar; we are not so. We need deep knowledge to understand their very basic alertness, and when dogs do not fit into our notion of what they should be or do, we can quickly turn against them in frustration and anger. Dogs, by contrast, are very reassuring when we become skeptical about them, when we lose our way in this realm of wordless language. We value skepticism, but they are clownish, foolish, and excessive in their desire to please and cooperate. When they are disobedient, it is often a sign that they, probably rightly, distrust our authority and intelligence. Yet they are very forgiving. "Dogs are in general more skilled at belief than we are" (1986: 60). Like forgiveness, animals are a gift: they come to us with their own beauty and dignity, and they plead for our patience and understanding. In turn, they give us more than we could otherwise have known about ourselves by allowing us to venture into a relationship that goes further, due to its very awkwardnesses and limitations, than the boundaries of human language normally permit. "The fact that animals are so generous in answering us is what makes it not only okay to train them but a human duty, one way we enact our gratitude to the universe that animals exist" (265). By accepting our overtures, dogs return the gift that we want to give them by demanding our patience and understanding as prerequisites to our knowledge. We are thus able to redeem our ineptitude by persisting at the negotiations of what can only be called friendship.

In *Bandit* (1992), Hearne's book on what she calls the pit-bull wars, she lashes out at the lack of imagination that North American discourse on dogs betrays. "We have replaced dogs with ragged ungrammatical words, traded awareness for an autistic, crippled, resentful, and violent language" (54). Arguing against the privatization of pets, she suggests that well-trained dogs should have greater access to the various forms of our public square. Unfortunately, we seem to be afraid today of dogs with strong temperaments and personalities, dogs who like challenges, who need obstacles—dogs who demand that we read them differently than we would like. "The difference between commanding a dog to sit and commanding him to retrieve or negotiate obstacles is like the difference between requiring mannerly behavior in a classroom and commanding the students to draw a picture or write a poem" (62). Maybe we just do not know what it is to command anymore, to assert warranted authority, to take responsibility for issuing an appropriate order. We seem to think that we must either consume animals or let them roam free, and there is no middle ground between these two attitudes.

Consequently, loving animals becomes a substitute for knowledge, which is born only through a shared activity of trust and commitment. "Love makes mistakes about this with animals. Love whispers at people like the very devil" (90). Brutality results from not wanting to know, from intellectual carelessness and from ethical shortsightedness (which are, for Hearne, the same thing). Tender mercies, she suspects, are too frequently cruel (Proverbs 12:10). She replaces the language of love and kindness not with the scientific pursuit of objectivity and its distanciation of testing and evaluation but with the participation of training and its emphasis on obedience and commands. For Hearne, dogs are work, not leisure, and training is an act of translation, not a poetic profusion. We have to work to deserve the right to a dog's obedience; otherwise, that obedience is tainted by our lack of moral courage to see through our own limitations and desires.[8]

Love, like learning, Hearne insists, must be earned. Nevertheless, Hearne's theology of good works and merit does not deny the role of pleasure in our relationship with animals. In her most recent book, *Animal Happiness* (1994), she says that her own happiness lies in the variety and independence of animal minds, while she also realizes that the happiness of animals, as when one's dog tips over the garbage can, often conflicts with our own.[9] What she resists is mystifying animals, "as if they were, like lovers or gold, more precious when uninterpretable" (167). She takes communication with animals as a given, which makes her response to Wittgenstein's lion comment, which I briefly discussed in the introduction, so interesting. Too often when we imagine an other animal we are merely imagining ourselves without language, and since we are defined by language, we can imagine nothing. Yet the lion's not talking does not deny that communication, even language is occurring. "The silence of Wittgenstein's lion is like many of Wittgenstein's own silences: there is something there" (169). She compares such vocal silence to the Kabbalah's notion of *zimzum*, God's voluntary withdrawal from the world. In fact, whenever a person meets a lion, the lion is tremendously present and hard to ignore, no matter how silent. But it is in the training situation where communication is most obvious. The lion and the trainer both know exactly what they are saying to each other.[10] The command "stay," in the context of the world created by the countless exchanges of training, means something quite specific: the lion's posture is its response to the request. Animals, especially wild animals, are reticent to read our behavior, to obey our signs, but when a relationship with an animal is established, we experience not some primordial innocence but rather the attainment of knowledge made possible by care and attention.[11] Concerning such training Hearne comments, "Nor is this a realm of love, a Christian realm. It is a realm, rather, of Respect" (173).

The priority of respect over love is reinforced in Hearne's insightful reading of the Book of Job. Chapters 39, 40, and 41 of Job contain vivid and exact descriptions of wild animals, including the wild goat, the unicorn, the peacock, the ostrich, the hawk, and the eagle. These descriptions demonstrate the author's remarkable knowledge of and admiration for animals. Job, as Hearne points out, was a successful herdsman, so he must have known domesticated animals well, and he complains (in 30:1) that he would not let the fathers of those who mock him handle the dogs guarding his flock, suggesting that they are too depraved to exercise the craft of dog training. In one remarkable passage, Job calls on the animals of the world to defend him by teaching his friends: "Go and ask the cattle, ask the birds of the air to inform you, or tell the creatures that crawl to teach you, and the fishes of the sea to give you instruction" (12:7–8, NEB).

Yet the Voice from the Whirlwind reminds Job that God's knowledge of all animals is so much greater than any human comprehension. Wild animals do not recognize human accomplishments of any form; indeed, the very fact of undomesticated animals strips us of our righteousness. "So when the Voice tells Job that the unicorn does not have a working temperament, it is reminding him that there is a vast world of significance, meaning and earthly—that is, ordinary—divinities that is outside of the nobilities, charities, and righteousnesses of Job's condition as an animal husbandman" (Hearne, 1994: 226). God is teaching Job the limits to his knowledge; animals give us humility if we properly receive their gift. Even more important for Hearne, God is teaching Job the limits to love. "You might say that what God tells Job is that he is not capable of being kind, of fully desiring kindness, toward the whole planet" (227). Humans have to be guided by what we know, which is tightly confined to our finitude and the world's complexity, and not by what we desire.

The constructive result of these investigations—"a rebuke to moral excesses" (238)—is as challenging to the animal rights movement as it is to Christian love. Hearne thinks that too often animal rights philosophers are more concerned about the capacity for animals to feel pain than about their abilities for creativity and imagination. Consequently, such philosophers too frequently want to protect animals by removing them from all human interference and interaction. "What I hear in this," she responds, "and in much of what is touted as a new concern for animals and for the environment, is despair at the possibility of the hearth, of what is secure, domestic, of what you might call a cozy rationality" (191). We do not have the luxury of leaving nature alone, she argues, so that training can teach us something about the burden of our responsibilities. Indeed, kindness, for Hearne, is never impersonal. Rights should be a result of relationships and obligations, not abstract laws, universal rules, and generalized feelings.

She thus argues that the state cannot give rights to animals because animals recognize only their owners, and it is owners who must speak for their animals. "Hence it is not an incidental or accidental but a central fact that in practice the only way a dog's rights are protected, against neighbors or the state, is *by way of an appeal to the owner's property rights in the dog*" (213). She realizes that many owners do mistreat their dogs, but she gets around this point by arguing that proper ownership means owning up to one's dog, being deserving of his or her loyalty. What she is afraid of is having others, whether the state or those who are against animal training, tell her what she can or cannot do with her animals. The misguided kindness of strangers is the worst kind of generosity. Yet her position seems to restrict the power implicit in our relationships with animals. Ownership limits the value of animals to the laws protecting property, dismissing or diminishing the transformative dynamic that intimate relationships with animals can evoke. Thinking of animals as gifts, not possessions, I have argued, not only urges the improved treatment of companion animals but also enables us to extend the pet relationship to wider and wider circles of animal care and concern.

Keeping the Other Other

What Hearne is looking for is a new kind of language within which we can frame our understanding of animals, a language to which the animals themselves would contribute. She relies on the language of animal trainers, but she also encourages a reevaluation of literature, of story telling, as a way of getting at animal otherness. For Hearne, animal stories should have a moral point, a lesson about the limits to kindness and the need to discipline our knowledge through the practice of attention and the following of rules. "Obedience is reciprocal, and you cannot get responses from a dog to whom you do not respond accurately; I have enfranchised him in relationship to me by educating him" (212). Animal stories certainly can illustrate moral lessons or rules. To the extent that they merely exemplify a general principle, however, they risk reducing the animal in the story to a means to some extrinsic end. The story about the animal becomes a story that is really about us. In other words, it is a story that could be told in some other way, about something else, but still with the same point or message.[12]

There is another kind of story that is in contrast to Hearne's celebration of the human ability to name animals, to call them into human society and interaction. These are stories that celebrate the animal's aloofness from human society. They represent animals as creatures that are valuable precisely because they do not need us. For example, in the climax to Jack London's classic *The Call of the Wild* (1903), the dog named Buck ascends in the Alaskan frontier into the atavistic and the primordial. Buck is masculine, rugged, courageous, and, when he finally leaves John Thornton, he joins the wolves and learns how to hunt. In the wild he is finally free. In Donald McCaig's *Nop's Trials* (1984), Nop, a Border Collie, loves his work more than human companionship, and that is what he returns to in the end. The dogs in Richard Adams's *The Plague Dogs* (1977) escape from research terror into the wilderness, suggesting these two scenes as the only alternatives to each other. Elizabeth Marshall Thomas employs anthropomorphism in order to enter into the world of dogs, not the relationships between dogs and humans, in the nonfiction work, *The Hidden Life of Dogs* (1993). Her book ends with the dogs building a secret cave and one dog disappearing into the woods. The author tries to find her, and indeed, "year after year our search continues" (138), but the dog (in fact, all dogs) cannot be found. "Our efforts were absolutely useless" (138). The point is that animals must leave us, and we must let them go. The pet in the dog is only (human) skin-deep. The most we can give our dogs is to let them be. In her most recent book, *Certain Poor Shepherds* (1996), Thomas tells the story of a dog and a goat who journey to Bethlehem on the first Christmas day but are in search of animal, not human, companionship. "No redeemer appeared for the animals; however, none was needed. The animals were much the same then as they are now, just as God made them, perfect according to his plan" (13).

From Melville's whale to Faulkner's bear and Hemingway's bulls, American literature, as Mary Allen (1983) has demonstrated, is especially full of realistic animals, powerful actors in human dramas, capable of interfering with human affairs. Wild animals represent the pure locomotion of individuality and freedom, the opposite of social constraint and domesticity; therefore, pets in American literature (in contrast to British literature, which is more sympathetic to domestic settings) are rare. Animals are praised in proportion to their distance from human manipulation and satisfaction. The animal rights movement tends to support this attitude when it propagates images and narratives that most often exemplify the genre of the horror story. All contact with animals, these stories imply, leads to cruelty and death; therefore, only by removing animals from human hands can they be saved. By emphasizing the predominance of human attempts to control and use animals by any possible method, the animal rights movement blurs together all human relationships with animals, leaving human absence as the only viable option for animal liberation.

In a short piece of fantasy fiction entitled "She Unnames Them," Ursula K. Le Guin imagines the radical, feminist reversal of Hearne's (by implication, masculine) process of naming and domestication (1987: 233–6).[13] In Le Guin's story, a new Eve begins to withdraw human language from the animal world, and few animals other than pets resist this return of the human gift. Although cats "steadfastly denied ever having had any name other than those self-given" (234), dogs insist that their names are a part of who they are and can be persuaded to part with them only when told that they could still be called anything they prefer. The process of unnaming brings the animals closer to the narrator, but not in any sentimental or suffocating way: "They seemed far closer than when their names had stood between myself and them like a clear barrier: so close that my fear of them and their fear of me became one same fear" (235). A primal unity ensues, and the narrator decides that she cannot make an exception for herself. She petitions Adam and gently gives back her name, while trying not to sound impolite or ungrateful. Adam, distant and preoccupied, hardly notices, and she departs with the animals, determined to make her words "as slow, as new, as single, as tentative as the steps I took going down the path away from the house, between the dark-branched, tall dancers motionless against the winter shining" (236). Her descent into nature is made possible by her rebellion against the tyranny of words, the ways in which nouns generalize away specificity, concepts attenuate complexity, and categories diminish vitality. She is drawn toward a silence that levels all conventional differences in the hope that more natural distinctions might be born.

The story is a wonderful fantasy of wordless communion with otherness. The fact that it is a fantasy, however, makes one wonder about the potential for a naming that does not capture and control. Does all naming imprison or betray the other? Is there an Edenic naming that is active, outward reaching, full of hopeful longing and trusting awareness? I noted in chapter 2 that domestication is not always controlled by human intention. Dogs, for example, are a kind of social parasite on humans. "Their survival," Stephen Budiansky writes, "has nothing to do with being rewarded for their utility to man. It has to do rather with their superb adaptation to human society" (1992: 36). In many cases of domestication, the taming goes both ways. Not all relationships are predator-prey; mutualistic, symbiotic relationships are common and ingenious throughout nature. Domestication should serve to remind us that freedom is not an absolute value; instead, community and belonging are also of utmost importance. Nature cannot be purified of human presence; instead, we must learn to name that which is more than us in order to call it forth even further into a mutuality that enhances and expands.

Reading Excess

In contrast to both Hearne's focus on discipline and Le Guin's defense of the wild and untamed, a third kind of story is often told about dog-human relationships in which the excessive nature of mutual devotion is itself the theme of the plot.[14] This is the kind of story that dog lovers tell every day, and admittedly, such stories can border on the sentimental and idiosyncratic. The love for pets has its own rhythm, its own rhetoric and grammar, as Wittgenstein would say. To use another Wittgensteinian distinction, perhaps the human-dog relationship shows us something that cannot be said or that cannot be said in any straightforward manner. These stories often have only private meaning; they demonstrate that the imagination seems always coupled with interests that limit our capacity to communicate our particular passions to others. Nevertheless, by relating the intensity of our commitments—by publicizing the domain of the private—animals can be inserted into the world of human affairs with a passion that is hard to deny or contain.

If style is connected not only to content but also to the virtue or the good that the narrative seeks to convey, then the exuberance of some animal stories will suggest a moral point that is in contrast to the economics of a language that seeks to organize, order, and utilize. Dog stories, for example, if they are true to their subject, cannot be anything but extravagant; otherwise, their form would betray their content, and they could not show what they have to say. Such rhetorical excess is the site of the animal's presence. Dogs appear, that is, not only as characters in dogs stories but also in the story's tone, its embellishments, and its gushing eagerness to persuade and please. Dogs are a form of excess, an embodiment of hyperbole, and thus they extend and amplify our emotions and perceptions along unpredictable and immeasurable paths.

The stories we tell about the animals we love, then, are not always simplistic and commonplace. Such stories can appear in any literary genre, but more often they constitute their own distinctive category, one which is marginalized by literary critics and connoisseurs alike. Nevertheless, the best examples from it show that in the divulgence of excessive attachments something powerful can be revealed. These stories are not fantasies, even though they often appear to be fantastic in their range of emotion and concern. Sometimes such tales of devotion can appear only in nonliterary genres, like the novelist T. H. White's confession of love for his dog, Brownie, which he could write about only in the privacy of a letter. "It is a queer difference between this kind of thing and getting married," wrote White; "that married people love each other at first (I understand) and it fades by use and custom, but with dogs you love them most at last" (1968: 182). Other depictions of animal love blend the biographical with the imaginary. Virginia Woolf's *Flush* (1983), for example, is the story of Elizabeth Barrett Browning's cocker spaniel, but it is also the story of Woolf's own dog. Woolf was afraid that the book would be praised and thus condemned for being "charming, delicate, ladylike" (quoted in introduction by Trekkie Ritchie to Woolf, 1983: xiii). The work does occasionally assume the dog's perspective through thick descriptions of both the blur of sensations and the distinctive smells and sounds of the dog's life, but it succeeds in avoiding triviality by keeping at the same time a certain distance between the human and the animal world. "The fact was that they could not communicate with words, and it was a fact that led undoubtedly to much misunderstanding. Yet did it not lead also to a peculiar intimacy?" (37).

Beat Sterchi's *Cow* (1988) pursues this same "peculiar intimacy" not through the process of simple identification but by the use of a parallel structure. Sterchi tells the story of an unwanted Spanish guest worker in Switzerland who is demoted from farm work to the slaughterhouse, where he is able to follow the entire life cycle of a cow for whom he has great respect. Although the guest worker does identify with the cow, it is not in any maudlin way. Instead, he sees his life shared by the cow's life, even as he is forced to participate in the killing of the cow, which is portrayed in a cruciform manner. Sterchi manages to draw together two very different lives in a manner that does not diminish the differences even as it suggests bold resemblances.

Finally, note the most honest and direct portrait of the dog lover's love, J. R. Ackerley's *My Dog Tulip* (1965), which pushes the human-animal identification as close as it can (respectably) go.[15] The book manages to be a story about a love affair in which the intensity and intimacy of the human-dog relationship does not appear as transgression or "bestiality." Ackerley pushes his dog passion so far that it becomes both hyperbolic and ironic, the irony balancing the hyperbole as it reaches a pitch of nearly hysterical proportion. He mixes careful observation ("Dogs read the world through their noses and write their history in urine" [43]), appropriate humor ("No matter how preoccupied her mind may be with other things, such as rabbiting, she will always turn back, before following me, to the place where she saw me relieve myself—for nothing that I do escapes her—to sprinkle her own drops upon mine. So I feel that if ever there were differences between us they are washed out now. I feel a proper dog" [55]), grateful admiration ("She had, after all, fulfilled a dog's most urgent need, she had managed to bestow her heart, and upon steady people whose dull, uneventful lives required the consolation of what she had to give" [125]), confessions of dismay ("The look in hers disconcerts me, it contains too much, more than any beast may give, something too clear and too near, too entire, too dignified and direct, a steadier look than my own. I avert my face. Raising a paw, she bangs me on the knee" [138]), sober sympathy ("I realized clearly, perhaps for the first time, what strained and anxious lives dogs must lead, so emotionally involved in the world of men, whose affections they strive endlessly to secure, whose authority they are expected unquestioningly to obey, and whose mind they never can do more than imperfectly reach and comprehend" [158]), and ultimate acquiescence to a bond that connects regardless of limitations and differences ("I listen, but I cannot act. How can I put her from me?" [139]). It is the combination of humor and curiosity that enables Ackerley to speak with such revealing passion without appearing too eccentric and ridiculous.

The best of these stories shows that self-indulgence need not turn into narcissism, nor does passion necessarily slip into sentimentalism. In a discussion of William James, Jacques Barzun declares that "sentimentality is no excess of anything; it is a deficiency of the imagination that should lead to action" (1983: 68). Sentimentalism, in its pejorative sense, betrays an indefensible gap between the intellectual awareness of suffering and concrete moral practice. Sentiment in a positive sense, the particularity of passion, if it is born from a generous imagination, can only spread outward, encompassing the other and transforming the self. The best dog and animal stories are the ones that embrace the oddness, the exuberance, the poetry of the pet relationship, and thus empower the reconceptualization of the human-animal relation that conceptuality itself cannot achieve. Indeed, if the difference between humans and animals, once it is articulated and conceptualized, always distorts an otherness that cannot be put into words because those words are all too human, then to understand otherness we need stories that capture something beyond the conceptual realm. We need stories that show what ordinarily cannot be said.

After all, animals are not *the other,* as if they are so different from us that we can never understand them. If that were the case, then petkeeping really would be a folly. True, animals are more different from us that we like to imagine, and this forces us to stretch our imaginations by telling better stories about them. The problem is that their difference from us is both distant and intimate, drawing us out of ourselves and toward that which we can never fully know. What I am after here is what Mary Midgley identified as something pointless. Indeed, what we need is a notion of excess, or hyperbole. Excess, I want to argue, is a different difference, a "more than" that reaches outward across the space where concepts and ideas flounder. Difference that is dependent on the logic of analogy sees the unknown only in terms of the known, giving us an otherness whose similarity is greater than its difference. The (il)logic of hyperbole constitutes a better otherness than analogy by imagining the other as much more than more of the same and yet sufficiently similar as to be sayable, in the form of stories about passion and care.

We need a public moral language appropriate to our relationship with pets that magnifies that relationship in practical and encompassing ways. We do not need harder and clearer rules that would define the common features of all animals that allow them to be included within our range of ethical action. Instead, we need a different rule, or a different kind of rule altogether, one that urges and galvanizes the extension and amplification of our care outward, in ever widening circles, in unsystematic and yet expansive rhythms of transforming concern.

I call this the rule of hyperbole, the way in which a relationship, like the human-dog relationship, which always entails a dimension of extravagance and excess on both sides, can empower our lives with an outward emanating care, can, in other words, hyperbolize our relationships with others. We can call hyperbole that which beckons us further than prudence and self-interest would advise. The rule of hyperbole states: begin where you are, with what you've got, and go not deeper, searching for some essence within that is shared by all animal others, some firm foundation from which a moral position can be launched, but look for moments or relationships in which something is given to you that you could not otherwise give yourself, and then try to give that (back) to others. Look for others who draw you out, however precariously, into new spaces that allow new perspectives, and from those vantage points learn to cultivate and expand your care.

Martin Buber, in his famous philosophy of encounter developed in *I and Thou*, witnesses to the rule of hyperbole in his meditation on the real otherness he sees in the look of animals: "The eyes of an animal have the capacity of a great language" (1970: 144).[16] He finds in domesticated animals a primary example of an exchange that liberates both partners. "Man once 'tamed' animals," he writes, "and he is still capable of bringing off this strange feat" (172). Taming, for Buber, involves an openness to the other: "On the whole this response is the stronger the more direct, the more his relation amounts to a genuine You-saying" (172). Only by saying Thou, by giving up the I, can domestication occur, as it occurs every time a human looks at and allows for the return look of an animal. It is questionable, then, whether domestication ever could have happened if animals had been treated merely as what Buber calls an "It."

When Buber talks about looking into the eyes of a cat, he does not suggest that the cat has received the eloquence of a glance from us. Furthermore, he is aware that the cat's look has changed due to domestication. It is now full of surprise and question. The cat now asks, "Can it be that you mean me?" and "Do I concern you?" (145). The eyes of all animals show an anxiety, "the stirring of the creature between the realms of plantlike security and spiritual risk" (144). It is precisely this anxiety, this pleading, that stirs a basic response of empathy and solidarity. Even Berger agrees that exchanging anxious looks with animals can empower us to see them anew: "The animal scrutinizes him [a human] across a narrow abyss of noncomprehension. This is why the man can surprise the animal. Yet the animal—even if domesticated—can also surprise the man. The man too is looking across a similar, but not identical, abyss of noncomprehension" (1980: 3). The anxiety of the question "What do you mean to me, and I to you?" or "What can we give to each other?" allows us to see in the other more than what we find in ourselves and to pass on this surplus to others in turn. In the look of the animal is a question, and we are compelled to give an answer.

Excess as More Than Other

Let me return, then, to a reflection on what I promised: excess and otherness as they relate to dogs. Most nonbehaviorist talk about dogs is condemned as anthropomorphism, and anthropomorphism is, in turn, often simply equated with exaggeration. Anthropomorphism was a term first applied to theology, meaning the act of attributing human traits to God. Theologians argue, mostly, that this is not an error but an inescapable limitation whereby we conceive of God as analogous to how we conceive of ourselves. As long as we realize the limitations of this language, we can claim to have knowledge that is more than a mirror reflection of ourselves. Later, this term (with all of its difficulties) got applied to animals. Can we have more than anthropomorphic knowledge of animals? Can we learn to read from them more than what we read into them? Is our projection of human terms onto the dog world an attempt to create them in our own image, or is it a donative act that tries to respond to the gratuitous with gratitude?

Dogs are by definition deformed: they have been bred, changed, their features exaggerated. In the words of a beautiful poem by John Updike, dogs have "no nonhuman word for love" (1993: 141). They are the most plastic of animals (as opposed to cats); cats relieve you of the burden of intervention, manipulation, and invention. The shape of the cat, for example, cannot be changed much through breeding. As Camille Paglia notes in her comments about cats and ancient Egypt, cats are geometrical; they have a sense of their own elegance and design (1991: 64–66).[17] Cats move alongside us, keeping their shape to themselves. Dogs, on the other hand, are more amorphous; they are, to a certain extent, what we have made of them, for various ingenious purposes. They are the product of human attempts to exaggerate nature, to stretch it out of shape, to remold and reinvent it. The transfigured shapes of dogs are, at their best, more like exaggerations than deformities; that is, they are distortions that make sense.[18] The body of the dog, then, is the shape of the figure of hyperbole, the material incarnation of that figure of speech, extending outward in extravagant ways but nonetheless retaining the integrity of an organic whole, of shape. The dog is a figure for a figure, but the dog is also an embodiment of the figure of excess in a more meaningful way. The dog is always more than we know, extending beyond our knowledge and calling on us to match his or her excess with acts of generosity of our own.

The gift that the dog is has not always been adequately returned. Indeed, in such a close relationship there is enormous risk. Familiarity and intimacy bring great danger in the forms of resistance and denial. Ritvo tells the story, for example, of the English fascination with and horror of rabies, which resulted in outbreaks of dog massacres in the early modern period. This usually occurred during the so-called dog days of summer, originally named after Sirius, the dog star, but also connected to these regular and ritualized killings. Ritvo suggests that the disease of rabies had more symbolic than real meaning: "At issue was control over the rhetorical arena in which the meaning of both the animals and the disease was defined" (1987: 171). The dogs most frequently targeted were strays, mongrels, and the dogs of the lower classes. Such killings involved the whole society: "The rhetoric of purity and contamination structured the discussions both of science and bureaucratic rationalizers and of their most ignorant and panic-stricken charges. Rabid dogs were viewed as not only dangerous, but also unclean; their disease was a kind of pollution" (174). These slaughters show how deeply ambivalent people can be about otherness, especially when that otherness is so near and close.[19]

The nearness of dogs—their being close at hand, in the sense of Heidegger's *zuhanden*—can also force them to function, of course, as a mere extension of the human ego. Much of the psychological literature on dogs, for example, treats them as diversions from the real world that might provide indirect health benefits but hardly deserve attention as ends in themselves. As James Turner remarks, "The pet encapsulates the virtues of the heart, unsullied by skeptical calculating intellect" (1980: 76).[20] By the very purity of their devotion, pets can provide an avenue of escape from the harsh realities of everyday life. When dogs and other pets are magnifications of the human ego, though, they risk losing any meaning in themselves, and thus they are treated as excessive in the sense of being irrelevant and wasteful.[21]

Indeed, there is a lesson here about rhetoric. Bad hyperboles give us a hyper-reality that is disconnected from quotidian reality, a symbolic level of meaning that can be manipulated, entered into, and enjoyed but leaves us unchanged, unaffected, and alone. Good hyperboles, by contrast, take us further than we could otherwise have gone and do not return us to the same place. Surely it goes without saying that dogs can be merely the repositories of our surplus feelings, all that is alienated during the workday, all of those emotions that could be channeled into social change or into bettering human relations. But good dog relationships, like good hyperboles, do more than this; they offer us more than we could ever find within, take us further than we knew we could go, and make us more than ourselves. As Turner's statement itself suggests, dogs are like a gift, a grace undeserved, that releases us into an economy of abundance, where the economic laws of scarcity and therefore competition no longer apply and where instead we feel ourselves the beneficiaries of a wealth that is actualized only as we give it away, and in giving we see something that we could not see before. In this way, dogs are part of the antieconomy of giving, generosity, and grace.

Revolutionary potential exists, then, for the dog-human relationship to embody not necessarily consolation but, more than anything, the joy of squandering, of experiencing the useless, the nonnecessary, the wasteful, and the hyperbolic.[22] If utilitarianism is too dependent on calculation to be a guide to human-animal relationships and rights theory is entangled in questions about the connection of responsibility to self-interests and contractuality, then my own approach allows for a fresh start on the issue of the ethical treatment of animals. I am arguing that we owe animals charity, not justice; this charity, however, is not something freely and arbitrarily given, from the goodness of our hearts. It is a giving that is mutual, a response to real otherness, the return of a gift of loyalty and affection.[23] Charity is born from its own kind of covenant, even if it is not the explicitly negotiated agreement that provides the contractual foundation for justice.[24] Such generosity is in complete opposition to the kind of economic thinking that treats animals as products to be efficiently processed in factory farms and laboratories.

How our covenant with dogs began is not a relevant question to the morality of this relationship. Dogs were domesticated from wolves sometime during the Stone Age (see Zeuner, 1953), but what prompted this interchange is impossible to ascertain with any certainty. Perhaps domestication began as an attempt to create a guaranteed supply of food or sacrificial victims. Perhaps wolves began to follow humans on their hunts, and their complementary hunting skills (their noses, our primitive weapons) made them worthwhile hunting companions. Perhaps the wolves were drawn by the humans' fires and began behaving in such a way as to obtain scraps and handouts. It is as possible that domestication began with a leap of identification, with a surprising sense of friendship, as it is that it began with more utilitarian concerns and motives. Whatever the origin, the lives of dogs and people are so intertwined that it is impossible to find a firm foundation of utility on which the relationship rests. The dog is evidence of our capacity to reach out to others as much as the dog is evidence of our desire to dominate and control.[25]

Such mutuality has its own dynamic, which circulates in ever- widening circles, and if we follow it, passing it on and giving it over and over again, we will see it unfold as a bounty of generosity that can never be limited to dogs alone. The rules of consistency would require us to treat similar animals in similar ways; following the gift of the dog leads in the same direction, but with its own logic of excess and extravagance. As Richard Ryder notes, "It is possible to see the growth of animal liberation as an expansion of the family circle; the perception of other animals as our 'brothers and sisters,' literally as our evolutionary kin to whom we feel 'kindness' "(1989: 317). After all, nature is becoming increasingly domesticated and decreasingly wild; the earth is one huge household in which all animals, including humans, must learn to get along with each other. Instead of idealizing a natural world disconnected from human intentions, we need to learn to deal with a world that is more and more dependent on us for its very survival. As Ritvo notes, "The concept of pet is not inevitably limited by species; pets do not even have to share our domiciles. Pets can also be understood as animals to which we maintain a certain relationship of domination mixed with responsibility and generosity. So defined, pets may prove to be nearly ubiquitous" (1988: 29). Animals do not need liberation. They need love. There is nowhere for them to hide from us, so the only question is how, not if, we will exercise our dominion over them. Power is not always instantiated in an economy of domination and control; sometimes power can be empowering, so that distance is not the only way to protect the other. Skeptics will demur, cynically creating dilemmas (What would you do if . . . ?) and slippery slopes (Where will it all end . . . ?) in which concern for animals raises unfortunate consequences or meets impossible implications. But as Rollin reminds us, "An ethic is a yardstick, a measure of where we are deficient, or a target to aim at that sharpens our skill" (1992: 23). All moral impulses, I would suggest, lead us into difficult situations; we can only trust in the passion that carries us and follow the gift that has already been given us.

Historically, philosophical justification for kindness to animals has been based on a cosmological principle, either the transmigration of souls, which appears to be the basis for the vegetarianism of Pythagoras (Pythagoras is said to have stopped a man from beating a dog because he recognized the voice of a dead friend), or a dualistic understanding of the relationship of spirit to matter and mind to flesh, which inevitably privileges asceticism, making vegetarianism an expression of strenuous moral achievement, as with the Desert Fathers, the Manichaeans, and Porphyry. Neither of these ideas emphasizes compassion or illuminates the ambiguous mixture of closeness and distance in our relationships to animals. More recent philosophical programs also seem irretrievably limited when faced with animal otherness. A philosophy of introspection (Descartes) can never do justice to the animal world. It begins with human self-consciousness as the unique avenue of knowledge; methodologically, then, human value is privileged in an exclusive manner. Observation, which tells us that animals are more similar to us than we would like to think, is demoted and circumscribed by self-reflection. Even the dialectic of the other and the same is of no help here, because, as demonstrated by Hegel, what is named the other is understood only in terms of its relation to the same, and thus a logic of identity precedes and controls the explication of difference.[26] Giving up these philosophies and taking a more scientific approach to animals, however, is no improvement. The sciences are built on the backs of animal sacrifices, and although Darwin would suggest more similarities than differences between animals and humans, the worldview of the sciences tends to subordinate ethical concern to the advancement of knowledge. The scientific worldview also emphasizes knowledge as the exclusive domain of and the reason for the infinite value of humanity alone.

What is needed are a philosophy and a theology humble enough to learn to listen to limits, to hear difference seep in through the cracks and crevices in the stories we tell about animals, to let go of metaphysics and embrace the recklessness of rhetoric, the passions in which we know our dogs, and to find in the extravagant gesture of petting, of bending down to touch, an act worthy of reflection, repetition, and amplification. Dogs' special position in the great chain of being allows them to be available both as examples of human ingenuity and as expressions of human compassion. This intersection, where the useful meets the useless, can seem impossible, a contradiction of economies or a clash of dimensions, yet it is also surely commonplace, so much a part of who we are that it challenges even as it consoles, instructs as it reassures.

We are creatures capable of tender mercies, gestures of love that can wound as well as heal. Somewhere in the heart of that wanton gesture, which is surely at the origin of the domestication process itself, lies an act of transcendence, even transgression, in which we reach beyond ourselves, in defiance of the rules of prudence and calculation, and endow the other, the animal other, with the affection that is not merely a diversion from a heartless world but an eschatological statement about who we want to be, a rebellious act against the restraints of moderation, and a claim upon some sort of truth that I cannot but help to understand as religious, as spiritual, as a reaching toward some encompassing realm of love, toward some concrete place where all excessive acts one day will be mutual, will circulate like endless gifts continually returned even as they are again given away—a mutuality born, sustained, and guided by a blessed excess.

PART III

A Theology for the Dogs

CHAPTER FIVE

Theology and Dogtalk

The Sensibility of Sentiment

How do we get from the passion of the canophile, which reveals animal feeling to us and yet situates that relationship in the context of a particular covenant, to a zoophilic compassion for all animals? How do we widen the closed circle of the family dog (an honorary human being) to the infinite circle of the family of all living beings?[1] The difficulty of balancing family, group and national loyalties with universal moral requirements is an ancient and familiar problem, especially to theologians, who must defend the particularity of revelation, the covenant, and the church within the framework of God's universal providence. Widening moral concern from pets to animals, however, does not have the same sanctions as the movement from, say, one's own children to all children. To express sentiments about all animals strikes most people as noble but futile, something easy to say (indeed, something that it is easy to say in exaggerated ways, something that lends or gives itself to exaggeration) but difficult to do (to translate rhetoric into action, to make excess go to work).

Admittedly, sometimes it is hard to get past the rhetorical flourishes of the typical so-called animal lover. It is hard, for example, to read the often quoted views of Albert Einstein without a smile of condescension or, even worse, warm admiration mixed with a cool sense of the impracticalities of which the genius professor was admirably but absently unaware.

> A human being is a part of the whole, called by us the "Universe," a part limited
> in time and space. He experiences himself, his thoughts and feelings, as something
> separate from the rest—a kind of optical delusion of his consciousness. This delu-
> sion is a kind of prison for us, restricting us to our personal desires and to affection
> for a few persons nearest to us. Our task must be to free ourselves from this prison
> by widening our circle of compassion to embrace all living creatures and the whole
> of nature in its beauty. Nobody is able to achieve this completely, but the striving
> for such achievement is in itself a part of the liberation and a foundation for inner
> security. (quoted in Wynne-Tyson, 1989: 76)

With no sense of the positive aspects of finitude, of the necessity for limitations,
of the emergence of morality in specific and exclusive relationships of responsibility, Einstein favors the unlimited over the limited, the open over the closed.
I do not want to defend Einstein's particular version of animal compassion, but
I am drawn to his notion of widening the circle of our care. Is this project
mere sentiment, a foggy mist of rhetoric and embellishment, without any connection to the practicalities of everyday living? What is sentiment, that it strikes
us as equal parts wisdom and foolishness, insightful and absurd?

Note how the two words "sentimentalism" and "squeamishness" tend to go
together, indeed, to depend on each other. These terms signify an attraction or
repulsion that seems more based in the imagination than in reality. Sentimentalism is a hasty extension outward, the reverse of which is squeamishness,
which turns one inward, away from something that becomes suddenly much
too real. If the sentimental object is treated as too familiar, the squeamish is
that which we do not want to touch at all. We need to be habituated against
both, which are overreactions that show a lack of prudence. The two can be
seen as one movement because only the person who goes too far in imagina-
tively identifying with the other can be surprised and shocked by the other's
very real pain and suffering. The person who is sentimental, then, is also squeamish. The sentimentalist literally and naively identifies with the other, in ways
that make the other's pain too much to take. To risk love is to be vulnerable to
identifications that discomfort and appall.

Unfortunately, in our post-Freudian universe, we believe that aggression is
more fundamental than kindness, so that we can imagine sentiment only as a
form of violence, no matter how refined. The exercise of sentiment challenges
well-defined boundaries, dragging the private into the public by expressing and
valuing something that for many people is better left (like pets) at home. The
sentimental cannot be the basis for public policy, not only because it is a private emotion but also because it recklessly goes too far toward the other. As
Vicki Hearne writes, "But the terror of sentimentality is no less an oppressive
and truncating force than any other form of hatred or terror, and results in as
much stupidity" (1994: 106). Sentiment goes outward too quickly, and so we
pull back from it, suspicious and leery. The squeamish should be bravely en-

dured or politely backed away from but not identified and internalized. Confronting the squeamish without sentiment is today a sign of courage, not denial.

Faced with the reinterpretation of sentiment as aggression and the acceptance of the squeamish as a sign of maturity, the love of animals seems neither possible nor realistic. It is crazy, surely, to spread our care so far and wide. To care is to make oneself vulnerable—to acknowledge the reality of the other's interests. To care for all animals is, consequently, a supererogatory act, something commendable but not obligatory, something reserved for saints but not required for the ordinary person. True, the dog lover already exhibits something of the saint's passionate inclinations and idiosyncratic excesses. The pet lover transgresses boundaries in order to attend to an other who can share both sorrows and joys. Nevertheless, something else is needed to bridge the love for the pet to the concern for all of the anonymous, unnamed other animals. We need a way of loving everyone who suffers; otherwise, our love threatens to be self-interest in disguise.

If caring is so risky, then how can we be prompted to care beyond the immediate relationships that make us who we are? Not only do animals represent rhetorical excess, but also they are in reality excessive, in the sense that there are too many of them, so that we do not know what to do with their pain and suffering. It is at this point that Christianity proves more worthy than some of its critics, as well as its own theologians, might suspect. Christianity suggests that grace enables relationships of mutuality through a special sensitivity to pain and suffering. Sharing occurs through our capacity to identify with the other's feelings, an empathy that can heal through the confidence that comfort provides. Our own pain strikes us as an excess that renders us confused and disoriented, but feeling the pain of others is, like receiving a gift, an excess that draws us out of ourselves and leads us into specific obligations and responsibilities. As process thought rightly insists, God feels what we feel, so that grace creates joy by carrying the other's burdens. God through Jesus Christ feels the pain of the entire world, allowing us to reconfigure the meaning of suffering. God not only alters our own pain by sharing in it but also shows us how grace can help us to reconsider the pain of all others. We are empowered to sympathize in radically open-ended ways because God too has taken this risk. Only the sentiment of grace, then, allows us to acknowledge the squeamish without denial or resignation.

According to traditional Christian belief, Jesus Christ took on the suffering of the world in a death often referred to as bestial and animal-like; he was tortured for no good reason at all and reduced to empty flesh, treated, that is, like an animal. This connection between human and animal pain is important. Pain reduces humans to an animal state; what people mean by this common observation is, I think, that extreme pain deprives humans of their distinctive

use of language. People moan and groan, scream and cry, but their words have
no referent, no object, and no coherence. Pain is, in the words of Elaine Scarry,
"an intentional state without an intentional object" (1985: 164). Pain levels the
distinctions that make humans human. As Bradford Stull notes, "Pain, at its
most destructive, disintegrates the human life-world as it disintegrates language: one's physicality is made so overwhelmingly present that one cannot
speak it; one can neither point to nor construct objects in which the pain can
be placed" (1994: 16). Even the animals can cry like this; even they have this
most minimal use of language, guttural screams born of terror and confusion.
I once followed a truck on a winding road that was transporting pigs to the
slaughter. They were two or three deep, suffocating each other, and their
screams were the most horrible sounds I have ever heard. I helplessly passed
the truck around a blind curve, frantically speeding away but furiously vowing
never to forget.

What else could I do? Perhaps the key reason we do not want to identify
with animal pain is that such identification forces us to admit that the most
primal and basic form of the language we use, the very language that separates
us from the beasts, is actually common among many species, and thus their
sounds of pain are recognizable even as we turn away. Nobody likes to hear
another human groan in pain; such groaning does sound like an animal. Perhaps when we recognize that animal cries are not so different from our own,
that animals share our most basic hopes and fears, then we will be less eager
to turn away from human cries, let alone animal pain. If animal screams are
within us, too—if we can hear the animal cries in Jesus' death—then how can
we pretend that the language of pain is something only humans speak?

Certainly, theologians have often pretended that animal pain has nothing
to do with the pain Jesus felt. Many follow Thomas Aquinas in arguing that
the irrationality of animals exiles them from the ethical sphere. "The love of
charity extends to none but God and our neighbor. But the word neighbor
cannot be extended to irrational creatures, since they have no fellowship with
man in the rational life. Therefore charity does not extend to irrational creatures" (*Summa Theologica,* II-II, Q. 25, Art. 3). Such attitudes allowed scientists
in the Christian West to torture animals with a vigor and detachment un-
matched elsewhere. In the seventeenth century, a time of great interest in the
rapid advances of physiology, dogs would be attached to boards with nails
driven through their paws and cut open, in the name of observation and information. According to Cartesian philosophy, their screams were nothing more
than the noise of broken machinery (Cartmill, 1993: 96). This was prior to the
development of anesthetics, so sometimes their vocal chords would be cut to
keep their shrieks from distracting the concentration of the vivisectors. Realdo
Columbo (1516–1559), who held the Padua chair of anatomy, reported that

high-ranking clergymen took great delight in his public displays of vivisection (the incident is related in Maehle and Tröhler, 1987). Once he opened up a pregnant bitch, pulled out a puppy, and tortured the pup in front of the dog, which began barking furiously. When he held the pup closer, she began licking it tenderly, being more concerned about her offspring than her own pain. The clergymen interpreted these experiments as confirming the presence of motherly love even in brute creation.[2] They were so impressed by the universality of the love of Mary for Jesus that it did not occur to them to worry about the dog's particular pain, yet that pain was necessary for them to make their theological point. They could both see and not see, the metaphor blocking their vision of literal suffering.

I should point out that among those instrumental in the beginning of the animal rights movement in nineteenth-century England were many Christians who followed their sense of compassion even though it was not given any theological or ecclesiastical support. It is also important to state the obvious fact that most animal pain is not caused by humans. Indeed, many people use the fact that suffering seems to be an inherent part of God's good creation to alleviate any human guilt or responsibility toward animals. Of course, we should not allow our sensitivity to and sympathy for animal pain to overwhelm our observation of animals' love of life. Animals live in the present far more than humans, so that their anticipation of death and their anxiety about the future is less than our own. Nevertheless, animal pain remains a stubborn aspect of creation not easily reconciled with the love of God. There is a glut of animals, and the multiplicity of life is part of the reason for such excessive pain in the world. How could God's extravagant love lead to such squandering of life?

If we do not know why God made the animals or what God feels about them, then how can we worry about what we humans should think or do? As long as theology is silent on animals, they will remain a mystery to the great majority of religious people in our culture, so that their pain will be impossible to comprehend. When C. S. Lewis wrote about this topic, he warned, "We know neither why they were made nor what they are, and everything we say about them is speculative" (1962: 129). What theologians call theodicy is the attempt to justify the ways of God to the ways of humans, and the creation of animals has always been a principle puzzle when wondering about the divine motivation. The ancient philosophical view of the great chain of being, the idea that God creates from a plenitude so that all possible levels of existence must be filled, was used by Augustine and other theologians to explain the variety of life. The idea of the fullness and balance of the cosmos has remarkable parallels to current environmental thought. Certainly nature is fecund, but the view that nature is perfectly full risks suggesting that this world is the best it could possibly be and thus needs no redemption. Moreover, from a Christian point of view the remarkable profusion of life does not solve the stubborn problem of animal suffering.

In response to this problem, theologians, like biologists, have argued that animal pain serves specific purposes. For example, Richard Swinburne argues that animal pain helps to educate humans. Since knowledge is based on experience, to have knowledge about the consequences of our actions we must have some experience of pain and suffering. Animal pain aids in that education: "Indeed a great deal of our knowledge of the disasters for man which would follow some action come from study of the actual disasters which have befallen animals" (1979: 209). Swinburne also argues that there is good reason that God has given to animals some power and knowledge to use for their own benefit but no free will and thus less responsibility than God has given humans. "There is a clear risk in having both [humans and animals] belong to the same world—that man will abuse animals, causing them much suffering or sorrow. But there are advantages. For both men and animals there is opportunity for responsibility and a new kind of co-operation and friendship" (197–98). Animals thus provide education and friendship to humans, but these observations solve the problem of animal pain only by treating them as instruments of human benefit.

There are a series of traditional answers to the problem of animal pain. Perhaps evil ultimately balances good in the end, although theologians traditionally have denied the afterlife to animals, so that their pain does not receive compensation or correction. Perhaps evil is largely a product of the fallen human will and thus a justified punishment for our wrongdoing. Evil as an unavoidable consequence of human freedom is the price we must pay for the goods that come with independence and autonomy. Calvin believed that the fall of humanity distorted the whole order of nature, but he did not infer from this belief that humans have responsibilities or obligations to nature. The problem is that animals existed long before humans, so the fall of humanity cannot explain their plight. Besides, why should they have to pay for our mistakes? Indeed, the distinction between moral and natural evil renders irrelevant many of the defenses of God's goodness in the face of immense human badness. Not only does some of the evil humans suffer come from sources beyond the reach of humanity's control (volcanoes and earthquakes, for example), but also animal suffering seems neither attributable to human mistakes nor redeemable on the basis of a plan that focuses on the human plight. Animals clearly do not deserve pain (they have not sinned), and they do not have the capacity to be improved by it either. Animal pain thus raises in the most troubling way the question of why God permits suffering in the world.

For C. S. Lewis, animal pain is so disconnected from the human sphere that it is only explainable in reference to a prehuman fall, an angelic being whose rebellion puts all of life off balance (1962: 134–35).[3] The idea of a pre-human fall goes back to Origen and earlier, and it traces the plight of both humanity and nature to a common origin in a prior fall of angelic beings. This myth has many advantages. It suggests that humans are not responsible for all of nature's problems, so that withdrawing from the natural world is not the answer to those problems. It also suggests that humans and animals share the same predicament and, by implication, the same hopes and destiny. Animals too exist in an interim; nature is not what it was meant to be. The Christian hope for liberation, redemption, and restoration, then, must encompass animal life as well. Somehow Christians must be able to find a way of seeing that the struggle of animals is not wasted in God's plan for the world.

Evolution and the Problem of Animal Pain

The final argument about animal pain for many theologians is an appeal to the mystery of God. Theologians argue that God's ultimate purposes for the world are hidden to us, so that, in the end, we simply must accept pain as part of the plan. Such excessive pain can be understandable, however, only if God has a design or purpose for the whole, of which we can see but a part. Evolutionary theory has diminished much of the mystery of animal pain and provides an alternative explanation. Natural selection does explain why animals suffer; animals must be motivated to act according to their best interests in order to survive. Without pain, animals would not defend themselves and struggle to dominate their environments. Evolutionary theory explains the function of pain, but questions for a theist remain: Could God have created a world where animals did not have to suffer quite this much? Is there a theological reason for so much suffering in the world? In fact, the theory of evolution makes animal suffering even more horrendous than the traditional doctrine of creation: think of the countless animals who suffered before humankind even entered the scene. Evolution makes animal pain natural, inevitable, and necessary, and thus it is all the more difficult to understand why God would call such a world good.

While theology provides an ultimate purpose for all things (say, the glory of God), evolutionary theory explains intricate adaptations on the basis of natural selection and random variation, not conscious intention or direction. Randomness is a difficult phenomenon to conceive. Teleology is deeply rooted in the human consciousness. We want to find patterns, reasons, and shapes, whereas things sometimes are just accidental and aimless. We resist the idea that luck and chance have played a significant, perhaps fundamental, role in the long history of who we are as well as the details of what we think and do. Before Christian theology, the Greeks believed that everything existed for a purpose.

For Aristotle, not only is everything caused by something else, but also everything exists *for* something else. Everything has a final cause, a goal that shapes that entity as much as any prior cause. Rain falls in order to make plants grow; objects drop in order to find their proper place.

Christian theology easily adapted Aristotelian science by arguing that everything does have a purpose, and that purpose is dictated by God. William Paley's *Natural Theology* (1802) is the classic expression of the argument from teleology. He made the analogy between the world and a clock; just as we know, intuitively, that there is a clockmaker for every clock, we also know that there is a worldmaker, a creator, who must be God. David Hume, in *Dialogues Concerning Natural Religion* (1771), had already attacked the philosophical reasoning behind this analogy. Why assume, he argued, that only one such worldmaker exists? Why assume, furthermore, that this creator really cares about creation? Why not assume instead that the world came about by chance since we have to stop looking for a first cause somewhere, and we do not know what brought God into existence? Nevertheless, for many people in Hume's day the analogy still made good sense; the world seemed too planned to be sheerly accidental.

Darwin radically changed all of this. Evolution is not directed by a mysterious guiding hand. "For Darwin," writes James Rachels, "there was nothing in the constitution of any organism that propels its development in any particular direction. Nor were there any 'higher' or 'lower' forms of life; nor any 'progress': there were only organisms adapted in different ways to different environments, by a process ignorant of design or intention" (1990: 116). Indeed, what seemed to consolidate evolutionary theory's superiority over the argument of teleology is the existence of vestiges of once-useful structures in biological entities. We would not expect an intelligent designer to include useless parts in an organism, but according to natural selection theory, some parts might survive in an organism even though they no longer play a useful role. Humans, for example, have muscles that no longer move ears, the remnants of a tail, and a purposeless appendix.

In point of fact, the world is not perfectly designed. Nature fits together in haphazard ways. Rachels explains, "Evidence of perfect, elegant adaptation would support the design hypothesis, while evidence of improvised, jury-rigged adaptation would support the evolutionary hypothesis. The contrast is between designs and contrivances; and the latter are what we actually find" (122). In his book about orchids, Darwin explains that nectar was originally an excretion of superfluous matter during chemical changes in the plant and only subsequently useful in attracting insects. The world seems put together by coincidence and chance more than intention and design.

The questions for theism appear overwhelming. Why would God design something with parts that did not contribute to the whole? Why would God work through chance and accident? Due to these questions, God has become a needless hypothesis for many post-Darwinians. God is an excessive belief; even if God exists, God serves no discernible function. Like a wheel that spins freely, unattached to the rest of the machinery, God is a superfluous part in the interconnecting whole of biology. Of course, some theologians, following Teilhard de Chardin, still want to argue that there is direction to evolution as a whole, that the process is not entirely random. It is hard to imagine ourselves, human beings, as products of a blind throw of the dice. Yet the idea of direction to evolution is awfully vague. Can we see it? Does it make a difference? Does the idea of direction explain things that the scientific theory does not? More pointedly, Jürgen Moltmann (1991) has argued that God, if God exists, must stand outside of, not within, the mechanisms of evolution. Redemption, which is conceivable only eschatologically, runs counter to evolution. Yet if God is God, then evolution too must come under God's ultimate concern. What does evolution, which spends life so easily and proliferates forms so messily, tell us about God? Can evolution be reconciled to belief in an ultimate order and goodness at the heart of things?

Interestingly, Darwin himself, who eliminated the need for extraneous elements in explaining the growth of life, valued the fleetingly emotional and the seemingly trivial as necessary aspects of a life most worth living. Simply put, Darwin loved animals. Stanley Edgar Hyman has described *On the Origin of Species* as a dramatic poem summing up the tragic action in which humanized animals are the main characters. The biblical comprehensiveness of the book contains a new morality: "Darwin's mystery is a kind of totemic brotherhood, a consubstantiality with all organic beings, resembling St. Paul's 'every one members one of another' " (1962: 42). Darwin could agree, with a slight twist of meaning, to the statement of St. Chrysostom that "surely we ought to show kindness and gentleness to animals for many reasons, and chiefly because they are of the same origin as ourselves" (quoted in Linzey, 1994: 11). Does Darwin himself point the way toward a morality, a philosophy, that takes seriously the love of animals?

For the most part, as James Rachels has shown, philosophers have been hesitant to infer any moral lessons from the theory of evolution. Since G. E. Moore's critique of the "naturalistic fallacy," in his *Principia Ethica* (1903), philosophers have avoided grounding ethical principles in questions of fact. What is the case cannot tell us what ought to be the case, as David Hume argued before Moore; therefore, biology has little relevance for morality. Much of the early reception of Darwinism, however, pivoted on this crucial issue of the relationship between evolutionary theory and the treatment of animals. People who were appalled by the idea that kinship with animals might force us to change the way we think about human dignity and uniqueness were closer to Darwin's own aims than those philosophers who tried to compartmentalize the sciences from morality.

Darwin was confident and thorough in his attempts to show the basic continuities between human intelligence and animal capacities. In *The Descent of Man,* Darwin displays an intense love and concern for animals that is now seen to be unscientific, even though he could not disconnect in his own work the emotional from the objective. And in his final book, *The Formation of Vegetable Mould, through the Action of Worms* (1881), he argues in favor of the case for intelligence in worms. True, Darwin lived in an age of anthropomorphism, but his basic point that intelligence is not an all-or-nothing affair is sound and his methods were thoroughly empirical. In *The Descent of Man* he attributes nearly every human characteristic to animals: from altruism to anxiety, animals have it all. "All animals feel *Wonder,* and many exhibit *Curiosity*" (n.d.:450). He is quite certain that animals have a moral sense, that is, that they have instincts that propel them toward the good of the community and not just their own survival. Animals have a social instinct that urges them to protect others, even at the cost of their own lives.

Darwin is especially attentive to the intelligence of dogs (which he ranks close to that of "savages"!). He clearly thinks that his theory, which stresses the commonality of all life forms, justifies the use of anthropomorphic language in reference to dogs. True, his observations about dogs are more anecdotal than scientific. When he speaks about dogs, he is almost forced to abandon the genre of scientific literalism for a mode of expression more appropriate to his topic. Some of his comments reside on the border of sentimentalism in the pejorative sense: "In the agony of death a dog has been known to caress his master, and every one has heard of the dog suffering under vivisection, who licked the hand of the operator" (449). Dogs can be generous ("A great dog scorns the snarling of a little dog, and this may be called magnanimity" [450]), and through their daily contact with humans, they can be considered moral agents: "Our domestic dogs are descended from wolves and jackals, and though they may not have gained in cunning, may have lost in wariness and suspicion, yet they have progressed in certain moral qualities, such as in affection, trustworthiness, temper, and probably in general intelligence" (457–58). Dogs even believe in supernatural agents, as when they detect movement without apparent cause and are disturbed by this. They have a primordial religiosity.

Darwin understands the fidelity of the dog to be an example of religious devotion and not just a projection of human wishes: "The feeling of religious devotion is a highly complex one, consisting of love, complete submission to an exalted and mysterious superior, a strong sense of dependence, fear, reverence, gratitude, hope for the future, and perhaps other elements. No being could experience so complex an emotion until advanced in his intellectual and moral faculties to at least a moderately high level. Nevertheless, we see some distant approach to this state of mind in the deep love of a dog for his master, associated with complete submission, some fear, and perhaps other feelings" (470). Darwin is here playing on the common thought that a dog looks upon his or her master as a god. It is more than an analogy; in this relationship we can experience the excessive longings and loves that also drive us to the divine. This relationship is not merely a clue to something else; it is itself an exercise of the passion that abides at the heart of every acknowledgment of mystery.

Just as Darwin shared with his fellow Victorians a great love of dogs, he also shared with them an incurable optimism about moral progress. Resisting the idea that we can know what we do not love, he firmly believed that the social instinct would grow along with humanity's intelligence: "Sympathy beyond the confines of man, that is, humanity to the lower animals, seems to be one of the latest moral acquisitions. . . . This virtue, one of the noblest with which man is endowed, seems to arise incidentally from our sympathies becoming more tender and more widely diffused, until they are extended to all sentient beings. As soon as this virtue is honored and practiced by some few men, it spreads through instruction and example to the young, and eventually becomes incorporated in public opinion" (492). We can smirk at his confidence in the inevitable expansion of the tribal circle of concern, his sanguine belief in progress and the victory of good over evil. After all, he reluctantly allowed himself to be influenced by friends into defending vivisection, an issue that shows knowledge and morality to be at odds with each other. But his description of the way morality works is persuasive. We begin with what we know and therefore love and learn to love what we do not know. We begin with what we are involved with and thus learn about otherness in terms that are intermingled with learning about ourselves.

Rosemary Rodd takes some of Darwin's insights into our biological kinship with animals even further. She argues that human-animal relationships are not abnormal. Part of what makes us human is our ability to befriend animals. Indeed, animal companionship is so common that there must be evolutionary reasons for it. We intuitively care for our companions even when that care gets in the way of our material needs and physical comfort. This is shown by the origin of domestication, which Rodd traces to the agency of female nurturing: "Before milk-producing animals were domesticated, human milk was the only suitable food available for raising very young wolf pups or lambs away from their own mothers. If women were the main agents in forming the original bonds between humans and domesticated animals, there is possibly a certain fitness in the present predominance of women in groups working for reform of the relationship" (1990: 228–29). We reach out to animals because we value otherness, regardless of how useful that valuing is. "Because we are the kind of biological entity which operates using intelligent consciousness, the value to us

of other consciousnesses who provide a social medium in which our consciousness can survive is much greater than their bodies' temporary value as raw
material. So it is only to be expected that defence of companions should be
one of our basic drives, not something secondary which is to be dealt with
after we have succeeded in satisfying the desire to reproduce" (237–38).

In fact, animal companionship is not biologically different from human
companionship. "If morality is a sociobiological phenomenon, then evidence
that human-animal relationships are often complex, requiring that the human
partners engage in social reasoning of the kind involved in inter-human relationships, will lend weight to the idea that ethical thought has an important
part to play in regulating such interactions" (223). Against those who would
idealize wild nature, Rodd urges the goal of an integrated community of animals and humans rather than vigorous separation of the two. "Recognition that
humans and domestic animals can form a true community offers the possibility
of a reformed relationship instead of the assumption that only wild animals
can have lives of real value, while the tame can be best served by their humane
extermination through birth control" (234). Pets are crucial: "Once one has
seen a *particular* animal as a friendly individual it no longer becomes easy to
regard another individual animal as a laboratory 'tool' " (185). She ends her
book by supporting a version of contractarian ethics, in which we must respond to the trust of animals in terms that honor that trust.[4]

Can we break out of an instrumental or utilitarian treatment of animals?
Evolution teaches us that life proliferates unbounded, leaving a competition for
resources among too many creatures. So much life, and so much misery, seems
to us to demand not just an explanation but a justification. We run up against
the limit question of why and persist in repeating that one word even though
we know no certain answers exists. William Paley argued in *Natural Theology*
(1802) that predation and disease were necessary in order to permit what he
called superfecundity, the way in which species overcrowd their environments
and reproduce prolifically. The agony of most animal life, however, is "a high
price to pay for the privilege of unlimited copulation" (Cartmill, 1993: 125).
Through the study of science we no longer believe the metaphysical idea that
nature's overfullness is a plenitude dictated by God's own fullness. Through
personal experience we also know that animal suffering is not merely a moral
lesson for us. We return again and again to the sheer excess of animal life, and
indeed, we are driven to reinterpret the very notion of wastefulness. If something does not seem amenable to the labors of our own conceptuality, then we
cannot find a place for it in our categories. We expel what we cannot rationalize. The crucial question, then, is: Can we find a place in the world today for
that which does not have a use? Can humans rise above the demands of utility
by loving that which seems to have no place or function?

Maybe their sheer excess is what animals have to teach us, in the end. In fact, nature itself seems to encourage the excessive and extravagant (see Webb, 1994). Animals do not serve a metaphysical or moral purpose; they are just there, splurges in the divine economy, embellishments, exuberant and prodigal displays of God's cunning and mischievous imagination. We can only pause to take delight in this world of multiple forms and various beings, and one of the best ways of doing that is with an animal who has become part of our world, an animal who has served us well but whose worth far exceeds any service or accomplishment.

Yet for theology, animals must be more than just waste; they are an excess that, paradoxically, serves a purpose. That is how animals can teach us not only about ourselves but also about their creator. Animals show us that God loves waste, that God identifies with complexity and excess and not just order and organization. God countenances that which is not necessary, that which seems accidental, trivial, and frivolous. The Christian message is that God loves that which seems without reason or place, that which is unserious, irrelevant, and excluded, that which is purposeless or anarchic according to the human standards of utility and value. Moreover, the Christian message is that to identify with the excessive is to risk pain and suffering, to risk humiliation in the eyes of human others who weigh every act according to the measure of cost and benefit.

Between the opposite claims that everything has a meaning and that nothing is meaningful, that everything has a place and that all things are out of place (*atopos*), is the phenomenon of those things that seem to occupy a place that is also at the same time placeless—beings who are marginal, both useful and useless. Perhaps they can tell us something about grace, about the power of God to love in spite of utility, to create in spite of efficiency, and to give in spite of the cost. To pet a dog is not such a bad way to practice theology. It is to acknowledge wonder as the impulse that drives us out of ourselves, and it is to witness reverence—as well as a plea for love and understanding—in the eyes of the other.

What is puzzling about evolutionary theory from the perspective of theology is that while it assigns pain a function, it also eliminates the purpose of life as a whole, so that the world seems more thrown and scattered than organized and conserved. Everything does not fit together for human edification and God's glory. In the light of the theoretical power of evolutionary theory, many theologians initially retreated in the direction of deism, which retains God as a first cause but eliminates any notion of providence. For Deists, God establishes the laws that govern the universe and then lets the world run on its own terms. God establishes the rules for the game and then lets luck and chance play their part. The problem is that God is left as an abstract hypothesis, hardly worthy of love or devotion. Deists seem to be saying that if God is a designer, then, given the harsh reality of evolution, God cannot be much of a lover, but what if God's love overflows and destabilizes our expectations for symmetry and harmony? Can we understand God's relationship to the world as one in which God is involved not as an organizer or structurer but as one who splurges in love, values even the valueless, and intimately supports all things no matter how they fit (or do not fit) together?

God transcends the mechanics of evolution, of course, so that we should not infer God's character from the course of natural development. Nevertheless, if nature does give us clues to how God works, then an adequate theological response to evolution is forced to separate theism from the design argument altogether. If God is the final source of power and direction in the evolving universe, then God must relish the fecund, the profuse, and the prodigious. If God creates through evolution, then God takes pleasure in the superfluous proliferation of life beyond all sense of order and purpose. Creation is, in the words of Annie Dillard, "God's spendthrift and neverending jubilee" (1982: 61). If so, the indecent bubbling over of divinity in the sumptuous dissemination of life invites us to cooperate with extravagant acts of our own. God loves even when and where such love does not seem to make a difference, and God enables us to love others, even other species, against the narrow concerns of the moment and the pressing anxiety of the future.

Descartes actually thought that his idea of animals as machines would benefit humans by relieving them of the guilt associated with inflicting pain on animals (see Linzey and Regan, 1988a: 45–52). It would indeed be convenient and fortunate if animals did not suffer, not only for those who harm animals but also for those who try to adjust their belief in God with animal suffering. Malebranche, a contemporary of Descartes, welcomed his theory precisely because it made the issue of theodicy less cumbersome. A theology that takes animals seriously will be much more difficult than one that maximizes the world's design by ignoring such a huge reservoir of senseless suffering. A theology for the animals must be at least a little absurd. To hope for complete redemption in the light of so much waste seems impossible. To have faith in God's love is an extravagant gesture in the midst of so much pain, not unlike the impulse to reach out to dogs and to accept their devotion.

Postmodern Western culture values irony and cynicism, attitudes that permit the disconnection between knowledge and feeling. We do not want to be caught believing too much; we would rather believe too little. We want to restrict our range of sympathy and care for fear of being foolish and naive. The most terrible deception, however, is to cheat oneself out of love. This is what cleverness, the opposite of sentimentality, accomplishes. Related to prudence, cleverness is a reservation to the risk of love that works only too well; cleverness believes that to fall short is better than to go too far. Prudence is a defense against the charge of hypocrisy because love can never accomplish what it expresses and desires. Love for animals is so simple and easy that the postmodernist mentality simply insists that it must hide some other agenda or obscure some deeper set of emotions. For those with faith, however, hope has the last word, even when it cannot be spoken. Robert Frost once said that politics is an extravagance about grievances while poetry is an extravagance about grief (1995: 904). Taking his thought one step further, I would say that theology is an extravagance about hope. God is the unspeakable hope that impossibly survives the unthinkable thought of animal suffering. Petting is one potent expression of this hope, even when it falls far short of words.

God as a Lover of Dogs

Darwin's love for dogs and the significant role that love played in his thinking about human responsibilities toward the natural world were representative of the Victorian mind. Talk about dogs and religion, however, is not completely absent in the course of Western theological history. In fact, some theologians have made a variety of comparisons among God, dogs, and humans, even though God is thought to be disembodied and dogs, like all animals, represent pure materiality. God is eternal, and the lives of dogs are always too brief. Nevertheless, everyone hears at a young age that dog is God spelled backward, suggesting a connection between the two that is more than wordplay to dog lovers. Is it so strange to claim that God loves us like we love dogs, indeed, that those two loves are the very same thing?

The Christian tradition often compares God (or Jesus or church leaders) to a shepherd, but this comparison is limited because the shepherd cares for the sheep from an interest in wool and mutton.[5] Jesus is not, in a way, a good shepherd, because he unprofitably lays down his life for the sheep; his giving breaks the economy of use value. The metaphor of the good shepherd is not one of predation or slaughter but one of the sacrifice of the higher for the lower. Building on Andrew Linzey's notion of a "generosity paradigm" for theology and animals, I want to compare God to the companion of a dog, somebody who cares just for the joy of caring. In a vivid and remarkable image, Psalm 104:27 portrays God as literally feeding the animals: "These all look to you to give them their food in due season." This image is repeated in Psalm 145:15–16: "The eyes of all look to you, and you give them their food in due season. You open your hand, satisfying the desire of every living thing." Jeremiah describes Israel as an untrained calf who needs the discipline of God (31:18). Isaiah contrasts Israel's failure to obey God with the way in which "the ox knows its owner, and the donkey its master's crib" (1:3). The image of God's love at its highest pitch naturally draws from the practice of petkeeping. To God, there are no wild animals because God claims responsibility and thus cares for them all.

The interconnections among God, humans, and dogs are rich. Both God and dogs love unconditionally, both God and humans are masters in their own realms, and both dogs and humans are creatures and servants. Humans are in between, both masters and servants, loved by God and dogs alike. God's venture across a great divide to identify with humanity is not unlike the human project of domesticating and adopting the canine species. Moreover, dogs, like God, are both infinitely close to us and mysteriously far away, everyday and unfathomable, immanent and transcendent. Hegel once tried to insult Schleiermacher's definition of Christianity as the feeling of absolute dependence by accusing it of turning the Christian into a dog, but perhaps he was not so wrong as his ridiculing tone tried to suggest.[6] Friedrich von Hügel took the dependence of dogs with utmost seriousness. In a discussion of our fickle yet intense love for God, he turned to dogs for a comparison:

> Our dogs know us and love us thus most really, yet they doubtless know us only vividly, not clearly; we evidently strain their minds after a while—they then like to get away from human company, the rich and dim, or (at best) the vivid experiences—the company that is above them, to the company of their fellow creatures, the company that affords so much poorer but so much clearer impressions—the level company of their brother dogs. And yet how wonderful! Dogs thus require their fellow dogs, the shallow and clear, but they also require us, the deep and dim; they require indeed what they can grasp; but they as really require what they can reach out to, more or less—what exceeds, protects, envelops, directs them. And, after a short relaxation in the dog-world, they return to the bracing of the man-world. (1923: 102)

Dogs are active partners in our relationship of love, and their seeking can teach us about the obligations imposed by desire. As David Hartley, an eighteenth-century psychologist, wrote, "We seem to be in the place of God to them, to be his Viceregents, and empowered to receive homage from them in His name. And we are obliged by the same tenure to be their guardians and benefactors" (quoted in Rollin, 1992: 32). Both relationships, God to us and us to dogs, are reciprocal, in spite of the asymmetry of power and intelligence.

Alister Hardy has argued that the connection between dogs and God is not just an analogy. Hardy insists that, because people and dogs are very close in their social behavior, the same biological factors involved in the dog's relationship to humans are involved in the human's relationship to God. In both there is a following that ennobles and expands. "The faithfulness, love and devotion of a dog for his master or mistress shows us, I believe, the same elements that make up the essentials of man's attitude to his personal God" (1975: 169).[7] Most theological reflections on dogs focus on their embodiment of devotion and fidelity, but our interaction with dogs also puts into practice our ability to communicate with an other beyond the realm of words. As Carol J. Adams provocatively asks, "What if trying to have a conversation with an animal is like trying to have a conversation with God? Would we then bring a discipline of attending to our relationships with animals?" (1994: 195–96). Literalizing the often-made analogy that God is to humans as humans are to dogs would have revolutionary consequences. Humans are not the only thing that God loves, but it was in God's special identification with humans that God most becomes God's self, and thus God is most able to identify with others. Likewise, it is in humanity's special identification with dogs that we can most come to terms with our own capacity to love beyond our species and our own fears and anxieties about identifying with the pain of animal others.

Philosophers too have trusted the dog as a guide to human knowing and loving. In Book II of the *The Republic* (which is about an ideal city that was meant to be, following Plato's conception of the Golden Age, vegetarian), Plato depicts Socrates discussing the guardians of the just city. Socrates says that the noble young guardian must be like a thoroughbred dog, brave and spirited. More than this, guardians must be fierce to their enemies and gentle to their friends. Is this balance of the emotions possible? Yes, Socrates argues, because the dog combines these characteristics. "The fact that a dog will be fierce with a stranger, though the stranger has never harmed him, while he will be gentle with one he knows, whether he has received any kindness from him or not. Has that never struck you as quite marvelous?" Socrates seems to be stating a commonplace, but he continues, "Surely, this is an admirable trait in the dog's nature. Indeed, it is this trait that makes the dog a philosopher" (1985: 72).

Now Socrates seems to be having fun at his listener's expense. Or is he? Is he using the dog as a metaphor for something human, or does the dog really exercise a virtue that philosophers need as well? "Do you not see that knowing and not knowing are the sole criteria the dog uses to distinguish friend from enemy? Does it not follow that any animal that verifies his likes and dislikes by the test of knowledge and ignorance must be a lover of learning?" (72). Most commentators do not take Socrates' argument very seriously. Socrates' dog, however, does not serve merely to illustrate an all-too-human point. Socrates is arguing for the connection of knowledge and love that might seem counterintuitive. Can't we love beyond what we know, and can't we know things that we do not love? Dogs let their desires be guided by their knowledge; presumably, the more they know, the more they love. When dogs get to know you, they love you naturally, automatically. This would be a good moral maxim: to know only what we love and to love all that we know.[8] No scientist could sacrifice an animal for the sake of knowledge if his or her knowing were so intimately connected to loving.

Many have argued that the love of animals is a test of character, and some have argued that for the Christian, the love of animals is a kind of dry run or rehearsal for relationships of graceful giving, a *praeparatio evangelica*. In the words of C. W. Hume, for example, "Relations with animals are simpler than relations with human beings, and therefore afford a less ambiguous test of a man's attainment in charity, humility, and ungreediness than his social relations do. Thus the attitude of professing Christians toward the less popular animals is an index of the sincerity of their profession" (1957: 83). Hume merely succeeds in theologizing the indirect duty arguments of Aquinas and Kant. I am suggesting, on the contrary, that our relationships with animals are graced with the same grace that blesses human society and the same grace that saves us all. This is the grace given to us by God through Jesus Christ, who embodies the pains and hopes of all living creatures and provides for us all.

The path I have tried to follow in this book is the expansion of what can be called a kind of sentimentalism or idealization. I am not suggesting that the romance of the dog and its potential amplification are peculiar to Western or Christian sensibilities. Nor am I suggesting that this is the only path that leads toward compassion for animals. It is commonplace to suggest that the emphasis on pets is a Eurocentric phenomenon, and this is not, of course, true. Nevertheless, other cultures do seem to be more aware of the vices of dogs, of their habits that limit human socialization as well as the ways in which they can coinhabit with humanity.[9] For the majority of the people in the Middle East, for example, dogs represent cowardice, dirtiness, and laziness (see Masri, 1987). Precisely because dogs try to scavenge human waste and surplus, they are thought to be out of place, neither wild nor human and thus something to be despised. Dogs lack shame in the persistence of their attempts to beg from and live off human excess, and dogs lack discipline and self-control in their perpetual search for food.

These very traits, however, can also be put to the religious quest for compassion and love. The Sufis, members of an Islamic mystical movement, were a decisive exception to typical Middle Eastern attitudes because they equated their own egos, their *nafs,* with the characteristic traits of dogs (see Nurbakhsh, 1989). The ego is an inward dog that needs more restraint than any real dog does. They also interpreted dogs' stubborn attempts at becoming part of human society as an analogy of the selflessness and persistence that is needed for any mystic to follow God's ways. Such analogies could lead to a literal identification with the dog: "I am the dog at the threshold of neediness. My collar is fashioned from fidelity to God" (57). More than a mere analogy, however, the Sufis took compassion toward dogs as a measure of one's humanity and godliness: "A man encountered a dog in the desert who was so thirsty that it was barely clinging to life. There being a well nearby, this man of meritorious practice made his cap a bucket and tied his turban to it to act as a rope. He readied himself and drew a draught of water for the helpless dog. Subsequently, word came from the Prophet that God was forgiving the man's sins" (23). The moral of this tale does not try to idealize the man's action or to place the dog's value on the same level with the worth of human life. Nevertheless, the moral is clear: "If you have been heedless, be mindful. Be devoted and practice generosity. God does not abandon one who does good for a dog; how then could one who does good for a worthy human be lost? Be as generous as you possibly can. The Keeper of the world never closes the door to blessings on anyone" (22–23). Two images come to mind. In one, God is like a dog, waiting at the door, but instead of guarding the threshold, God always lets everyone in, eagerly welcoming those who want to enter into God's abode and become part of God's family. Likewise, God treats us like one who has adopted a dog—extending kinship lines in unexpected and extravagant directions, quick to comfort and care, and never counting the cost.[10]

CHAPTER SIX

The Sacrificial Economy of Christian Theology

Economics and Sacrifice

Dogs emphatically give themselves to us, and we respond in kind. Such excess makes our moral concern both particular and expansive. The problem of framing and understanding this excess, however, can be exceedingly difficult. Indeed, the language of mutual acts of extravagant giving is in danger on two fronts. On the one hand, it is often claimed that all interactions are regulated by self-interest and thus economic rationality. The secular world seems not to know any alternative to the economizing mentality. On the other hand, the language of sacrifice is often used to justify animal killing (as well as human suffering). Sacrifice originates in a religious worldview, but its assumptions are now widely shared and voiced. It is important to understand the interrelationship between these two concepts in order to begin to formulate a vision of sacrificial giving that is shorn of an economic framework.

To say that economic calculation governs our relationships not only with things but also with other people is a trivial truism. In all of our acts we are trained to calculate the cost and the benefit of our expenditures, minimizing one and maximizing the other. We think habitually in terms of investment, interest, and income. Even in activities removed from the arena of work and livelihood, like art and play in all of their splendid shapes and forms, we think about what we want to put into and get out of time spent relaxing or enjoying. Simple pleasures that have no productive point, like entertainment or playing games, have been made into commodities for trade and profit, so that no area of our life is unaffected by the economy. We even make a game of economics, taking pleasure in economizing our resources or gambling on the economy itself. Like a game that serves no purpose, profit becomes an end in itself, something to be pursued for its own sake. Indeed, economic thinking is so pervasive in our modern, Western, postindustrial culture that thinking itself is organized in terms of efficiency, specialization, and production. Not only can we not avoid thinking about economics in conjunction with all of our activities, but the very form of our thought is economical through and through.

Many have complained about the negative effects of such economic thinking on various aspects of our culture. The reduction of human experience to the rigid rationalism of *Homo oeconomicus* has been connected to the erosion of communal values and the diminishment of human freedom and individuality. The consequences of such thinking on our relationship with animals are rarely investigated. A persuasive case can be made that the greatest victims of economic thinking have been nonhuman animals. Animals are treated as a renewable resource that can be used without limit and without end. In fact, the only limits to their use are economic. Not only are they bought and sold for everything from zoos to scientific and industrial research, but the pressures of the free market have turned farm animals into products that must be raised as efficiently as possible. Over 100 million cows, pigs, and sheep and more than 5 billion chickens are raised and slaughtered in the United States each year under conditions that treat animals like protein machines converting plentiful feed into precious flesh (see Coats, 1991). Animals are merely part of the costs that need to be *cut* in order to make a profit.

The language of sacrifice is equally pervasive in our culture. Feminists have criticized this language because sacrifice, although preached by men, is often most required of women. Indeed, women are portrayed in our culture as naturally adept at sacrifice, so much so that submission, rather than selfishness, is their tempting vice (see Plaskow, 1980). The feminist effort to enable female self-assertion, then, frequently comes into conflict with the logic of sacrifice. What is not as commonly investigated is a similar connection between sacrifice and animals. The language of voluntary and generous acts of sacrifice is imposed on animals, who are sacrificed, obviously, against their will. Animals are defined by sacrifice: that is their purpose. In continuity with the animal sacrifices of the Hebrew scriptures, Christians thank God for the animals at their meals, covering the taking of these lives with gratitude (eyes closed, not seeing) for God's giving them in the first place. Scientists often speak of research animals as sacrifices, and many people think that, no matter how tragic animal suffering is, it is a necessary evil for the acquisition of essential human goods or even justifiable for the satisfaction of trivial human pleasures.

Any discussion about the value and the role of sacrificial ideology today must focus on animals as the most prominent exemplification of that ideology. Sacrifice and economic rationality reinforce each other. Both assume that relationships are based on a zero-sum game: somebody must lose for somebody else to win. Both envision the world in terms of scarcity and competition, so that suffering and hardship are necessary byproducts of progress and advancement. Consequently, human profit is paid for in the currency of animal suffering since animals count for so little and thus can be spent so freely. Can Christian theology reimagine and literally reconstruct the world in terms of abundance and grace instead of scarcity and sacrifice? What is the Christian economy of (animal) sacrifice?

Karl Barth's Sacrificial Economy of Animals

The doctrine of creation is one of the three topics in which theologians most frequently discuss animals (the other two are the nature of humanity and the problem of evil). Karl Barth's response to Albert Schweitzer's demand for respect for all life is an honest and revealing exposition of how this doctrine can be used to subordinate animals to humans. Schweitzer was frequently accused of exaggerating the significance of animals for moral reflection, perhaps because he defined morality itself as a kind of exaggeration: "Ethics are responsibility *without limit* to all that lives" (quoted in Linzey, 1988a: 119). He insisted on the absolute principle that all life is holy, but he also could urge, in a more practical vein, the gradual extension and amplification of ethical concern to include all living things. "Until he extends the circle of his compassion to all living things," Schweitzer wrote, "man will not himself find peace" (quoted in Wynne-Tyson, 1989: 316). The quick response to Schweitzer is to argue that he provides no criterion by which distinctions and thus judgments can be made among the incredible variety of forms of life. Barth, in *Church Dogmatics,* his multivolume reflection on a Christian theology grounded in the revelation given to the church, does not take this easy way out. Indeed, even those who know Barth's work well are sometimes surprised to discover that he addresses in complete seriousness this issue of the value of animal life. Unlike many theologians, Barth was willing to admit that the problem of animals is complex: "It may well be insoluble and barely tangible, but it is genuine and cannot be ignored" (1961: 350). Barth intuitively felt the problem of animal suffering, even though he did not think that theology could easily respond to this problem.

Barth is best known for the Christocentric focus of his theology: all theological doctrines must be interpreted in the light of Jesus Christ. Thus, his reflections on the doctrine of creation, the origin, purpose, and destiny of the nonhuman world, are subordinated to a concern with the activity of God's saving grace through Jesus Christ. Jesus Christ is the Word of God, which is spoken to those who can hear it, that is, human beings. The Word takes various shapes—revelation, church proclamation, and scripture, in addition to the event of Jesus Christ—but as a form of address its audience is limited. The Word is not primarily the *logos* of creation, the "indescribable gift" (2 Corinthians 9:15) that unites all things in God's sustaining activity, but the specific exchange between God and humanity. What the Word speaks is the election of humanity to God's grace. In Jesus Christ, God is united with humanity even before the world begins. The drama of God's relationship to Jesus is thus the foundation of everything else, from the creation of the world to the salvation of humankind.

Keeping with this Christological focus, creation, for Barth, is that which makes God's giving in Jesus Christ possible and productive. In Barth's formula, creation is the external basis of the covenant of grace, while redemption is the internal basis of creation. Creation is the "corresponding space" (1958: 44) that allows the drama of election to unfold. While humanity has a dual status, being elected in eternity but also created in time, nature has a single status only. This does not mean that Barth devalues nature. He agrees with God's judgment that nature is good, but he rejects this statement as an abstract claim or as a description of the way things naturally are. Nature is good only because it is a necessary prerequisite to God's plan for the election of humanity. Humanity is the whole point and goal of creation. "That God's creation has the character of benefit derives everywhere, as we have seen, from the fact that its fundamental purpose lies in the covenant between God and man" (332). Humans are to be stewards or caretakers of creation because it was made for them. This privileged position does not, however, give humans the right to do whatever they want with the natural world. Indeed, Barth sees domesticated animals as a particularly promising sign of the kind of partnership that can develop in the context of stewardship: "It is said of a good horseman that he is so completely one with his horse that he always knows exactly to take out of it no more and no less than what it can not only give but is willing and glad to do so. If this is correct, in this respect a really good horseman cannot possibly be an ungodly person" (1961: 352). Training an animal is a paradigm of the exercise of proper (God-given) authority and power.

At this point in an analysis of Barth's doctrine of creation, it is common to accuse him of an overly anthropocentric view of the universe. For those who want to find in nature something good in itself, without regard for human valuing, Barth's vision is inadequate. As H. Paul Santmire comments, "From the perspective of Barth's theology, the master builder must be pictured as rejoicing in his establishing and shaping only because of something *still to be added* to his work, something for which his work is the occasion or means" (1985: 128). Santmire wants a doctrine of God that portrays nature as something valuable independent of the human quest for meaning or the history of the drama of salvation. Santmire values a world void of human presence, but from my perspective Barth does not permit enough human-nature encounter rather than too much. The problem is not with his anthropomorphic recognition of humanity's central role in God's plan for the world but with his limited understanding of the dynamic of giving. Barth does not go far enough in analyzing nature as a gift, a gift that demands as well as benefits. In fact, Barth does not envision creation as a gift in itself; it is only the preliminary preparation for the giving of Jesus Christ.[1] He affirms the gifted character of the world only when it is construed as an aspect of God's giving to us of Jesus Christ. We know that creation is good and that the world makes sense only on the basis of God's gift of Jesus Christ.[2] Without this primary gift, nothing in nature can be experienced as a gift. Thus, Barth rules out the possibility that animals can contribute something decisive to human reality, that animals can be a gift on their own terms. Animals are on the side of nature, not history, and thus they cannot contribute directly to human reality. The creation of animals is the "dark background to the true work [the creation of humankind] towards which the [creation] narrative hastens" (1958: 291). If nature is the scenery on which redemption takes place, animals are at best props, useful items or object lessons given only for humanity's physical needs and spiritual education.[3]

Even though this seems to portray animals in a purely instrumental light, Barth is at least sensitive to the possibility of treating animals as ends and not means alone. He insists that we should not dismiss Schweitzer's position as "sentimental" (1961: 349). Indeed, "Those who can only smile at this point are themselves subjects for tears" (349). Barth is willing to listen to the claims that nonhuman life presents to us, through the extremist rhetoric of poets, mystics, and other eccentrics. He even has a fine ear for the specific qualities of the language of animal love. "It is hardly an accident that in those who speak along these lines there is usually something strange and even excessive" (350). He knows that the rhetoric of animal compassion strikes many as marginal and yet compelling, something that can only be spoken in extremist terms. On this peculiar issue, Barth complains, we find ourselves at the furthest limit of both what can be thought and what can be done. Although he condemns the "quite enough human stupidity, severity, caprice and irrationality at work and needing to be curbed" (352), Barth draws back from this limit. Animals, he writes, are provided for humans to use. They are less like a gift than like something loaned, now owned, that can be disposed of at will.

Barth, however, is too dialectical to dismiss animals this easily. Drawing on the first two chapters of Genesis, which portray a primordial vegetarianism, and Paul's words in Romans about the whole world groaning for liberation, Barth admits that when a human kills an animal, as opposed to the sensible use of the superfluity of plants, it is "at least very similar to homicide" (352). In fact, Barth surprisingly grants that, given ordinary conditions, there can be absolutely no sufficient reason to kill an animal. Much of Barth's discussion about the importance of animals belies his disagreement with Schweitzer. He argues that on a biblical basis animals are the forerunners and companions of humans, share humanity's blessings and burdens, and will in their own way be freed from bondage in the end. Moreover, the animal "needs the Word of God even in respect of the living acts which it spontaneously accomplishes. It needs not only the presence but also the accompaniment of the powerful Word of God" (1958: 174).

Other passages are also worth quoting: "Man's salvation and perdition, his joy and sorrow, will be reflected in the weal and woe of this animal environment and company. Not as an independent partner of the covenant, but as an attendant, the animal will participate with man (the independent partner) in the covenant, sharing both the promise and the curse which shadows the promise. Full of forebodings, but also full of confidence, it will wait with man for its fulfillment, breathing freely again when this has taken place provisionally and will take place definitively" (178).[4] And this: "It is not said, and cannot be said, that the beasts belong to man, for 'the earth is the Lord's and the fullness thereof, the world and they that dwell therein' (Psalm 24:1)" (205). These comments go much further than most theological treatments of this issue. What, then, keeps Barth from simply agreeing with Schweitzer? Barth has come almost too close to saying what he does not want to, and so he must quickly search elsewhere to justify carnivorous practices. "The sense one gets in Barth," writes Andrew Linzey, "is that the issue is too vast and too demanding for appropriate human response" (1987: 92). Barth wants deliverance from this issue rather than deliverance for those who need it.

As with all of his theological arguments, Barth finally appeals to the grace of God. He states, "The slaying of animals is really possible only as an appeal to God's reconciling grace, as its representation and proclamation" (1961: 354). Our freedom to kill animals, then, is really the burden of a great responsibility. We can only take that which has been given to us, and killing it must be a form of return. A human can only kill an animal knowing that "it does not belong to him but to God, and that in killing it he surrenders it to God in order to receive it back from Him as something he needs and desires" (355). By implication, when we do kill an animal, it must be done as "a deeply reverential act of repentance, gratitude and praise" (355). God, in other words, still owns the animals, and by killing them we give them back to God (the giver and the taker of all life), who in turn lets us benefit from their death. Justified killing must take the form of both gratitude and guilt because it confirms God as the source of both life and death. Indeed, Barth's admission of the guilt involved in taking animal life begs the question of whether such killing can ever be justified, so he must search deeper for a theological basis for flesh eating. As a priestly act, he finally argues, animal killing is a recognition of the power of sacrifice, which is ultimately expressed in the death of Jesus Christ.

Only by recapitulating the crucifixion can this precarious frontier of killing animals be crossed. Only by saying grace before a meal can the gratuitous gift of animals be accepted (that is, consumed) with the proper mixture of gratitude and guilt.

This is surely a strange exchange of gifts. Why would God want us to return dead what he has given us alive? How is killing a form of giving? What is the gift of Jesus Christ, that its repetition or representation includes further loss of life? These are questions I will return to in chapter 7. Barth, as always, tries to anticipate his critics. In a crucial passage, he admits that vegetarianism "represents a wanton anticipation of what is described by Is. 11 and Rom. 8 as existence in the new aeon for which we hope" (356–57). Barth opts for moral realism rather than perfectionism, not wanting to burden Christians with impractical demands that can only cause frustration and resentment. Vegetarianism smacks of Pelagianism to Barth; it is the earnest work of the self-righteous, not a practical and natural expression of gratitude. Not only is it ironic that Barth charges vegetarian eating habits (which restrict and improve one's diet) with being wanton (prurient, unwholesome, craving), but Barth's use of this term also reveals a puzzling hesitation or reservation in his thought. Is vegetarianism wanton because it goes too far on the side of the good, or does it try too hard in the face of human limits and weaknesses? Is vegetarianism really too eagerly eschatalogical, or is it an appropriate return of God's gift of abundant life?

There is something wanton, I want to argue, in our relationship with animals, a giving that urges us not toward sacrifice but toward further giving. Barth outlines one possible economy of relationships among God, humans, and animals, an economy in which what is given must be utilized, consumed, and destroyed, both as a sign of respect for the giver and as an acknowledgment of the sacrificial nature of all giving. This model of our relations to animals leads directly to the factory farms where animals are treated as renewable resources to be produced as efficiently as possible. I want to outline another kind of economy, as well as another form of sacrifice, one in which the given is splurged, abundantly given over to us, so that we can kill but we can also receive, cherish, and return, in a parallel manner, that which is excessive and thus strangely compelling. We can give animals back to God by receiving them as gifts in themselves, and we can give to them (and here dogs are so important) as they give to us. In sum, they are not given to us, but we are given for each other.

Hebrew Sacrifice and the Covenant

To be fair to Barth, what he actually tries to retrieve, although he does not make this explicit, is the Hebrew notion of ritual sacrifice. It is important to put that practice of sacrifice in context in order to make sense of Barth's insistence that animals can be killed in order to express gratitude to God. Many ancient cultures have rituals of thanks and apology that precede the killing of animals for food. As the poet Gary Snyder writes, "Other beings (the instructors from the old ways tell us) do not mind being killed and eaten as food, but they expect us to say please, and thank you, and they hate to see themselves wasted" (1990: 20). The religious beliefs that require and sanction these rituals vary, but clearly ancient cultures had the sense that in taking animal life something was being desecrated—perhaps the home of the resident deity—and thus appropriate measures must be taken for placation and compensation. The animal, in other words, must be thanked for offering itself. It is thus possible to argue that hunting lies at the origin of animal sacrifice.[5]

The Hebrews, however, thought all creatures existed according to the authority of only one God, so sacrificial ritual did not placate the animal spirit. Instead, it acknowledged and gave gratitude to the single origin of all life. The theme of animal sacrifice in the Bible is thus a humble and grateful reverence for life, implicitly recognizing that the taking of life can occur only if the life of the animal rests ultimately in God's, not human, hands. Sacrifice is a complicated attempt to kill animals without degrading them, and to understand that practice, the relationships among God, humans, and animals must be examined in their broadest biblical context.

The Hebrews had a sense of the very particular obligations humans have toward the natural world that is lost or minimized in Christianity. It is exceptional that a pastoral people who lived on meat, dressed in animal skins, and wrote on parchment (although it should be noted that there is remarkably little hunting in the Bible, and Jewish law forbids sport hunting) should bequeath to the world a vision of an original and an ultimate vegetarianism. Even the animals in the Garden of Eden do not eat meat (Genesis 1:29–30). The Hebrew scriptures persistently portray all of creation as a blessing, thus envisioning animals as a gift from God. As the Wisdom of Solomon states, "For all existing things are dear to thee and thou hatest nothing that thou hast created—why else wouldst thou have made it?" (11:24, NEB). The breath of God sustains all living creatures; indeed, God "save[s] humans and animals alike" (Psalm 36:6). Salvation for the Hebrews is nothing if it is not inclusive and total (Isaiah 11:6–9; Hosea 2:18). It is reasonable to wonder at the insistence on animal compassion and redemption in a world that was so dependent on animal labor and consumption. How could such provocative ideas have become an integral part of the Jewish tradition? Moreover, how many more testimonies to animal concern have been lost in the development of the Jewish tradition, ideas that were thought to be too radical or challenging to be included in the stories passed down through the generations? Fortunately, enough scripture remains to demonstrate God's overwhelming concern with the animal world.

Of course, human agents are the primary focus of the Hebrew scriptures, but animals are never completely left out of the picture. Scholars debate whether the Hebrew covenant with God is conditional or unconditional. What is clear is that it includes the whole world. The covenant begins with Adam and Noah, and thus it is universal before it is particularized with Abraham. All of creation is a partner with people in God's comprehensive purposes. The Abrahamic covenant involves the land, and the Mosaic covenant is connected to the righteousness of the Israelites. Clearly, the covenant demands the cooperation of the Israelites before promising to bless their land and their animals (see Deuteronomy 7: 12–15). When the writers of the Hebrew scriptures discuss the fate of this or that city or people, they usually include their animals with them because they understood animals and the earth to be a part of God's overall concern. What is important to emphasize is that the covenant is as much a dream, wish, or passion as it is a contract or statement of intentions. It gestures to the future as much as to the past.

Many Christians, eager to justify their meat eating, zealously point out that the covenant with Noah legitimates precisely this practice. After all, Noah's first response to God after the flood was to offer burnt offerings of "clean" (noncarnivorous) animals. That God is moved by this act to reverse and obliterate his initial anger leads some readers to conclude that God takes delight in the gratuitous death of animals, even though the theme of the story is that God's covenant, which includes animals, is one of compassion and care. Indeed, God states that God will never again kill every living creature (Genesis 8:21). God's subsequent acknowledgment that the animals will fear humans seems like a mournful description of a world still fallen, not a benefit given to humans. Only at this point in the Genesis narrative does God grant permission to humans to eat meat, a sanctioning that reads to vegetarians as a begrudging and provisional concession. In fact, in the very next verse God seems to demand blood revenge (a life for a life), suggesting that God is trying to deal with humans by adjusting the divine purpose to a violence that has threatened to become endemic and pervasive. God has learned, for now, to compromise. The question is, how long did God intend to condone and overlook unnecessary violence to animals?

Traditional common explanations for God's permission of meat eating at this point in the biblical narrative include, first, that after the flood there was nothing else to eat (because all the vegetation had been destroyed!); second, that God accepted a lower standard of morality, seeing that humans could not live up to God's expectations; and third, that Noah had a new relationship with animals—having saved them, he now had the right to take them as food. For Jewish and Christian traditions alike, this permission to eat meat gradually becomes a custom and finally is taken as a commandment. Others read it differently. As Gary Comstock notes, "To me, the passage reads less as divine permission, more as divine curse; less as God's preferred norm for human-animal relations, more as God's grim prediction of what will happen to human-animal relations" (1993: 113). This is especially the case when just a few verses later (Genesis 9:8–11) God makes a promise to the whole of creation, including animals, never to destroy all life again. About the Noachic covenant, Jay McDaniel writes, "God *chooses* to enter into covenant with animals *after* having first recognized and empathized with their plight" (1993: 91). Surely it is not unreasonable to infer from this story that God permits something that nevertheless is neither encouraged nor thought of as a permanent state. In any case, the Noachide laws, which the Talmudic rabbis insist are the universal element of the Jewish faith and thus apply to all humankind, include a prohibition of cruelty to animals.

Later in the narrative, when the Hebrews were in the wilderness for forty years on the sojourn out of Egypt, they ate manna, a vegetarian bread (it looked like coriander seed, according to Numbers 11:7). There was no need to struggle to obtain it because no matter how much was gathered, each had enough (Exodus 16:17–18). The Hebrews, however, grew tired of the original food of God and longed for the flesh-pots of Egypt. Some exclaimed, "If only we had meat to eat!" (Numbers 11:4), complaining of their lack of strength on this new diet. (This story shows how old the superstition is that only the protein from the muscle of animals can build human muscles.) God, in response to the gluttony and rebellion, relents and gives them quail for a month, enough to eat, as God says angrily, "until it comes out of your nostrils and becomes loathsome to you" (11:20). Later, God regrets this decision and strikes the people with a great plague, so that they had to bury "the people who had the craving" (11:34). The place where the plague occurred was called "the Graves of Greed." Gluttony was an insult against the simple and plentiful diet God had provided. The moral of this story is that God seems to accommodate reluctantly human meat eating because it is one of the most obstinate and tenacious symptoms of human sin.

The eating of meat was not only habitually practiced by the Hebrews but also given religious sanction. As Richard D. Nelson notes, sacrifice may be seen as "a natural ritualization of the prosaic act of slaughtering and eating a domestic animal" (1993: 67). Any discussion of the role of animals in the Bible always returns to the animal sacrifices God seems to demand. What are we to make of these animal sacrifices today? The Hebrew scriptures never explain the purpose or the origin of animal sacrifices, so this practice gives rise to much unfettered speculation. There is reason to be wary of appropriating animal sacrifice as a legitimation of meat eating. Instead of viewing animal sacrifice as something the vegetarian must explain or apologize for, it is possible to see animal sacrifice as a constraint put on meat eating, a preliminary step toward vegetarianism that Christianity circumvented.

In point of fact, the cultic context definitely limited the amount of meat the

people could consume, and the gluttonous eating of meat is frequently condemned in the Hebrew scriptures. Leviticus treats the slaughter of animals outside the precinct of the altar of the sanctuary as murder, and no king of Israel
is ever described as participating in a hunt. Although not all meat eating was
the result of animal sacrifice and not every animal sacrificed was eaten, meat
eating and sacrifice were very closely connected, so that sacrificial ritual served
to place slaughter in a context that mitigated the wanton taking of life. Ritual
slaughter, while it provides religious justification for meat eating, also disciplines and controls that eating in ways that are totally disregarded by Christians
today.

Sacrifice among the ancient Jews is a complex topic not easily summarized.
At first animals could be sacrificed at solitary altars scattered throughout the
countryside or at altars attached to the various local temples. However, animals
were not to be eaten without the ritual of sacrifice. In early Israel, then, "every
meal where the family's own beast was eaten was thereby a ritual occasion, on
which consecrated flesh was eaten and blessing was received from the deity"
(Houston, 1993: 229). Gradually, sacrifices were consolidated in the Jerusalem
Temple, built by Solomon around 950 B.C.E., making other temples obsolete
(see Haran, 1978). King Josiah of Judah forbade all sacrificial worship outside
the First Temple in a series of edicts issued in 622 B.C.E. (recorded in 2 Kings
22–23), thereby instituting pilgrimage as an integral aspect of ritual slaughter.
With this consolidation, priests, traditionally a hereditary class of religious ex-
perts, became increasingly important in their office of attending to the Temple
and its sacred tasks. Another consequence of consolidation was that altars outside of Jerusalem were no longer permitted. It was thus necessary to develop
the distinction between sacrifice and nonritual (or less ritualized) slaughter for
food. This distinction is absent in Leviticus (Leviticus 17 requires all animals
to be brought to the tabernacle for sacrifice and specifically forbids the slaughter of domestic animals apart from sacrifice) but is discussed elsewhere, most
notably in Deuteronomy 12. Nonetheless, ritual (and gradually Temple-based)
slaughter remained both a standard practice and an ideal that served to place
meat eating in a restricted and covenantal context. Returning the blood of the
slaughtered animal to God exonerates the butcher from any defilement and
distinguishes an act of gratitude from a plain barbecue.

Animals were not the only sacrifices made by the Hebrews. They also
brought offerings of first fruits, wheat, and barley to the Temple. However, the
fact that about 150 of the Torah's 613 laws deal with animal sacrifices under-
scores the seriousness with which the Hebrews treated the killing of animals.
Some sacrifices were made every morning and afternoon, and to this day, the
morning and afternoon religious services commemorate these daily offerings.
Other sacrifices were gift-offerings or acts of atonement for violations of Torah
laws. In nearly all animal sacrifices, there was a laying on of hands before the

killing, perhaps a gesture of identification and substitution. Generally speaking, at least some part of the animal was burnt on the altar (the fat in particular), and the blood was sprinkled or smeared on the altar. After the sacrifice, some parts of the animal were eaten by the priests, while other parts were returned to the person who brought it. One kind of sacrifice, known in English as a holocaust, involved the burning of the whole animal. (I will discuss the most famous Jewish sacrifice, the paschal lamb of the Passover, in chapter 7.)

Louis A. Berman summarizes the rules involved in ritual sacrifice. First, human sacrifice is banned. Second, animals are limited to those deemed fit for consumption (clean land animals had cloven hoofs and chewed their cud, which eliminated carnivorous animals). Third, only Temple priests can conduct an animal sacrifice, and the theme is one of atonement and thanksgiving. (In the early part of the history of the Hebrews, any male adult could slaughter an animal at an altar. Later, only Temple priests could perform this important act.) Fourth, carcasses are eaten by the worshippers, but within limits: no drinking of blood, and no gorging on fat. Fifth, animal sacrifices are supplemented by the offering of doves and pigeons, so the poor can participate. And sixth, they are also supplemented by vegetable offerings of cakes baked with fine flour. Such regulations hardly make meat eating habitual and ordinary. Berman concludes, "Animal sacrifice, once an occasion for indulging in magical, sadistic, and gluttonous impulses, is transformed into a rite of atonement performed by Temple priests" (1982: 24). The result is an attempted reconciliation between the appetite for animal flesh and the worship of a loving and merciful God. Only by giving a portion of the animal back to God can humans use the rest. Only by putting reverence for life at the center of the act can animal killing be distinguished from murder.

The sacrificial system came to an end with the destruction of the Second Temple in 70c.e. In the mourning that followed this catastrophe, many ascetic groups formed, some of which were vegetarian (see Berman, 1992). The Babylonian Talmud, in the *Baba Batra* tractate (60b), records a debate among the rabbis about whether to eat meat after the destruction of the Second Temple. "The rabbis taught: When the Second Temple was destroyed many turned to asceticism, committing themselves not to eat meat and not to drink wine. R. Joshua approached them and said, My children, who do you not eat meat and drink wine. They replied to him: Shall we eat meat which used to be offered on the altar as a sacrifice, and now has been voided?" R. Joshua, however, argued, "Not to mourn altogether is impossible, because it [the destruction] has been decreed. But to mourn too much is also impossible, because we must not impose a decree on the community that the majority find unbearable." Moreover, "R. Ismael said: Since the Temple was destroyed, by right we ought to decree against ourselves not to eat meat and not to drink wine. But we do not impose measures on the public unless the majority would find them bearable" (Bokser, 1989: 196–97). The priority of solidarity and survival, coupled with the idea that vegetarianism might make survival more difficult, led the rabbis to reject vegetarianism as obligatory on the entire people of Israel. Nevertheless, it was an option that carried much weight and had to be carefully considered. Their compromise was to set aside the nine days preceding the anniversary of the Temple's destruction (Tishah B'Av) as meatless. Through this observance and in many other ways, the Temple was not forgotten.

Rabbinic writings continued to discuss with great care the particulars of animal sacrifice and to mourn the passing of the sacrificial system. The Temple was also sometimes metaphorized, by being portrayed as a Heavenly Temple, a cosmic allegory for earthly knowledge and prosperity (see McKelvey, 1969). Indeed, the transcendentalizing of the Temple began early in Jewish history. During the exile following the destruction of the First Temple, the Jews began to hope for a new Temple that would restore and unify all of Israel, but the building of the Second Temple did not serve as a substitute for these hopes. Thus, there was a continuing contrast between the empirical Temple and its counterpart in the new age. The heavenly Temple is the companion of the earthly Temple and, some believed, will one day replace it. Early Christians continued this line of thinking by arguing that Jesus and the church have become the new Temple. The rabbis also followed the path of spiritualizing the Temple, increasingly putting forward prayer, obedience, charity, and penitence as forms of or substitutes for animal sacrifice.

Later, during the Diaspora, in which Jews faced daily existence deprived of their Temple and its specific rituals, the oral tradition codified by the rabbis into the Talmud served to provide unity and structure for Jewish life. More specifically, the dietary laws of Leviticus (*kashrut*) emerged as a refinement and replacement for animal sacrifice. In order to continue the Temple tradition of killing animals only as an act of thanksgiving and repentance, the Temple priest was replaced by the *shochet,* the ritual slaughterer. Although there are no *shochetim* in the Bible, the rabbis maintained that the slaughter rules *(shechita)* of the *shochet* were given orally by God to Moses and passed down to their own generation. The strict rules for the *shochet* include specifications about the sharpness of the knife and the placement of the cut, which make the animal's death swift and minimize pain. A delay in the stroke, which causes needless suffering, renders the meat unkosher *(trayf)*. Given the fact that many ancient cultures commonly thought that meat would taste better if animals were tortured before their death, these slaughter rules, which continue the Mosaic emphasis on compassion, should be seen as nothing less than a revolutionary development in human history. Moreover, the *shochet* is supposed to be of blameless character and repute, which signifies the difficulty and gravity of the act of slaughter. For Judaism, animal killing is a holy act, something that can be accomplished only in fear and trembling before the grace and majesty of God.

By deritualizing sacrifice, the Christian tradition made the butchering profession secular, thoughtless, and debased. The killing of animals is something to do as quickly as possible, out of the public eye and with little scrutiny or oversight.[6] Historically, in Christian communities, butchers have been held in suspicion, not esteem; they were the subject of rebuke and stereotyped as merciless men. Indeed, they were supposed to be excluded from English juries convened for capital crimes because their long association with blood inured them to the taking of innocent life. It is as if the meat-eating population transfers its guilt and resentment onto the butchers, making them scapegoats, sacrificial victims of their own sacrifices. Judaism has guarded against this tendency by elevating the position of the slaughterer to that of a priestly role. The ritual not only makes the killing as painless as possible but also keeps the killers from becoming brutalized by the slaughtering process. Yet Gentiles continue to resent ritual slaughter, refusing, unlike Barth, to see any value in it and even arguing that it is more inhumane than more modern methods.

One of the controversies for Gentiles is over the bleeding of the animal. Jewish tradition teaches that the animal's blood is the essence of life (Deuteronomy 12:23) so it should be returned to God, the giver of life. Thus, the slaughtered animal must bleed completely, and Jews are forbidden to eat meat that still has the blood in it. Indeed, Orthodox Jews soak their meat in water to drain away the blood and then spread salt on it to draw up any remaining blood. Jewish law also requires that animals be conscious at the time of slaughter, perhaps to insure their bleeding as they die. Consequently, Jewish tradition prohibits the stunning of animals for slaughter, which is contrary to the development of the shackling and hoisting method, begun in 1906 because the U.S. government did not want animals to fall onto the bloody floor. The enforcement of shackling and hoisting regulations for kosher slaughterhouses meant that animals killed by ritual methods were subjected to increased pain (that is, they were hoisted without being stunned). Increasingly, countries are allowing ritual slaughterers to keep the animals in holding pens rather than using shackling and hoisting. Since stunning is often rushed and inadequate, it is argued that the expert cut of a ritual slaughtering in a holding pen is actually more humane than the stunning, shackling, hoisting, and cutting in secular slaughterhouses.

No single moral exists that can be drawn from the practice of Hebrew animal sacrifice. Although the Hebrew scriptures offer no theory of this practice, they do not refrain from criticizing it. To Christians, the antisacrificial texts are arguably too well known (see Amos 4:4, 5:21–26; Hosea 6:6; Isaiah 1:10–17; Micah 6:6–8; Jeremiah 7:21–22; and Psalms 40:6, 50:12–13, 51:16, 56:13), and older scholarship, under the sway of the Protestant doctrine of justification by grace alone, interpreted these critiques as attacks on the Hebrews' attempt to control their own salvation. Protestant scholars, with their belief that God is not affected by what we do, thought that the prophets rejected animal sacrifice for its Pelagianism. More recently, scholars see these criticisms as offering a renewed emphasis on right conduct and social justice as the necessary prerequisites for effective ritual. Certainly the prophets dealt with the problems of organized religion—the relationship between ritual and morality, action and emotion, God's grace and our response. Seldom, however, are the prophets placed in that line of Hebrew thought, beginning with Genesis, that is concerned about animal suffering.

Many scholars, anxious to find continuity, not discontinuity, in the development of Judaism, insist that these prophetic condemnations are relative and dialectical; they seek to reform, not revolutionize. As Godfrey Ashby notes, "To have condemned all offering of sacrifice would have been, in effect, to have condemned all public worship" (1988: 45). Animal sacrifices were a kind of prayer service for the ancient Jews, their most popular way of worshiping God. Thus the Jewish tradition teaches that prophets coexisted (with conflict but not contradiction) with the priests. Consequently, the prophetic teachings were absorbed into the mainstream of Judaism and did not constitute a radical departure from the sacrificial focus of the Jews, even though they later helped Judaism come to terms with the loss of the Temple. Indeed, as Judaism evolved, many Jewish groups grew more and more distant from animal sacrifices, viewing them as a primitive stage in their religious development. The prayer book of Reform Judaism, for example, ignores the subject altogether, while the Conservative prayer book refers to animal sacrifices only in the past tense. Only the Orthodox prayer book continues the hope that the Temple will be rebuilt and sacrifices offered there again. (This hope is shared by some Christian fundamentalists who think that the Temple must be rebuilt as a sign of the Last Days before the return of Christ.)

Although their meaning is ambiguous, the prophetic teachings continue to inspire those who see in them not just a critique of the formality of rituals but also a defense of innocent victims. As Jeremiah writes about the Temple, "Shed no innocent blood in this place" (Jeremiah 7:6, NEB). In Second Isaiah we find, "Whoever slaughters an ox is like one who kills a human being; whoever sacrifices a lamb, like one who breaks a dog's neck" (66:3). And in Habakkuk a fascinating divine pronouncement turns violence to animals against the perpetrators: "For the violence done to Lebanon will overwhelm you; the destruction of the animals will terrify you—because of human bloodshed and violence to the earth, to cities and all who live in them" (2:17). By focusing on compassion, the prophets, at the very least, showed that the covenant as a dream of ultimate harmony was still unfulfilled. They opened up a tension between the covenant of grace and mercy and the ritual sacrifice of animals, a breach that made Christianity possible.

The prophetic spirit is also still very much alive in contemporary Judaism (see Green, 1992: 87–89). One of the most fascinating reflections on ancient Judaism and animals is from Rabbi Abraham Isaac Kook (1865–1935), who was the chief rabbi of Palestine prior to the establishment of the State of Israel. Rabbi Kook argues that "the free movement of the moral impulse to establish justice for animals generally and the claim of their rights from mankind are hidden in a natural psychic sensibility in the deeper layers of the Torah" (1978: 317). In the beginning, he suggests, humanity's moral sense included animals, but it became necessary after humanity "suffered a setback and was unable to bear the great light of its illumination" (317) for people to focus their moral concerns on each other and to withdraw fellowship from the animals. It was essential that humans be separated from the world of animals and be given a feeling of superiority in order to elevate humans into the realm of morality. But the time is coming, he proclaims, when meat eating will be seen as an interim in humanity's spiritual evolution and our moral impulses will again enter an expansive and inclusive state. "The thrust of the ideals in the course of their development will not always remain confined" (318). Rabbi Kook takes a thoroughly historical view of moral development. Every moral insight has its own proper time, and sometimes it needs to be suppressed "in order to gather up its strength for future epochs" (318). Thus, meat eating, like war, is a necessary detour along the long road of humanity's spiritual growth. It is "a tax for passage to a more enlightened epoch, from which animals are not exempt" (318).

What prepares the way for this moral amplification are the laws of the Torah. Rabbi Kook suggests that if the lust for animal flesh had been completely prohibited, it would have burst the boundaries of morality and turned against all living things in an undifferentiated orgy of violence. Animals had to be sacrificed not for divine benefit but for human benefit. Meat eating thus could only be tempered, patiently pointing to future possibilities. The Torah commandments did exactly this. The commandment to pour out the blood of hunted prey and cover it with earth (Leviticus 17:13) means that hunters should be ashamed and should hide their shame. The sensitivity to family attachments among animals (do not slaughter animals and their young on the same day [Leviticus 22:28]), the prohibition against eating animals killed by other animals or that have died a natural death ("Be compassionate at least on the unfortunate ones, if your heart is insensitive to the healthy and strong" [Kook, 1978: 321]), the prohibition against eating fat ("When the savage luxury of eating fat and blood—one can always find room for a delicacy—is forbidden, it takes away the worst element of this cruel gluttony" [Kook, 1978: 320]), and the prohibitions against mixing wool (which is stolen) with flax (which is cultivated) or milk (which feeds the vulnerable young) with meat (which feeds the lustful instincts) all point to the fact that "the silent protest will in time be transformed into a mighty shout" (Kook, 1978: 319). Rabbi Kook firmly believed that to make the soil of Israel holy, to have a vital national existence under the reign of God, God's covenant with the animals could no longer be ignored. Christians who think that the Torah is irrelevant for the modern world should see that the Torah, for Christians and Jews alike, needs to be read again, as if for the very first time.

The End of Sacrifice

What is the relationship between sacrifice and animals, and how can Christians speak the language of sacrifice without perpetuating animal sacrifice? Sacrifice is a notion deeply rooted in Western culture. Although ritualized animal sacrifices have been abandoned by Christianity, the idea that something must be given up in order to approach God remains a first principle of many theologies and religious sensibilities. Sacrifice is now a metaphorical discourse that draws on ancient practices in order to illuminate the ethical sphere. The spiritualization of sacrifice has made it commonplace, even though its religious roots now strike many people as bizarre and disagreeable.[7] Even in secular culture, the value of sacrifice is accepted as a given. As a metaphor, it legitimates real suffering for a higher cause, and thus it offers to make pain meaningful and purposeful. Especially at times of crisis, leaders call on the language of sacrifice to justify the use of force to achieve specific ends, making sacrifice a crucial part of any civil religion. Although the concept of moral sacrifice today seems far removed from the context of animal sacrifice, animals are often its victims since they are used or killed in order to advance the human good.

Sacrifice is a language, a kind of discourse between God and humans. The word itself means simply "to make holy" (*facere sacer*), an attempt by the Romans to use one word to cover a wide variety of acts. Scholarly debates about the origins and purposes of animal sacrifice have been complex and inconclusive. In the past, scholars have sought an Ur-sacrifice, an original sacrifice from which all other forms have developed. Some (including Maimonides) have hypothesized that animal sacrifices began as a substitute for human sacrifices, but now most scholars do not try to unite all rituals in one category or history. Perhaps the most basic description is that a sacrifice puts things right between people and the divine. It can avert danger, propitiate an angry deity, or expiate guilt or sin. It can be a petition or a bribe, a calculated transaction or a praise of thanksgiving. Some have argued that it is a tribute offered to an invisible authority figure in order to insure good fortune. Others have argued that it began as a way of feeding the gods. J. G. Frazer, in *The Golden Bough* (1922; first published in 1890), speculated that ancient peoples thought that the animal sacrificed became divine in the ritual and then passed on divine powers to those who ate it. Some have emphasized the cathartic aspect of the ritual, which leads to a joyous meal. The sacrifice does dramatize the entire process of a crisis and its resolution, providing a rite of passage through suffering, death, and renewal. In some definitions of sacrifice, the animal is hardly mentioned at all. According to Ashby, "Sacrifice is not primarily a death rite. It would be nearer the truth to say that death is incidental" (1988: 8). [8] Yet animals do seem to be an essential aspect of many ancient sacrificial rituals, and their death is the whole point of those rituals. Free-flowing blood is dangerous, but giving up blood to God is a way of representing and controlling the precarious line separating life from death.

Spilling blood is also a way of exercising power and authority. Perhaps the most provocative theory of sacrifice is Nancy Jay's thesis that connects it to the establishment of lines of descent from father to son. Sacrifice, for Jay, is a way for men to compete with childbirth. Since biological paternity is never certain, men are hesitant to build social structures on it. The only way men can wrest from women control of reproduction and the intergenerational organization of the family is by imitating and transforming female reproduction. "What is needed to provide clear evidence of social and religious paternity is an act as definite and available to the senses as is birth" (1992: 36). Biological descent is thus replaced by social and religious descent; the young man is not really born until he can sacrifice or participate in an animal sacrifice. Sacrifice is thus a remedy for the male anxiety of having been born of a woman. Moreover, it not only usurps the role of women but also creates a society that transcends biology altogether. Those who sacrifice, and especially the priests who control the sacrifice, transcend mortality by the same process that they transcend biology. Sacrifice establishes a male priesthood that mediates between man and God and organizes that priesthood in a unilineal and eternal descent. It is no accident, then, that women are almost always excluded from animal sacrifices. Only men identify themselves with the eating of meat (and even today, men often cut and cook the meat, leaving the preparation of the rest of the meal to women). Analyses like Jay's point to the continuing need to criticize and transform sacrificial practice.

Like all languages, this one has changed throughout the course of history. The Hebrews themselves were able to mandate acts of love and kindness to animals alongside a sacrificial ideology. The New Testament continues and sharpens this tension by simultaneously characterizing Jesus as against all acts of violence and portraying the death of Jesus as a kind of sacrifice (see Young, 1975). What cannot be denied is that the New Testament constitutes a revolution in the actual practice of animal sacrifice. Unlike Buddhism's vegetarian critique of Hinduism,[9] however, Christianity never made explicit the compassion toward animals that undermines the sacrificial system.

Indeed, it is very difficult to determine on historical grounds what attitude Jesus had toward the practice of Temple sacrifice. The Gospels were written by Christians with little or no actual knowledge of the Temple. For these writers, the destruction of the Temple was a symbol of the triumph of Christianity over Judaism. This feeling of vindication, along with Christological embellishments and anachronisms, is projected back into the Gospel narratives, vitiating their reliability as historical documents. Some scholars argue that Jesus really had no major disagreements with his Jewish contemporaries, while others portray him as a Prophet who criticized ritual abuses and excesses from the standpoint of compassion and mercy. When Jesus is recorded as criticizing Jewish practices, the interpreter must be careful, because Jesus was, after all, a devout Jew with no intention of founding a separate religion. By the time the New Testament was written, Christians were struggling to establish their identity in contrast to their Jewish roots, so later conflicts are superimposed on the Gospel stories. Tragically, many of these passages have been taken out of context to support a terrible history of anti-Semitism in Christian theology.

The evidence about Jesus' attitude toward the Temple is not clear or consistent. He attended the Temple and encouraged his followers to do likewise, although he is never shown participating in a sacrificial ritual. After healing a leper, Jesus told him to go to a priest and to sacrifice as Moses commanded (Mark 1:40–45), and he warned his disciples to make peace with their brothers before they brought their gifts (sacrifices) to the altar (Matthew 5:23–24).[10] Scholars debate whether Jesus intended to disconnect morality from cultic matters, but he did pronounce the forgiveness of sins prior to rather than subsequent to ritual sacrifice.[11] Indeed, he never requires sacrifice as a means for becoming righteous. He also challenged the power of the Temple in more direct ways, telling the woman of Samaria, for example, that true worship takes place "in spirit and truth" (John 4:21–24). Most significantly, Jesus provocatively entered the Temple court during a crowded national holiday (Passover) and aggressively confronted the very heart of animal sacrifice, overturning tables and driving out those who sold animals (Mark 11:15–18, Matthew 21:12–13, Luke 19:45–46, John 2:13–22). In Mark, Jesus justifies his actions by saying that the priests have turned a house of prayer for all nations into a "den of robbers."

The Gospels portray Jesus as predicting the destruction of the Temple (Mark 13:1–2), and they attribute to his accusers at his trial the testimony that he threatened to destroy the Temple (Mark 14:58). During his crucifixion he is taunted as one who threatened to destroy the Temple (Mark 15:29). It is possible that some of these negative sayings reflect the later Christian community's attempt to retroject the destruction of the Temple back into the life and thought of Jesus, but the inclusion of the so-called cleansing of the Temple in all four Gospels leads many historians to argue that this incident was a crucial symbolic gesture of Jesus' ministry and that it precipitated the events leading to the crucifixion. What is striking is that readers and interpreters of the struggle in the Temple rarely if ever think of Jesus as acting out of compassion for the animals, even though such an interpretation, admittedly a "strong" reading of the text, is at least as plausible as others.[12] The Gospel of John, for example, emphasizes that Jesus freed the doves and drove out the oxen and sheep from the Temple (2:12–16), an action that is often placed in the shadow of his overturning the tables of the money changers and expelling the traders in animals.

The usual explanation of this event is that Jesus was angry at the money changers for cheating the people (doves were used as sacrifices primarily by the poor), and thus he tried to cleanse the Temple of corruption and abuse.[13] However, as E. P. Sanders explains,

> In the time of Jesus, the temple had long been the only place in Israel at which sacrifices could be offered, and this means that suitable animals and birds must have been in supply at the temple site. There was not an "original" time when worship at the temple had been "pure" from the business which the requirement of unblemished sacrifices creates. Further, no one remembered a time when pilgrims, carrying various coinages, had not come. In the view of Jesus and his contemporaries, the requirement to sacrifice must always have involved the supply of sacrificial animals, their inspection, and the changing of money. (1985: 63)

Sanders points out that the animals are the focus of the Temple cult, which makes it at least plausible that Jesus' action was not unrelated to the animals themselves. As Sanders makes clear, sacrifice necessarily involves an economy, a network of offerings, journeys, priests, clothing, crafts, music, and consumption. Bruce Chilton explains: "The sacrificial cultus brings to paradigmatic expression those goods that a community cherishes, because just those goods are spent in the act of sacrifice and its corollary activities" (1992: 32).[14] The currency of expenditure in the economy of sacrifice is the lives of animals. Was the cleansing an indirect and symbolic statement about the intersection of religion and economics, or is it just as reasonable to think that Jesus saw the animals and was drawn to their liberation?

Scholars continue to debate the purpose of the action. Sanders, for example, interprets Jesus' action as a symbolic demonstration that the Temple was soon to be destroyed and rebuilt in the context of the eschatological restoration of Israel. Indeed, many scholars agree that it was a symbolic communication (a kind of parable in performance) of the Kingdom of God that Jesus envisioned and that it would have been seen as hostile by the Temple priests and leaders. What is important to note is that if Jesus intended to make a statement about the coming destruction or transformation of the Temple and its replacement with a heavenly Temple, then we would need to consider more concretely what eschatological Temple Jesus had in mind. Unfortunately, we do not know the answer to this question, but by placing Jesus in the prophetic context we can surmise that the Temple he envisioned would have granted more immediate access to God, bypassing the suffering of animals. Certainly the Temple that Jesus desired or imagined would have been consistent with the rest of his teachings and practices. What was distinctive about Jesus' message, as Sanders insists, is that it offered inclusion in the Kingdom of God to sinners without requiring sacrifice as a prerequisite.[15]

In fact, Jesus' placement of ritual in a broad context of compassion seems to have caused tension with some of his contemporaries. His sayings and teachings urged a reversal of the usual order of things (the first shall be last, and the last shall be first), and he was particularly concerned with those marginalized by social customs. For Jesus, as for all Jews, eating defined and illustrated the notion of purity, and his willingness to have an open-table fellowship was a proleptic celebration of the coming of God's inclusive kingdom. The unclean eat with and are purified by Jesus and his banquet of abundant grace, not the sacrifices of the Temple; consequently, the whole distinction between clean and unclean is radically altered (Mark 2: 15–17; Matthew 9:13, which cites Hosea 6:6). The kingdom is promised without stipulations and conditions. Jesus asked only that he be followed, his message proclaiming the good news that God pursues the sheep who are lost, at enormous risk to the rest of the flock (Matthew 18:12–14; Luke 15:3–7). The kingdom in this way is like a feast that includes "both good and bad" (Matthew 22:10). Following Jesus and accepting his message thus competed with the sacrificial requirements of the law, an offense made graphic by Jesus' action in the Temple as a way of pointing toward the Temple of the new age "not made with hands" (Mark 14:58).

As Christianity grew, the relationship between Christians and the Temple became even more complex.[16] Stephen, in a decisive event for the early church, preached against Temple worship as a form of idolatry (Acts 6, 7). He continued Jesus' teaching concerning the destruction of the Temple (though he did not predict a new Temple). Yet Peter and James maintained their Jewish practices, and Paul made sacrifices in the Temple (Acts 21:23–26). Paul also, however, calls the financial aid sent by the Philippians a "fragrant offering" (Philippians 4:18) and equates sacrifice with moral dedication and obedience (Romans 12:1; see also Romans 15:16, Philippians 2:17; and 1 Peter 2:5). For Paul, the Temple is the people of God, as a whole or individually. Indeed, for much of the New Testament, sacrifice takes place in the activity of the Christian, thus moving this term from the ritual to the ethical sphere. Nevertheless, the term "sacrifice" continued to resonate with more ancient connotations just as it was used to illuminate new ideas and actions. This mixture of sacrificial metaphors, combined with both critiques and defenses of sacrifice, persists throughout the early history of Christianity's development and displays a deep ambivalence toward sacrifice. The problem is that sacrifice was an assumed backdrop to all religious developments in the early Christian era, so its meaning was rarely debated or clarified.

Although Christianity began as a sect within Judaism, it quickly became a separate religion, so that Christians did not long for a restoration of the Temple and its sacrificial system like some Jews did. Indeed, the New Testament basically transfers what the Hebrew scriptures say about the Temple to the person and work of Jesus Christ. The Letter to the Hebrews talks about a heavenly Jerusalem where the blood of Jesus creates a new, nonsacrificial covenant (see Hebrews 12:22–24), and Revelation envisions a future earthly city of Jerusalem (21:2), but this city is shorn of its Temple (21:22). No Christian writers, even those chiliasts like Tertullian who expected a thousand-year reign of Christ and literally located this future kingdom in Jerusalem, hoped for or imagined the restoration of the Temple. The dominant theological tradition, represented by the allegorical genius of Origen, decisively distanced Christian eschatology from the Jewish longing for the restoration of the land and the cult (see Wilken, 1992: chap. 4).[17]

Thus, the spiritualization of the sacrifices, as articulated in the prophets but also in the rabbinical response to the destruction of the Second Temple, found an easy home in Christian thinking. Early Christian theologians by and large also accepted the Greek philosophical critique of animal sacrifices, in addition to the Jewish polemic against idolatry, which enabled the Christians to treat the public religious rituals of the Romans with contempt. The refusal of the early Christians to participate in public Roman sacrifices exposed them to persecution. After all, their rejection of sacrifice had very concrete implications for the Roman economy (see, for example, Acts 19:24–27). Thanks to Christian influence, today we live in a world almost totally void of animal sacrifice, but as a result, the language of sacrifice is more vague, diffuse, and amorphous, and thus the need to interrogate the logic of sacrifice is all the greater.

Indeed, the early Christians rejected the practice of sacrifice, but they continued to utilize its framework and vocabulary. How that vocabulary affected Christian beliefs is complex and uncertain. Disconnected from both their pagan neighbors and the Temple tradition, patristic theologians did not systematically reflect on the idea of sacrifice, so the theology of the crucifixion was not fully developed and clarified until the work of Athanasius in the fourth century. Instead of a doctrine of sacrifice, Christianity promulgated a wide mixture of metaphors. Juridical, military, commercial, and moral-obedience images were used to describe Jesus' victory on the cross. Jesus' death is a bargain with the devil, the payment of an otherwise impossible debt, the acquittal of guilty defendants, or the appeasement of an infinite anger. Following Paul, the language of the law courts or the market seemed to make sense as illuminations of the atonement, but the connection between the crucifixion and animal sacrifice was never clearly stated. The language of martyrdom is perhaps the crucial link between the two. Like the Jewish martyrs of the Maccabean revolt, early Christian martyrdom was interpreted as a form of sacrifice, helping to shape the interpretation of the death of Jesus. Notice how Ignatius, on his way to a gruesome death in Rome, conflates the language of martyrdom and animal sacrifice in his Epistle to the Romans: "I am the wheat of God, and let me be ground by the teeth of the wild beasts, that I may be found the pure bread of Christ . . . that by these instruments I may be found a sacrifice to God" (Roberts and Donaldson, 1950: 75). By giving all to Christ, the body of the Christian is reduced to food for the beasts, freeing the soul for its ascent to heaven.

Although the doctrine of the atonement was never officially clarified in the early church, the idea that Jesus was a sacrifice exercised a subtle but pervasive influence. After the destruction of the Temple, it became possible to argue that Jesus was himself a sacrificial victim who replaced the Temple cult. The Letter to the Hebrews, probably written for an audience of Jewish Christians who were tempted to return to Judaism, portrays Christ as the high priest and the victim, both the sacrificer and the sacrificed, who thus permanently repairs the covenant and renders all other acts of sacrificial mediation unnecessary.[18] In the minds of many Christians today, some version of this argument is still the basis of how the atonement is understood. God was angry with sinful humans, and the Jews tried to appease God by offering animals as symbols of their own guilty selves. Jesus, perfect and innocent, died as a substitute for the Jewish rituals and accomplished once and for all what the repetition of earlier rituals could not achieve. This reading of sacrifice not only fails to do justice to the Hebrew context of the covenant, in which God is merciful and the sacrifices acknowledge God's prerogatives, but also portrays God as stubborn and spiteful, a portrait at odds with the main thrust of both the Hebrew scriptures and the New Testament. This argument also legitimates animal sacrifice as an inadequate but otherwise reasonable way of pleasing God. Jesus is the substitute for the animals, but this is read not as a liberation of animals but as a critique of human effort in the light of God's prevenient grace. The reading of God as a tyrant who demands slaughter for God's satisfaction allows us to project our violence onto God, to see violence as an unavoidable and inevitable dimension of reality, and to rationalize our own acts of violence as tragic but necessary.

Early Christian, Jewish, and Greek thinkers alike criticized ritual sacrifices as incompatible with the doctrine of God. Just as people gradually came to realize that the gods did not need to be fed or bribed, the argument was also made that gifts to God should be worthy of the divine character. For the first-century Jewish philosopher and historian Philo, we can only give to God what God has given to us (see Daly, 1978: 104–10). Sacrifice is thus symbolic and consists of moral virtue and spiritual offerings. For Justin the Martyr, the second-century

Christian theologian, God does not demand the destruction and waste of God's gifts but rather their proper use and distribution. The neoplatonist Porphyry argued in his *De Abstinentia* that killing animals itself is morally wrong, so it is impossible to think of the gods as requiring an immoral act as worship. A spiritual being needs only spiritual gifts. Moreover, since God needs nothing, God demands only our gratitude and moral transformation. Most interesting is the argument of Clement of Alexandria that carnivorous eating habits were the origin of sacrifices (see Ashby, 1988: 54). Sacrifice was thus invented as a pretext for flesh eating. He recommended vegetarianism as a way of controlling sexual desires. Finally, Augustine shows how far Christians were from the connection of animals and sacrifice when he argued that "the true sacrifice is offered in every act which is designed to unite us to God in holy fellowship" (1984: 379). Augustine is clear that a true sacrifice must advance both the love of God and the love of neighbor.

Even though God no longer demands animal sacrifices, humans do, and our demands are often cloaked in the language of religious ritual and belief (see Gorringe, 1996). Although Barth is not quite this crude, notice how a certain Rev. J. Price justifies animal slaughter by the continuity he perceives with Christology: "The principle of vicarious suffering pervades history, some suffering and dying for the good of others. . . . Is it not in accord with this great principle that animals should play their part by sometimes suffering and dying to help in keeping Britons hardy, healthy, and brave, by providing healthful recreation for so many, in providing the means of livelihood for many thousands?" (quoted in Clark, 1984: 144). The voluntary assumption of suffering by Jesus Christ is here used to justify the forced sacrifice of unwilling innocents. Moreover, animals are sacrificed to humans, while both the Jewish and Christian theological traditions argue that only God is worthy of sacrifice. Certainly the loose talk about sacrifice by theologians through the centuries has created much confusion about the relationship between humans and animals. When theologians talk about sacrificing the lesser to the greater, and when they talk about the need to sacrifice the flesh to the spirit, they reinforce (perhaps unintentionally) the conviction that the very purpose of animals is to be sacrificed for human pleasure and profit. Animals are defined by a sacrificial logic that Jesus intended to reverse and destroy.

When the theological move that justifies animal suffering on the basis of the death of Jesus is made explicit, its absurdity is recognizable by all, and thus a transformation of the theological tradition is made possible. Simply put, the suffering of Jesus makes animal suffering more horrific and unacceptable rather than easier to understand and perpetuate. What we desperately need today is a different kind of sacrificial relationship with animals, a way of acknowledging their divine origin and returning them to the purpose of that source that is more congruent with our recognition of their capacity for both satisfaction and suffering. Sacrifice in this sense is, according to Eugene Masure, "the return of the creature to him who has made it for himself so that it may find its end and therefore happiness in him and for his glory. To sacrifice a thing is to lead it to its end" (quoted in Linzey, 1986: 130). The end of animals, as with all creatures, is a relationship of mutuality and reciprocity. With Jesus, the higher is sacrificed for the lower, and the medium of sacrifice is love, not blood. God voluntarily condescends to lower himself to us, which should be the model of our relationship to animals. God gives up privileges in order to make possible relationships of mutual giving and growing.

More than any other theorist of sacrifice, René Girard enables a rethinking of the crucifixion that frees it from perpetuating animal sacrifice. Girard's theory of sacrifice (1977, 1987) belongs to a well-developed tradition, originated by Emile Durkheim, which argues that this ritual creates and maintains community. Social cohesion, for Girard, is a precarious balance of competing desires that can easily collapse in violence and chaos. Desire, in fact, is socially constructed, both mimetic and acquisitive. We desire what others desire, so we are both models and obstacles for each other. We alternately worship and despise our rivals, who must be both beaten and assimilated. This basic situation for humanity, what Girard calls mimetic rivalry, keeps social groups always on the edge of conflict. Mimesis can easily escalate to aggression when everyone wants the same object. The solution to mimetic desire is to replace the opposition of all against all with the opposition of all against one. It does not matter who the victim is. Although usually chosen randomly, the victim is given the signs of the outsider or stranger. What matters is that the identification of the sacrificial victim is the enabling force that draws together and establishes all group identity. Only by projecting violence onto someone who can be identified as different can social chaos and competing desires be overcome and healed. The return to a calmer state of affairs allows the community to convince itself that the victim is the one and only cause of its problems. Indeed, the fact that the death of the victim seemingly bestows good fortune on the community leads, in the myths of ancient societies, to the elevation of the victim to a sacred status. The violence of the scapegoating mechanism thus founds all culture, and it is the origin of the sacred as well. Rituals are the attempt to organize and worship this founding violence as a way of perpetuating the precarious order of peace.

For Girard, we never recognize scapegoats as such; instead, we always believe in their guilt. We believe that they cause, and thus have the power to remove, our problems. Jesus Christ has the potential to change all of this. Girard's reading of the death of Jesus (1986) gives us a portrait of an involuntary sacrifice, in fact, a murder plain and simple. For Girard, the death of Jesus does not magically restore our relationship to God by absorbing our guilt. It is not something God demanded to appease the divine anger. Nor does Jesus' sacrifice represent the moral necessity for self-denial. Instead, the cross reveals to us the desire to prosecute the innocent that lies at the very heart of mythology and religion. Religious leaders, politicians, and the crowd all get swept up in the desire to scapegoat. Of course, they do not know what they are doing. Even today, theologians argue that Jesus had to die for some higher purpose, that sacrifice is necessary and inevitable. For Girard, the scandal of Jesus is that he sides with all victims by demonstrating the mechanism of victimage itself. Violence is divested of its sacred character.

The murder of Jesus Christ exposes once and for all the sinful nature of all human desire, especially the desire of the righteous. To believe in Jesus Christ is to side with the victims and against the persecutors, even the persecutor within our own selves. For Girard, the cross actually is the last and final sacrifice, because in it all other sacrifices are not only disclosed as evil but also shown to be directed against the ultimate reality of love and forgiveness. The institution of sacrifice ordinarily conceals, justifies, and propagates violence, but this sacrifice reveals, illuminates, and ends violence. The truth that God suffers, that God has been and is being humiliated by our violence and aggression, and that we ourselves, good religious people, contribute to that humiliation, is a difficult truth to accept. The church often teaches that murder is somehow necessary, even while proclaiming the power of love. Jesus Christ inaugurates an age of forgiveness, unleashing the only power that can overcome the collective force of desire and conformity. In the eucharist, we do not sacrifice another, nor do we rationalize what is allegedly inevitable. Instead, we proclaim our intention that he be the last victim, or rather, we acknowledge that he is, in fact, the final victim, the ultimate refusal of the unbounded ego which nevertheless restores the ego to itself, free from slavish imitation.[19]

Sacrifice is brought to an end, although the demystification of sacrifice is a long and gradual process, not always aided by the followers of Christianity.[20] Although Girard does not say this (indeed, he seems not to be interested in animal suffering), it is easy to see, once one thinks about it, that animals continue to be scapegoats, even though their deaths have been deritualized. Instead of sacrificing them to the gods, we sacrifice them to science and to our own appetites, proud that their deaths are no longer cloaked in ritual. What is not ritualized, however, is hidden from view, turned mindless and brutal, so that our progress away from the ancient cults of blood and violence has not taken us very far. If it was wrong for Jesus to die on the cross, if through our persecution of the good we all share responsible for this event, then it is also wrong to kill animals in the name of God. Unfortunately, today we do not even think about what the term scapegoat literally means. The ritual from which we derive this term is described in Leviticus 16, where a goat is driven into the wilderness for the expiation of the sins of the people, but the word is most often used now to refer to people being victimized, not animals.

The basic point of Christian theology is that the cross does not take away but instead reveals our sin, so that repentance, not celebration, is the only possible response. The cross says no to our amazing and infinite capacity to make violence meaningful. The implication for animals is enormous. Christ saves by freeing the scapegoat, the animal who must be our victim in order to vanquish violence from the world. We no longer have to disown and project our worst impulses onto those who are close enough to us to suffer but far enough away so that their complaints can be ignored. Animals, after all, represent instinct, and thus they are the perfect receptacles for the disposal of human instinct in its most vulgar and immediate forms.[21] It is time that we make friends with the animals, and thus become better friends to ourselves, and in the process achieve something of the grace that God gives so abundantly by enabling us to embrace the suffering of the other and to find in the heart of that suffering the love that is God's own being in the world. Christianity offers us a way of opening ourselves to others that permits ultimate vulnerability by providing for the hope of ultimate reconciliation. We can say yes to animal pain because we know that God is even there, in the midst of immeasurable silent suffering. Only the infinity of God's love could redeem, and indeed render conceivable in the first place, the infinity of animal suffering.

Significantly, the pet relationship is the opposite of scapegoating. Instead of projecting negative emotions onto the animal and allowing the animal to carry the burden of human guilt and aggression, we transfer to the pet excessive positive emotions, an act that embodies the potential for idealization but nonetheless subverts the desire to blame, negate, and destroy. If animals are not to be bought and sold, and if they are not to be sacrificed for a greater good, what are they for? Indeed, it is pets who raise the question of what animals are for in the most focused and provocative ways. They point to an ensemble of relationships that do not completely eliminate the notion of sacrifice but rather remove sacrifice from the economics of competing interests and the clash of desires. Pets give us a sacrifice that is antieconomical, based on a surplus of emotions and affection in which we give up something for the other in order to let the other become more than it otherwise would be rather than asking the other to give up its life so that we can benefit from it. What pets are for is, decisively, the end of the reign of animal sacrifice—the sacrifice of sacrifice— and the beginning of a different kind of laying on of hands.

CHAPTER SEVEN

Jesus Christ and the Future of Animals

A Vegetarian Eucharist

Interpreting the crucifixion as the demand to end all nonvoluntary sacrifices necessitates a rethinking of the central Christian ritual, the eucharist. For the Jews, food laws were one of the most fundamental expressions of personal and social identity. What you ate, when you ate it, and with whom were a direct reflection not only of social relations but also of the relation between humanity and the divine (see Feeley-Harnik, 1994). God's blessings and punishments came through the provision or withholding of food, and eating prohibited food was tantamount to committing idolatry. Jesus and his followers also used food to establish the distinctiveness of their movement. For example, Jesus often talked about banquets when he portrayed the Kingdom of God (see Matthew 22:4 and Luke 14:16). Because Jesus communicated his radical message through food—breaking social boundaries and reconfiguring the relationship between humanity and God—he was called a glutton and a drunkard (Matthew 11:18–19). His most radical message of all was his use of a meal to interpret his death, identifying the bread and wine with his very own body and blood.

One of the oldest laws in Judaism is the prohibition of consuming blood, dating back to the covenant God made with Noah, which was applicable to all humankind (Genesis 9:4). Even foreigners were not exempt from it (Leviticus 12:10–12). Saul built his first altar for the Lord because his army, faint with hunger, ate meat with the blood still in it (1 Samuel 14:31–35). Shared by both humans and animals, blood as the essence of life belongs to God alone. It must have been shocking, therefore, when Jesus presented the cup of wine to his followers during the Last Supper as the blood of a new covenant. What does it mean that Jesus gave his life as the seal of his teachings and then refigured his message through the symbols of bread and wine?

The communion meal embodies both memory and promise, a way of reinterpreting the past and the means for imagining a new future. The eucharist does this by connecting the crucifixion to animal sacrifices, although the comparison between these two rituals is only indirectly made in scripture and was rarely analyzed by early theologians. Today most scholars think that the Last Supper of Jesus and his disciples was a modified and transformed Passover.[1] The synoptic Gospels place the Last Supper on the same evening as Passover, and Paul in 1 Corinthians 5:7 calls Jesus the paschal lamb. The testimony on this issue is not unanimous. John has the death of Jesus coincide with the slaughter of the lambs in the Temple (they were killed there but eaten at home), suggesting that the crucifixion replaces the sacrifice required by law, but the lambs were supposed to be slaughtered the day before Passover was kept.

If the Passover is the context for the eucharist, its message becomes crucial for understanding the New Testament narrative. The Passover reenacts and celebrates the drama of the liberation of the Israelites from Egyptian bondage and slavery, from the crossing of the Red Sea to the birth of Israel and her wedding to her God. In Exodus 12 we learn that each household of Israelites in Egypt killed an unblemished male lamb, sprinkled some of the blood on their doorstep, and ate the flesh with bitter herbs and in haste. God then passed over these houses, while he plagued the Egyptians. In the time of Jesus, the Passover was celebrated again in a situation of bondage and with yearning for freedom, this time from Roman rule. A large goblet was kept for the prophet Elijah, in case he should come back, and these thoughts must have been part of the background for Jesus' own reinterpretation of the meal. Interestingly, there is no record of Jesus actually eating lamb in the Last Supper, and Christians gave up that aspect of the ritual not only as a way of distinguishing themselves from the Jews but also because early Christians seemed to understand that eating meat was not an appropriate way of remembering the vivid and brutal death of Jesus.[2] (Meat has returned in the commemoration of Jesus' death in the North American tradition of serving ham on Easter, a way of emphasizing the difference between Christians and Jews as well as compensating for the exclusion of the lamb in the eucharistic meal.)

Although there is textual evidence in the Gospels that Jesus' death was thought of as a substitution for the Passover lamb, it would be a mistake to think that the crucifixion merely continues the logic of animal sacrifice. Indeed, literally linking the crucifixion to animal sacrifice is an unhelpful exaggeration. Jesus' body on the cross was not broken, and his blood was not spilled (except in John's account, where he is bled after his death); he died, most likely, of asphyxiation. We should not link the bread and wine to the act of slaughter but to the nourishment Christ provides, here and now and still to come. Bread, after all, is the symbol of life, and wine is the symbol of joy. The eucharist, as the central ritual of Christianity, should embody the deepest and broadest Christian vision of what life under God's grace should be. Clearly, Christ is the lamb in the sense that when God sees his suffering he will pass over not just the homes of the elect but the whole world, sparing all from the divine judgment and wrath. In any case, Jesus identifies himself in the Gospel of John with the vegetarian manna, the "true bread from heaven" (6:32–35), making clear that the nourishment he gives does not involve the taking of life.

Even though Christians call it the Lord's Supper, it is hard to imagine today's eucharist as a meal; it takes place in the morning, and so little is eaten. Perhaps one of the reasons that the communion service has become such a token ceremony is that for many it does not seem like a real meal because no meat is served. The real meal takes place at home, after the pretend meal of the bread and wine or juice. It is also hard to think of this ritual as a celebration; it is usually treated as an occasion for somber contemplation, as if one can only be happy and grateful for a meal that includes meat. Nevertheless, Christians believe that this ritual condenses and articulates the basic message of the Gospel's proclamation of the good news of grace. The gift of food and the solidarity created by eating together are the most basic expressions of the Word of God. Like all celebrations, the eucharist creates a sense of comfort and community, and in my own tradition (Disciples of Christ) of open table fellowship no one is turned away because all are invited. The eucharist is a ritualistic meal that literally gives what it symbolizes: the strength of peace and the nourishment of grace.

If the eucharist is a celebratory meal, precisely what kind of nourishment does it offer? True, when the early Christians practiced the eucharist as a full meal, meat might have been served; some scholars think that it originally consisted of bread and fish, but through Paul's influence, who might have been influenced by the vegetarians he speaks about in Romans, it became bread and wine. However, I am interested in the theological logic of this meal, what it should and can represent, not how it might have been practiced in its earliest form. My question is the following: Could it be possible to argue that this meal is both literally and figuratively vegetarian, that is, that by remembering the suffering of Jesus in the context of the covenant of God with all of creation, it anticipates the total reign of God in a world of complete harmony, void of all strife and suffering? Is the eucharist not only a meal in which suffering is remembered but also a meal in which pain is not inflicted in its preparation and in which the abolition of all suffering is confidently hoped for and expected? Do the bread and wine of the eucharist replace the flesh and blood of a meal of meat? I want to argue that a certain future is already breaking into the present in the communion meal and that this meal locates compassion for animals in a new horizon of God's suffering presence and future redemption.

The eucharist makes Jesus' suffering present for our participation and gratitude. It comprises all three modes of temporality: the present recollection of the past shapes the expectations of the future. Theologians have long debated just how precisely Jesus Christ is present in this ritual. The question I am interested in pursuing is not the mode of Christ's presence in the eucharist, but how this meal both perpetuates and revolutionizes the notion that it is acceptable to sacrifice animals. The relationship between the eucharist and meat eating is directly related to a long tradition of debates about the role and relevance of the category of sacrifice in the theology of the eucharist. Protestants worry that a sacrificial interpretation of the eucharist contradicts the theme of justification by faith. They do not think that anything can be added to God's work of grace, and moreover, the event of Jesus Christ's death is unique and unrepeatable. The eucharist is God's offering to us, not our offering to God. Yet if our response to and practice of this ritual do not add anything to it, then we risk reducing it to a magical formula that works all by itself, automatically. Most traditional theologians have wanted to argue that the eucharist is efficacious, that is, that this ritual really gives us the message and the person of Jesus Christ, so that our reception of it transforms our lives. What does the eucharist accomplish, and how is that accomplishment related to what happened on the cross?

Even the vegetarian food of the eucharist embodies the theme of dying and rising. The wheat must be ground and baked and the grapes crushed and fermented. Nevertheless, biological transformations occur that make the wheat and the grapes more full of life, so that life is not taken in order to be given. Literal considerations aside, this communal meal, inclusive and joyous, means that sacrificial victims are no longer needed. The eucharist is connected to animal sacrifices in the sense that it puts an end to all sacrifices and places the economy of God's relationship to the world in the framework of graceful giving, not the shedding of blood. The remains of Jesus are inedible as body and blood because that body is resurrected and ubiquitous, intimately identified with all suffering flesh. Jesus' words, take this and eat, thus serve as a warning; they mean, do not eat—do not eat what can feel the same pain that I feel. As you eat your memories of me, eat life and peace, not violence and death.

Carol J. Adams (1993) to this date has made the most sustained argument for a vegetarian eucharist. She is interested in the ways in which the foundational ritual of the eucharist shapes the daily rituals of eating. She points out that meat eating is already ritualized in our culture, in contrast to those who think that meat eating is plainly natural. The raising, processing, packaging, and marketing of meat and even the prayers given over meals deflect attention from the violence meat production necessitates (farm animals are not given individual names). Our power over animals is so diffuse that it seems invisible, a matter of common sense, not a careful social construction. The eucharist could serve to fight a ritual of absence with a ritual of presence, forcing upon our attention suffering we would rather ignore. Unfortunately, this rarely happens. In the eucharist the brutality Jesus passively experienced is separated from animal pain, so that the scope of his healing love is limited to humans alone.

To understand the eucharist as revealing the divine grace in the midst of all suffering, we need to discern patterns of justice in Jesus' life rather than look for some absolute judgment about meat eating in the Bible. The resulting Christology would not be "concerned with whether Jesus was or was not a vegetarian just as feminist theology rejects the relevance of the maleness of the twelve disciples" (Adams, 1993: 155). The only meat we are told that Jesus ate was fish, which is arguably a less significant moral act than the killing of mammals, especially in a situation (such as probably occurred in Jesus' time) of scarce protein.[3] Some have argued that Jesus might have been a vegetarian to the extent that he was influenced by the ascetic Essenes. The apocryphal Gospel of the Ebionites, written by a Jewish Christian group, provides one of the earliest portraits of a vegetarian Jesus. It even suggests that John the Baptist ate bread, or manna, instead of locusts (James 1975: 8–10). This Gospel also explicitly rejects the idea that Jesus ate flesh on Passover. Some scholars (see Schneemelcher, 1991: 168) think that the vegetarianism of the Ebionites originated in a protest against the impurity of the Temple cult. Moreover, the Ebionites seemed to have thought that Jesus came to end all animal sacrifices, thus making vegetarianism a requirement for all Christians.[4]

Even more interesting, some apocryphal material emphasizes Jesus' special concern for the animal world. The Gospel of Pseudo-Matthew portrays Jesus as a new Adam who is adored at his birth by the animals, who recognize in him their master. This same Gospel tells the story of lions and panthers accompanying Joseph, Mary, and Jesus on their sojourn to the desert. The lions and panthers "showed their submission by wagging their tails" (Elliott, 1993: 95), like dogs, and these wild animals befriended the oxen, sheep, and asses. None of the animals hurt each other, which fulfills, this Gospel explicitly argues, the prophecy of Isaiah. At one point in the Gospel Jesus says, "All the beasts of the forest must needs be docile [or should grow tame] before me" (95). This theme is continued in the apocryphal Acts of Philip, where Philip and his sister are worshipped by a leopard. The leopard says that he seized a goat intending to eat it, but the goat pleaded, "O leopard, put off your fierce heart and the beastlike part of your nature, and put on mildness, for the apostles of the divine greatness are about to pass through this desert, to accomplish perfectly the promise of the glory of the only-begotten Son of God" (Elliott, 1993: 515). The leopard is tamed by these words, and when he addresses Philip he asks him to transform his beastlike nature. Philip prays, "Now therefore, Lord Jesus

Christ, come and grant life and breath and secure existence to these creatures, that they may forsake their nature of beast and cattle and come to tameness, and no longer eat flesh, nor the kid the food of cattle; but that men's hearts may be given them, and they may follow us wherever we go, and eat what we eat, to your glory" (516). The animals, then, become vegetarians, just as the Apostles are clearly portrayed as vegetarian, and the animals give thanks to God for taming them.[5]

The life and words of Jesus can provide a model for compassion in all of its forms, but we cannot expect events and people in ancient history to have the same categories and concerns of the modern world. After all, the word "vegetarianism" was not coined until the 1840s. We also need to keep in mind that until relatively recently most people thought that the consumption of some animal flesh was utterly necessary for human survival and that many people in the ancient world did not have sufficient nonanimal protein alternatives. Apart from the heroic discipline of asceticism, vegetarianism for most people is possible only where an abundance of food exists, so that some food can be voluntarily precluded. Throughout most of history, the poor could not afford to give up any food opportunities, no matter how seldom they actually ate meat. Indeed, in the ancient world, vegetarianism was usually connected to a cosmology that envisioned this world as beyond redemption, using diet as a way of freeing the soul from the body. Andrew Linzey has argued that given the historical context, for Jesus to have been a vegetarian "it could well have meant associating himself with a Manichaean philosophy of asceticism which would have been inimical to his teachings as a whole" (1994: 133). Vegetarianism meant something different 2,000 years ago (it expressed life-denying rather than life-affirming values), so that what we mean by vegetarianism today was not really an option for Jesus then, even though the case can be made that the shape of Jesus' life (combined with better information about the sufficiency of plant protein) makes it a compelling option now.

Linzey shows how speculation about the past is surely beside the point. To be a disciple of Jesus is to treat him as both a model of the human and a disclosure of the divine, but it does not necessarily entail the belief that Jesus was perfect in every detail. A totally perfect and unique human being would be so disconnected from the historicity and finitude of humanity that it would be hard to know what to make of (and it would certainly be impossible to conform one's life to) such a docetic outline of personhood. (Besides, no diet can ever be perfect. Whatever we eat, we compete with animals and thus contribute to their suffering, so that, even though some diets are better than others, self-righteousness on this issue is necessarily precluded.) To detach Jesus from his environment is to deny his humanity altogether, something the church has always considered heretical. No one life story can plot all of the myriad possibilities of self-giving love. Moreover, this particular story will come to a climax only when its eventual universal meaning is disclosed, a stretching of the Gospel plot beyond what any of us can now imagine. What must be emphasized is that Jesus was not just the product of his time. Instead, he challenged his age in ways that we should continue and intensify today. Following Jesus is a creative process that appropriates the ways Jesus redefined the attitudes and ideas of his contemporaries in order to apply his life and death to situations and problems the early church could not have anticipated. What was once permitted due to a perceived necessity should now be condemned as a waste of life and resources.

Jesus lived for others, and the early church interpreted his victory over death as the way to make suffering meaningful. A Christology sensitive to his acts of healing, his stories of the unexpected and inclusive Kingdom of God, and the gift of his death that enables us to affirm life would have a lot to say about the use and abuse of animals. Adams pinpoints the place to start: "A Christology of vegetarianism would affirm that no more crucifixions are necessary, and insist that animals, who are still being crucified, must be freed from the cross" (1993: 156). Indeed, the uselessness of animal suffering is a parody of the efficacious suffering of Christ. "The suffering of animals, our sacrificial lambs, does not bring about our redemption but furthers our suffering, suffering from preventable diseases related to eating animals, suffering from environmental problems, suffering from the inauthenticity that institutionalized violence promotes" (156). Vegetables should represent grace because they are grown and harvested without animal suffering and because they are more than enough for what we need.

In an essay written with Marjorie Procter-Smith, Adams draws the parallel between the dangerous memory of Jesus Christ and the disruptive acknowledgment of animal suffering. Both overturn the presumption of human confidence and self-righteousness. But the connection between the two goes deeper. The suffering of Jesus, like animal pain, is difficult to fully recognize and confront. The two modes of suffering are also interconnected in ambiguous ways because the death of Jesus is mediated by the symbol of the sacrificial lamb. Adams and Procter-Smith see a confusion in the use of lamb imagery. Instead of Jesus replacing or at least transforming the role of the lamb, Jesus frequently becomes identified with or is portrayed in literal continuity with the lamb.

They blame this confusion on the emerging understanding of the mass as a repetition of the original sacrifice and thus a meal based on the consumption of that which was killed. "The tradition of animal sacrifice continues to exercise its influence on the symbolic language which came to be applied to the eucharistic meal and its nonanimal food elements. As the identification of the bread and wine with the presence of Christ becomes more and more the focus of theological reflection, the language becomes increasingly reminiscent of the eating of meat" (Adams and Procter-Smith, 1993: 306). The idea that the eucharist is a sacrifice was slow to develop in the church, but by the Middle Ages the priesthood was firmly identified with its exclusive power of sacrifice. The Fourth Lateran Council in 1215 defined the eucharist as a meal of flesh and blood, just as heresy and the rejection of meat were becoming more popular and more interconnected. In the theory of transubstantiation, the bread becomes body and the wine becomes blood, which draws attention to the similarities rather than dissimilarities with Hebraic animal sacrifices. The priest celebrated the eucharist with his back to the congregation, serving the body and blood to God, not the people, and it is difficult not to see the smoke wafting from the censer as an imitation of the smoke from the fire of an animal sacrifice.

Vatican II made possible a whole range of nonsacrificial interpretations of the eucharist, but the logic of sacrifice persists among Protestants as well as Roman Catholics. Indeed, the problem goes deeper than transubstantiation. From the very beginning, Christians were accused of cannibalism by outsiders who took their symbols literally, but such charges hide the fact that the eucharist, understood as a sacrifice, justifies the eating not of human but of animal flesh. Identifying Jesus as an innocent and spotless "lamb" can, as Adams and Procter-Smith suggest, lend credence to the idea that it is acceptable to sacrifice those who are blameless and voiceless. Indeed, sheep are ideal victims because they do not protest. Sacrifice thus rationalizes and becomes indistinguishable from murder. As the advocate of creation spirituality, Matthew Fox, insists, "one of the laws of the Universe is that we all eat and get eaten. In fact, I call this the Eucharistic law of the Universe, even Divinity gets eaten in this world" (quoted in Linzey, 1994: 119).

The eucharist risks turning a voluntary act of self-donation into a metaphor for the food chain. The lower must be consumed by the higher. "The lamb in Christian communion becomes doubly removed, first by being slaughtered and then by being resymbolized as a human male" (Adams and Proctor-Smith, 1993: 307). Communion thus reimagines vegetarian food along the lines of meat eating. In a carnivorous diet, vegetable food is animalized: animals take and transform grains with their entire bodies, which are then taken and eaten. "But in communion, not only is the vegetable food animalized, it is masculinized through the imagery that this is the body and blood of Jesus" (308). The final result is that the eating of real lambs, not humans, is normalized. An early Easter hymn (from the fourth to sixth century) exemplifies the confusion of meat eating and the literal presence of Jesus: "We are looking forward to the supper of the lamb . . . whose sacred body is roasted on the altar of the cross. By drinking his rosy blood, we live with God. . . . Now Christ is our passover, our sacrificial lamb; His flesh, the unleavened bread of sincerity, is offered up" (Bynum, 1987: 49). If the death of Jesus can reinvigorate our spiritual lives through this meal, how much more can the death of lambs give us physical strength?

Too often the eucharist is a way of taking God for granted by accepting too easily the formula that sacrifices are necessary for the common good. Jesus had to die, unfortunately, but thank God that he did! Likewise, animals have to die, unfortunately, but they taste so good! In both cases, the sacrificial victim is objectified as a necessary means to some extrinsic end. The victims are appropriate because they were meant to be delivered unto human hands. As Adams and Procter-Smith write, "Whether the 'appropriate victim' is a battered woman, an abused child, a political prisoner, or a nonhuman animal destroyed for food or some other purpose, in each case a process of objectification is necessary to protect those who offer the sacrifice from the necessity of feeling guilty" (1993: 307). To eat a meal of sacrifice, it is almost impossible not to think that the inevitable has occurred, thus relieving one of responsibility and obligation. The eucharist that repeats Christ's sacrifice (and puts the liturgist in the role of the sacrificer) confirms us in our belief that sacrifices of innocent lives for our own good are good in themselves.

A vegetarian eucharist would eat against these alleged necessities. To eat in memory of the sacrificed Jesus is to acknowledge our role in inflicting pain on others, while it is also to state our intentions not to participate in such cruelty in the future. To thank God is to eat freely and without guilt, not because God has magically removed our sin but because we know that God is making possible a world of peace, and our meals are a sign, no matter how small, of the world that is yet to come. Avoiding meat does not restrict the traditional theological theme of Christian freedom by subjecting God's grace to legalistic requirements. Instead, it continues the Jewish insistence that all of life should be related to God's intentions and guided by God's compassion. All aspects of life should express gratitude to and worship of God. To emphasize the vegetarian shape of the communion meal, feminists sometimes reclaim the bread as bread and replace the wine with water, thus disconnecting the elements from any thought of ritualized killing. Jesus is our bread and water because Jesus literally sustains us, but such sustenance need not be mediated by yet more suffering and death. Feminists want to stress that the eucharist does not participate in a sacrifice all over again but rather provides a concrete symbol of God's care and an opportunity for a communal celebration of our gratitude. This is an important move, but the connection of the eucharist to suffering should not be denied. The eucharist shows us that God is with us in our suffering and that suffering is taken by God so that we do not have to inflict it on others.

Feminists are right to point to the simplicity of this meal. In the early church lavish meals would be permitted on saints' days, but the eucharist retained its plainness and frugality while still being connected to images of fullness and plenty. Although it differs from pagan banquets—the eucharist is not a bacchanal, not a carnival—it still represents fecundity and satisfaction. It modified the Jewish Passover by making it public and inclusive. The eucharist creates community on the basis of God's infinite giving, but it does not waste food by eating in excess of what is needed. Paul criticizes those who partake of the eucharist while disregarding their hungry brethren (1 Corinthians 11:17–34), and the author of Hebrews writes, "Never forget to show kindness and to share what you have with others; for such are the sacrifices which God approves" (Hebrews 13:16, NEB). One way to better distribute food resources is not to consume meat, which takes a tremendous and inefficient amount of grain, land, and water to produce. A meal of thanksgiving that wastes God's resources by utilizing grain in the production of meat for the elite few may be not a gift from Jesus Christ but the execution of divine judgment. Such meals will be as bad for the body as they are for the spirit. Meals of greed create barriers, while the communion meal breaks them apart.

The greediness of the rich, whose meals are a sign of luxury and power, causes disunity, and historically, the key sign of a luxurious meal, as we have seen, is meat eating. Interestingly, the Bible uses the image of a feast not only to portray God's abundance but also to display God's judgment. The feasts of judgment in the Bible are frequently connected to flesh eating. Isaiah 34:1–6 describes the slaughter of the people of Edom in the terms of animal sacrifice, a connection that is also made in Jeremiah 46:10. Micah condemns the rich rulers of Israel by using the figure of a butcher and meat eating (Micah 3:1–3). Carnivorous feasts, where predators prey on the sinful, characterize the judgment and wrath of God in Revelation 19:17–18 and Ezekiel 39:17. Contrary to meals based on destruction, in the eucharist God wishes to feed the poor, welcome the stranger, and include all who are hungry in the body of Christ (see Grassi, 1985). The eucharist treats the world's resources as God's good gifts, which are to be cherished and passed along to those in need. Animals can be excluded from what this meal represents only if we think their hunger, which is a great equalizer, is not real. Eating, after all, is an expression of joy that is very basic, creaturely, and not at all unique to the human species.

Fasting should be the complementary side to the fullness of the eucharistic meal. Following the cross means making sacrifices for others, not just accepting the sacrifice of God. While the eucharist should not be idealized by purifying it of the association with suffering, it should be connected with voluntary, not involuntary, acts of self-sacrifice. Just as the eucharist bonds us with each other as equal recipients of God's grace, fasting acknowledges our vulnerability to the elements and connects us to those who do not have enough. Throughout the Middle Ages, not eating meat on Fridays, the day the death of Jesus put an end to animal sacrifices, was one of the chief penitential signs of being a Christian. Although abstaining from meat was rarely advocated from the perspective of animal compassion, an acknowledged connection existed between eating meat and lust and aggression. Gluttony, one of the original seven sins, was never linked to the overeating of vegetables, grains, and fruits (for an example of its condemnation in the Bible, see Proverbs 23:20–21). Historically, meat eating, the essence of feasts and festivals, has been a conspicuous consumption that only the wealthy and powerful could afford, and though our democratic culture is proud that almost everybody can afford a regular diet of meat today, meat eating is still a costly indulgence for the environment, our health, and the animals themselves.

Today, we can think of vegetarian eating as a kind of continuous fasting, and not because it gives up something that is tasty. Rather, the vegetarian meal recognizes that meat eating is not a just or adequate use and distribution of resources. By practicing vegetarianism, we literally feed the body of Christ by contributing to all who are dependent on a more fair use of the world's resources. Indeed, in a vegetarian meal an interplay of plenty and frugality nicely captures the Christian double emphasis on celebration and compassion. The vegetarian eats well, even as he or she eats so that others may eat better.

In the end, what is most important about the eucharistic meal is that it looks forward as much as it looks back. As Jesus said, "I have food to eat that you do not know about" (John 4:32). Recent scholarship has tried to recover the eschatological dimension of the eucharist, a recovery that is necessary for my interpretation of the eucharist as vegetarian. As Horton Davies notes, "This recovered emphasis seems an important rectification of eucharists in the past that have stressed the agony and death of Christ with an excessively retrospective look, and that transformed the marriage feast of the lamb into a funeral repast" (1993: 90).[6] The image of the eschatological feast comes from Revelation 19:9. Christ as the lamb of God is employed no fewer than twenty-eight times in Revelation, and it evokes John 1:29. Christ is patient and sinless, and his death is efficacious. Yet Revelation connects not only his death but also his consummation of all things in the end time to the image of the lamb and thus the drama of the Passover. Weaving together the eucharist with the exodus and eschatology, Gustavo Gutiérrez and other Latin American liberation theologians have argued that this ritual is empty action unless it contributes to solidarity and the end of exploitation (see Balasuriya, 1979). The exodus, like the resurrection, negates an act of injustice and restores what was destroyed. The eucharist should symbolize the ultimate exodus, the liberation of all life from every form of bondage and violence. For liberation theologians, praxis is more important than theory, so that it is pertinent to argue that our very eating should, as much as possible, follow the biblical model of liberation. As Carol J. Adams writes, "Our goal of living in right relationships and ending injustice is to have grace *in* our meals as well as *at* our meals" (1994: 178).

The eschatological aspect of this meal permits the introduction of the theme of justice. The eucharist is promise as well as remembrance, and this promise must be in continuity with the covenant of the Hebrew scriptures. Instead of dwelling on sacrifice and legitimating killing as a means of communicating with God, the eucharist should look forward to the restoration of all things to their original unity. "Proleptically, we taste—no more—the meal that is to be," Davies writes, "the meal that is the pledge of the resurrection of the friends of the risen Lord" (1993: 235). In the Gospel of John, Jesus is not only the lamb but also the bread of life, a clear allusion to the vegetarian manna that fed the wandering Israelites in the wilderness. To eat the bread of Jesus is surely to anticipate life in his cosmic body, in which all who are hungry are fed and all who are needy are comforted. Jesus also offers us wine as the promise of the celebration of the kingdom, and he says that he will not drink wine again until he can drink it in the kingdom (Mark 14:25). A meal of bread and wine is both simple and joyful. As Davies observes, "There is no question that our western worship at the Eucharist has become far too dolorous, dominated by the cross rather than the Resurrection" (1993: 121). Jesus, after all, was a kind of holy fool, a jester who satirized authority and customs and frequented dinners and parties, and in the end his own claims were mocked and caricatured (see Cox, 1970). It is not hard to imagine that the meal in his honor should be a meal (vegetarian) that is marginalized and even ridiculed today and that meals of dead animal flesh are merely a further continuation of his mockery and suffering. If the eucharist is a messianic banquet, and if the eschaton means total harmony, then the eucharistic anticipation of the end time simply must be vegetarian. What we eat is what we believe, so that to eat otherwise as a Christian is to declare one's lack of confidence in God's ability to redeem the whole world by restoring it to an original peace and blessing.

In sum, when Christians partake of the body of God in the eucharist, it surely is not as a commemoration of an animal slaughter but as an admission to our own guilt in slaughtering and destroying others, our own identification with Jesus in all of his animal cries and pain, and our own affirmation of the struggle to work to overcome such pain. Literal meat eating, then, is a parody of the vegetarian supper of the eucharist, and giving thanks for servings of dead flesh is an affront to the suffering of God in Jesus Christ. How else could Nietzsche's Zarathustra satirize the Last Supper by serving the meat of two good lambs as a substitute for the bread, thus ludicrously literalizing the metaphor of Jesus as the lamb of God: "But man does not live by bread alone, but also of the meat of good lambs, of which I have two" (1968: 396–97).[7] By spiritualizing sacrifice, Christianity too hastily ignored thinking through the link between sacrifice and animals and thus missed the very material lesson of the cross that bodies matter and that the unnecessary infliction of pain on all bodies only continues the crucifixion of God. It is only at this most vulnerable point of pain, uttering unintelligible cries, that God redeems all suffering and asks for our participation in the end of sacrifice.

The Cosmic Christ and the Church for All Creatures

By showing the source of all of our nourishment and sustenance, the eucharist reveals Christ not just as a personal savior but also as the Cosmic Christ, the one who was present at the beginning of all things and will bring all things together in the end. The theme of the Cosmic Christ, frequently neglected or undervalued in Western theology, can be found in Romans 8, 1 Corinthians 15:22–28, the Gospel of John, and the Letter to Hebrews. It is most prominent, though, in the books of Colossians and Ephesians where, as Paul Santmire explains, "the intense expectation of the future dawning of the last day in its fullness, which so captivated the minds of Jesus and Paul, has given way to a profound, even serene, confession of the present rule of God and his Christ, throughout all things" (1985: 203). From this perspective, God's providence is spatial rather than temporal. The prophetic and apocalyptic traditions are complemented by an emphasis on the hierarchic interconnections that bind all of reality together, extending from the earth upwards to the angels and the eternal heavens. The world is a web of connected parts held together by grace. This vision is not, however, complacent. Christianity added to this portrait of the great chain of being the insistence that the cosmos was fragmented; the spatial links that connect the here and now to the heavens above have been broken and need repair for spiritual and social stability and for the soul's journey up the heavenly ladder. The key to this restoration is not so much the crucified Christ but the exalted Christ. The body of the resurrected Christ is the sign that the original unity is both already present and still to come.

Perhaps some theologians are hesitant to embrace the Cosmic Christ because the idea belongs to a syncretistic worldview. The Cosmic Christ can seem needlessly speculative and complicated, especially when compared to the simple message of individual salvation so often preached in our churches today. There are certainly elements of gnosticism in it, with hints about the multiple levels of divine power, secretive knowledge necessary for illumination and salvation, and the theme of a descending and ascending savior figure. However, the New Testament vision does not fall into the trap of dualism, pitting the spirituality of the elect against the materiality of the damned and reducing the world to a stage for the drama of an esoteric knowledge intended only for the elite. Instead, Jesus as Lord reigns over all powers so that the whole world will be restored to him. Everything will be filled with Christ's saving power.

Indeed, the exalted Christ enables the whole cosmos to be the church.

Christ is the vitality and unity of creation, so that cosmos and church, exalted Lord and crucified Savior, creation and redemption, are seen to be one and the same thing. The creative Word of the Father and the redeeming Word made flesh are unified. Christ, then, is the power not only of the beginning but also of the end. This emphasis on "all things" (*ta panta*) in the vision of the Cosmic Christ abolishes the distinction between the spiritual and the physical, the invisible and the visible. Creation is one; it is not dualistically divided into living mind and dead matter. All things are capable of responding to God's love; nothing is self-contained, mechanical, and predetermined by fate or destiny. The body of Christ demonstrates that the spiritual end of all things transforms but does not obliterate the materiality of the world in which we live.

The Cosmic Christ forces Christians to alter their attitude toward the natural world. In his admirable account of the role of nature in Christian theology, Paul Santmire (1985) isolates two biblical themes, migration and fecundity, that contrast and complement each other. The first is a temporal movement, dynamic and active, while the second is a spatial image, connoting fulfillment and rest. In the first, Christ is that toward which all things strive, in order to find themselves, and in the second, Christ is presently in control, whether that presence is acknowledged or not. Both themes are present throughout the Bible, so it is impossible to isolate them or even to work them against each other. Certainly, after the early Christians recognized that the parousia, the climactic return of Jesus Christ, was to be postponed, the migration theme became dominant. The church came to focus on its own survival and its missionary outreach, treating the world not as a home but as a passing phase or means to a greater goal. This mindset cannot be ignored by any theological reflection on nature or animals; Christians have a sense that they are moving through the world, saving bits and pieces of it but not giving the world their ultimate loyalty.

Nevertheless, the church is not just an alienated body in the midst of a sick world. The church is a representation of Christ in a world created and still full of God's presence, so that it can bear witness to God's glory by shaping the world as God intended. Ultimately, the church and cosmos are one, so that what the church gives refuge to is everything, just as the fate of the church is dependent on the future of the natural world. Our beatific vision should be full of animals, like Noah's journey, because redemption fulfills creation, and the church celebrates the power that is already present, as well as the power that is still to come. Christianity, like the exodus, is a migratory movement, but the goal is a new world—inclusive, comprehensive, and complete—that can be glimpsed even now.

To say that the incarnation has relevance for animals will strike some as sacrilegious blasphemy. Jesus was God, some will cry, not an animal. That he was also human merely demonstrates the centrality of the human in God's plan. Indeed, it is tempting to suppose that since God became incarnate in a human being, then human form limits the efficacy of God's redemptive work. "God's eternal Son and Logos did not will to be an angel or animal but a man," Karl Barth observes. "This and this alone was the content of the eternal divine election of grace" (1958: 18). Indeed, Barth argues that humanity and animals are different only because humanity "is the animal creature to whom God reveals, entrusts and binds Himself within the rest of creation, with whom He makes common cause in the course of a particular history which is neither that of an animal nor of a plant, and in whose life-activity He expects a conscious and deliberate recognition of His honor, mercy and power" (1961: 351).[8] The image of God reflected in the creation of humanity is none other than Jesus Christ, so that the doctrines of Christology and creation are interdependent. As a result, Barth implies that God says yes to humanity only by saying no to animals.

It is possible to argue that animals are redeemed regardless of the incarnation due to their sinlessness. It is also possible to argue that something like the incarnation might or will occur for animals in a way similar to the embodiment of God in humanity. Paul Tillich, for example, recommends that we leave open the question of

> possible divine manifestations in other areas or periods of being. Such possibilities cannot be denied. But they cannot be proved or disproved. Incarnation is unique for the special group in which it happens, but it is not unique in the sense that other singular incarnations for other unique worlds are excluded. Man cannot claim that the infinite has entered the finite to overcome its existential estrangement in mankind alone. Man cannot claim to occupy the only possible place for Incarnation. (1957: 96)

Indeed, in the allegory of Narnia C. S. Lewis imagines the divine logos as incarnate in the mighty lion, Aslan.

Other theologians, in a less speculative mood, have wanted to emphasize the capacity of the incarnation in human form to include animal creation. As Athanasius writes, "When the Word visited the holy Virgin Mary, the Spirit came to her with him, and the Word in the Spirit molded the body and conformed it to himself, desiring to join and present all creation to the Father, through himself, and in it to reconcile all things, having made peace, whether things in heaven or things upon the earth" (quoted in Linzey, 1994: 10). This is something saints and mystics have always known, with women frequently leading the way. Two English mystics and theologians are good examples. Julian of Norwich (1342–1416?) writes, "For when he was in pain we were in pain, and all creatures able to suffer pain suffered with him" (1978: 142–43). And we are told about Margery Kempe (c. 1373–1440) that "when she saw the crucifix, or if she saw a man had a wound, or a beast, whichever it were, or if a man beat a child before her or hit a horse or other beast with a whip, if she saw or heard it, she thought she saw our Lord being beaten or wounded, just as she saw it in the man or in the beast, either in the fields or in the town, and alone by herself as well as among people" (1989: 104). Jesus, as with all humans, certainly could feel and identify with the suffering of animals, so God's experience of suffering through Jesus is not limited to the human species alone.

The crucial distinction that needs to be made is between the form (which is necessarily limited) and the range of efficacy (which is unlimited) of the incarnation. In fact, the incarnation is formally limited in many ways that do not constrict the mission of the church. God, after all, chose a Jewish male for this special point of contact. Gentiles and women, therefore, are distanced from the form of the incarnation, just as animals are. (Even today the Roman Catholic church argues that only men can be priests because they share a physical resemblance with Christ.) Arguably, however, animals are a part of the incarnation because traditional Christology combines the divine and the human without subtracting anything from the physical or material aspects of creation, and humans are mammals, flesh and blood creatures with bodily needs and functions.[9]

People, however, want to think of God as the same as us; indeed, people want God to appear in their own specific image, including the specifics of race, gender, and age. Western Europeans, for example, have long tried to portray Jesus as Northern European-looking, denying the otherness of Jesus. The idea of the *imago dei* likewise has been used to define some quality, like intelligence, that identifies humans with the divine and separates humans from animals. The Genesis story suggests that the image of God means that humans can exercise the same capacity as God can for compassionate responsibility for others. Surely the image of God is Christlike love, not the specifics of human shape; God, after all, transcends all images, and furthermore, no representation of God could include everybody. William C. Placher observes that "humankind divides along any number of lines, and all of us are in some ways like Jesus and in other ways not" (1994: 114–15). The point is that Jesus does not save us by becoming exactly who we already are. The incarnation identifies God with hope in the midst of suffering, not a particular type of body. The patristic principle that what is not assumed in the incarnation is not healed in the redemption forces us either to restrict the range of God's power to redeem or to broaden the meaning of God's embodiment in Jesus Christ. The ubiquity of God's presence should force us to conclude that God participates in and therefore will heal the suffering of all flesh. Cruelty is thus a heresy, the denial of God's good intentions in creation and God's power for comprehensive reconciliation.

In the New Testament, significantly, the body of Christ is not limited to the specifics of a human body. This is true in a trivial sense because we simply do not know what Jesus looked like. More profoundly, the body of Christ is—whether literally or metaphorically—present in the eucharist, the shape of the body of believers called church, and identified with the body of the whole cosmos groaning for restoration. The body of Christ includes the purely material in an utterly inclusive spiritual vision, and so it transgresses all species categories. Christology is not only anthropology but also cosmology. Why, then, are we reluctant to say that in this body God also feels and redeems animal bodies, that the body of Christ includes everything that suffers regardless of its stage of evolutionary development? The body of Christ, after all, was insulted, and through that trauma God identifies with the least among us, those who can feel but cannot defend themselves, those who suffer but cannot speak. No theologian would want to deny that God through Jesus Christ feels the pain of those humans who, whether due to age, illness, or physical challenge, cannot think or speak. If the body of Christ is the furthest reach of God's love, then it seems arbitrary to limit that love to only one species of creation. God's love is limitless in scope and depth; wherever suffering is, there God is also.

The Cosmic Christ strives toward a cosmic reconciliation. That Christ is an eschatological figure implies that aspects of Christhood are not yet revealed in the historical Jesus. There is more to come; discipleship is not static imitation but creative appropriation, on the basis of both what once was and the hope for what yet will be. The Cosmic Christ does not strictly correspond to the created order. "For the revelation of God in Jesus is such as to intensify rather than diminish the puzzle of the created order. For Jesus stands against as much as for the order of nature as we now know it. The natural processes of sickness and death and disease, even indeed the vagaries of the weather, are subject to the power of God in Jesus Christ" (Linzey, 1993: 137). In many of the miracle stories, Jesus tames nature and brings it into submission, just as God controls and subdues the primeval ocean as one of the first acts of creation (Genesis 1:2, 6). Throughout Western history the mark of a holy man was his ability to charm a ferocious beast. Christ is the true Adam, exercising God-given dominion in the form of service and solicitude, which we can imitate in our own treatment of animals.

The Hebrew scriptures insist that one of the blessings of wisdom is to stand in peace even with the wild animals (see Job 5:22–23). Perhaps this is why the Gospels portray snake handling as a sign of faith (Mark 16:16; Luke 10:19; see also Psalms 91:13). By acting as if one of nature's most dangerous animals is actually tame, the believer leaps, albeit wantonly, into the eschatological future by turning the clock back to before the fall. The snake handlers grasp the biblical message that nature is not meant to stand alone, unrelated, in a state of conflict and disunity. They try to make peace with the animal who, according to the Genesis myth, is most inimical to human gardening. In doing this, they are following a biblical pattern. The comfort that God gives Zion, for example, is to turn her wilderness into an Eden and her thirsty plains into a garden (Isaiah 51:3). The paradise that stands at each end of history is a garden—tamed, domesticated, and ordered (see Gottfried, 1995). The word "paradise," in fact, is a Greek adaptation of a Persian word for an enclosed park, orchard, or pleasure ground. The origin of botanic gardens, so crucial to the development of modern science, was an attempt to re-create the Garden of Eden (see Prest, 1981). Gardens are a place of rest and meditation, providing an encyclopedia of plant life where people can commune with the innocence of a fruitful and perpetual spring. Gardens also serve as a reminder, because they have to be defended from pests and separated from most animals, that the human search for Eden will continue to be tragically limited until our visions are broad enough to encompass all living beings.

Today, Christianity is frequently criticized for legitimating the exploitation of nature and for not sufficiently celebrating the beauty of the wild. Undeniably, much of Christian history is driven by the desire to cultivate the wild, both spiritually and physically, making of it a refuge from the world and a foretaste of the world to come. The image of the garden is crucial in Christian history, being progressively applied to the church, the monastery, the medieval university, and finally to theological seminaries in the new world of America, which itself was construed as a kind of paradise by early settlers (see Williams, 1962). The Bible portrays the wilderness, unsown land, as the realm of demons and death. The early Christians saw themselves as Israelites being led out of the wilderness and into the promised land of a redeemed community with its sacraments. Baptism itself was the analogue of passing through the Red Sea, the eucharist was connected to the bread from heaven, and the church was a provisional paradise sent into the wilderness of the world to complete the restoration of all things to the divine order. After the success of the church in the Roman Empire, some devout Christians thought the triumph led to corruption, so that paradise could be found only in an ascetic escape to the desert, where the holy could appease lions and tame wolves.

Paradise, then, is not a geographical place as much as it is a spiritual journey. The garden is a powerful metaphor for Christianity because it teaches that creation is still in the process of being created. God is still planning and cultivating, bringing creation to its peaceful Sabbath rest. To believe that redemption will be limited to the human sphere is to deny the fall, that is, to accept parasitism and animal suffering as good, as creation as God intended it to be, not in need of transformation and liberation. If nature is fallen, morality cannot appeal to what is in order to envision what should be. Christian morality sees in Jesus the beginning of a whole new creation, a garden that requires our own efforts and stewardship. To think Christ against the faults of the present world is to think the suffering of Jesus and animals together.

The church, then, is both a particular institution, the people who follow

Jesus, and the sign of the body of Christ, which has no limits. It is difficult to keep both of these visions in sync with each other. At the very least, we should recognize that the church is more than the people of God, but Christians have long found it difficult to talk about animals in church. "When in 1772 James Granger preached against cruelty to animals, his sermon, he tells us, 'gave almost universal disgust to two considerable congregations.' 'The mention of horses and dogs,' he continues, 'was censured as a prostitution of the pulpit' " (Passmore, 1975: 200). Yet animals are an important part of the lives of those who worship. As Jay McDaniel writes, "There is something very abstract, very unbiological about this way of thinking. If we eat animals, for example, they do indeed become part of us. When we arrive for worship, we bring them with us, albeit in decomposed form. How is it that we should think of them as 'outside our communities' even when they are 'inside our bodies'?" (1993: 94). Human community is material, embodied, and mixed. Pets, for example, are now admitted to be members of human families, but they still are excluded from the household of faith. Although some churches set aside a day to bless the animals, a day when laity are encouraged to bring their pets to church, most churches have not changed their attitude about animals since the seventeenth century, when the office of the dog-whipper was invented in England to keep dogs out of church. Before that, dogs were common in many English churches, and the practice did not desist completely until the nineteenth century.

The message of Christianity expanded the family structure to include the whole human species, so that all men and women are siblings. We now know that the idea of separate human races is a myth. Any superficial differences that exist among human groups do not alter the consistency and trustworthiness of God's providential care. The Christian dynamic extends outward and equalizes relationships; perhaps it is this dynamic that is the background to the growing importance of pets in the Western world. This process of inclusion can and should continue, so that all animals are brought into the human family, not as equals but as dependents whose needs are worthy of respect. Pets, of course, do not belong to one religion or another. But they do pray by seeking freedom from pain, and they praise creation by their playing and resting. Psalm 148 depicts all the animals as praising God, and Tertullian wrote, "Cattle and wild beasts pray, and bend their knees, and in coming forth from their stalls and lairs look up to heaven, their mouths not idle, making the spirit move in their fashion" (quoted in Linzey and Regan, 1989: 7). Animals should not be baptized because they do not sin, but this does not mean that they are not in need of God's grace. Redemption is not from sin alone. It is from everything that distorts fulfillment, including pain and premature loss of life.

Animal Afterlife

These comments about the Cosmic Christ and the inclusive church bring up a
topic that many people like to discuss even though theologians find it unnerv-
ing. Indeed, the topic of animal afterlife, which involves speculation that theologians (who otherwise rarely are known to limit their powers of speculation!)
find to be odd or embarrassing, is actually quite common and widespread.
Dogs, for example, have long been connected to images of an afterlife. Their
very being is at the threshold, alternately welcoming and warning, so it is not
surprising that they are often linked to images of the transition from this life
to the afterlife. There is Cerberus, the three-headed hound who guarded the
entrance to Hades, the Greek underworld and land of the dead, and there is
the Egyptian Anubis, the god of the dead who conducts the soul from this
world to the next. We now recognize such myths as attempts to depict the
unknown in terms of the known. But questions still remain: Is thinking about
dogs as accompanying the dead to the next life a story that eases fear and
anxiety, or do dogs really play a role in the world to come? Do all dogs go to
heaven?

Pet burial makes us uncomfortable, and it is often parodied, as in Errol
Morris's 1978 documentary about pet cemeteries, *Gates of Heaven*.[10] Why care
about the dead bodies of beings who have no souls? We all drive by dead
animals on the side of the road. Who can afford the time to worry about that?
Although we do not like puppy mills because we do not want dogs raised under
the same conditions as farm animals, we also do not acknowledge that millions
of pets are killed each year in "shelters." Pets are put down, put to sleep, eu-
thanized, and sacrificed for science, euphemisms for "murdered" or "killed."
Pets are rendered (made into tallow), not buried. True, the urban denial of
animal death is part of a wider refusal to confront the reality of human death,
but the process of dealing with animal death is not given public support or
sanction. Mourning for the death of a pet is a display of excessive grief for
which many feel ashamed. In the last few years there has been a growing recognition of the need for public rituals of the expression and management of such
grief. In some ways, people are more free to mourn for the death of a pet than
for the death of a human because such grief is simple and lacking any ambivalence; moreover, we do not feel like we have to hold ourselves together for
others. But such feelings are expected to be brief, and normal activity should
resume almost immediately. Many of these bodies, after all, are indirectly eaten
through chicken and pig feed.

To think about animal resurrection means that these bodies are valued and
will be restored; it means that their lives, as well as their deaths, will have to
be treated with respect. For this reason, few Western theologians have taken
animal afterlife seriously. Because we cannot reward or condemn animals in

this life, Maimonides argued (and many others have repeated this argument) that animals will not have access to the afterlife. Animals, being morally neutral, will have neither future pleasures nor future pains. Of course, we do treat some animals as moral agents, training them to respect their environments and those around them and holding them responsible for their behavior, so the notion of animal morality is more complicated than Maimonides assumed.[11] But the more important response to Maimonides is to challenge the very connection between the afterlife and moral agency. This connection, it should not go unnoticed, also denies the afterlife to human patients, those who, whether infants or severely mentally handicapped, also are morally innocent. The Jewish and Christian traditions, however, have long recognized the intimacy of God's relationship even with those who are not sufficiently developed to be responsible for their actions. In fact, it could be argued that animals, by their very blamelessness, share a closeness with God that sin denies to humanity. As Father Zossima says in *The Brothers Karamazov,* "Look at the horse, that great beast that is so near to man; or the lowly, pensive ox, which feeds him and works for him. . . . It's touching to know that there's no sin in them, for all, all except man, is sinless. Christ has been with them before us" (1957: 270). All of us know what theologians often forget, that love and moral agency are not necessarily connected.

Animals share not only in God's grace but also in the sufferings of the world. That animals are morally innocent does not mean they do not need redemption, if redemption means deliverance from suffering. Only if the afterlife is imagined solely as a place of judgment does moral capability play such a determining role. What if heaven is not about reward and punishment but rather redemption and consolation? What if heaven allows for the completion of what is left incomplete in this life? This would connect the afterlife to the notion of justice, not the psychology of the fear of death and the desire for more living and infinite pleasure. Keith Ward has spoken eloquently about animal afterlife. "If there is any sentient being which suffers pain, that being—whatever it is and however it is manifested—must find that pain transfigured by a greater joy" (1974: 223).[12] Indeed, that justice demands an afterlife for those unable to make the best of their situation in this life is the best reason to believe in an afterlife for humans as well.[13]

Like many others, C. S. Lewis hesitated to address the topic of animal afterlife, lest he find himself "in company with all the old maids" (1962: 136). It is a topic that is most often raised by children and thus easily ridiculed and ignored, even by those theologians who discuss issues of equal absurdity and impracticality. Lewis points out that the silence of scripture on this topic is not important since revelation is not meant to be a comprehensive system answering all questions, and furthermore, the idea of the afterlife is very late to develop in Jewish history. A more important difficulty is that many animals, those who lack self-consciousness and live through a mere succession of sensations, would not recognize themselves in the afterlife, so it would have no meaning for them or their pain. Redemption is for those who remember their pain, not entities that live only in the instant, without a coherent sense of past, present and future. As John Hick explains, "It is extremely doubtful whether even a zoological paradise, filled with pleasure and devoid of pain, could have any compensatory value in relation to the momentary pangs of creatures who cannot carry their past experience with them in conscious memory" (1977: 316). Of course it is possible that God so greatly enjoys variety, and that all creatures so greatly enjoy their own existence that all life will share in the final restoration of the cosmos. It is not unreasonable, though, to assume that God, like us, is most concerned with the higher animals, those with a sense of their own selfhood.

Lewis pushes this argument even further, suggesting that God cares about only those animals that humans care about. "Man is to be understood only in his relation to God," he writes. "The beasts are to be understood only in their relation to man and, through man, to God" (1962: 138). Humans, already part animal and part spirit, intercede for the animals, just as Jesus intercedes for us. Animals were created as companions for humans, so that Christianity does not glorify the wildness of nature. "The tame animal is therefore, in the deepest sense, the only 'natural' animal—the only one we see occupying the place it was meant to occupy, and it is on the tame animal that we must base all our doctrine of beasts" (138–9). Tame animals obtain their sense of self through their masters, and so when we think of human resurrection, we should include in that thought the resurrection of those who depend on humans and who complete the life of humans.

While I think that the afterlife should extend to all of the more developed animals on the basis of justice, not just human companionship, Lewis does make a good point. Martin Heidegger once argued that animals do not have a spirit because they do not have a world; he meant that animals have an immediate experience of the world that does not allow for shaping, creating, and reflecting on the environment (1959: 45).[14] I have argued that animals do have a world, and it is the world they share with us; moreover, some animals learn to be very aware of our shared world. It is this relationship, Lewis is suggesting, that permits animal experience to be cherished and preserved. The animals will be saved because they contribute to a community worth restoring, a community that must include not only all those who feel pain but also all those who can matter to others.

Carol J. Adams has criticized Lewis for perpetuating a hierarchical and thus patriarchal theology of animals, and she is right that Lewis is concerned with maintaining humanity's centrality to the universe (1994: 181). Lewis certainly resists the idea that God would care to compensate for absolutely all creaturely suffering. Even Lewis's friend Evelyn Underhill was not sympathetic to his argument:

> You surely *can't* mean that, or think that the robin redbreast in a cage doesn't put heaven in a rage but is regarded as an excellent arrangement. Your own example of the good-man, good-wife, and good-dog in the good-household is a bit smug, don't you think, over against the wild beauty of God's creative action in the jungle and deep sea? And if we ever get a sideway glimpse of the animal-in-itself, the animal existing for God's glory and pleasure and lit by His light, we don't owe it to the Pekinese, the Persian cat or the canary, but to some wild free creature living in completeness of adjustment to Nature a life that is utterly independent of man. (1943: 301–2)

Lewis is wrong to imply that God cares only for domesticated animals, but he might be right that the best way to imagine how God loves the animals is to look at how people love pets. Moreover, Lewis is correct in sensing that all animals will increasingly conform to the model of the pet as the wilderness shrinks and human need and technology continue to grow. Adams seems to suggest that loving relationships are incompatible with all forms of hierarchy and authority, but properly ordered relations are made possible only by acts of care and sacrifice that signify different levels of power and responsibility. If human involvement in managing the wild is inevitable and necessary in this life, then why is such involvement so difficult to imagine in the next life? Why do we want to imagine that the ultimate destiny of wild animals is to remain in the wilderness, turned against each other and against us in strife instead of living with each other and us in harmony and community?

Christians believe that the blessing given to humans is one day to stand in the presence of God, in a relationship of dependence and yet fulfillment and joy. Lewis argues that the animals who depend on us surely will be included in God's final embrace of the world. God must love what we love, and in the midst of such infinite love, the differences between humans and animals begin to diminish anyway. More and more animals are becoming dependent on us every year, and all animals depend on God for their very existence, just as people do. When God redeems the world with a final reconciliation, if animals are part of such a reconfiguration, it seems warranted to imagine their participation in that world more along the lines of domesticated pets than wild beasts. After all, Isaiah envisions the lion as lying down with the lamb, in a tame and restful state, joining with those creatures who do not need to kill but do need caring and attention. Isaiah seems to imagine that both in this life and in the life to come the destiny of lions is to become more like lambs. Of course, it is hard for us to imagine lions eating hay and not other animals, but it is hard for us to imagine much that religious hope points us toward.

Although some people have used Psalm 49:12 and Ecclesiastes 3:21 to deny animal afterlife, other biblical passages confirm Isaiah's vision. Hosea construes the peacefulness of animals as the consequence of the end of human violence on the day that God will make "a covenant on behalf of Israel with the wild beasts, the birds of the air, and the things that creep on the earth, and I will break bow and sword and weapon of war and sweep them off the earth, so that all living creatures may lie down without fear" (2:18, NEB). Ezekiel too imagines the new creation as void of wild but not domesticated animals (34:25–28). And Zachariah imagines the new Jerusalem populated with animals (2:4). These images imply more than a hope for peace from dangerous animals; they guide the theological vision to the hope for a peace with the animals. By implication, at the very least we should not romanticize animal violence. "I think the lion," Lewis writes, "when he has ceased to be dangerous, will still be awful: indeed, that we shall then first see that of which the present fangs and claws are a clumsy, and satanically perverted, imitation" (1962: 143). Our imaginations were once obsessed with mysterious creatures and ferocious and threatening monsters. Now the geography of our imagination is a domesticated landscape, populated only by the fear of what we can do to the earth, not what nature can do to us. Perhaps something is lost in Lewis's tranquil portrait of the consummation of God's kingdom, but regret for untamed wilderness can only stem from idealization and nostalgia, not a realistic examination of how life lives off life in the natural world. The telos of all things is God, which means that freedom is formed and founded in loving relationships and not in the destructive isolation and competition of the parasitical world. All creatures will one day find their freedom in dependence, in rightly ordered and yet mutual relationships of giving and gratitude, authority and trust.

If there is a resurrection of the human dead, then it is accomplished by a purely graceful act of God in order to right what was wrong and complete what was not completed. Such a resurrection is not based on anything humans have or are. Nothing in us predisposes us to the afterlife, no biological trait or characteristic. We do not consist of something immaterial (say, a soul) that God needs in order to work the miracle of resurrection. Neither is the soul a bit of matter that only humans have; the soul is just a sign of what matters, and everything matters to God. Nothing we possess enables God to give us more life, because all life in its entirety is a gift from God. Only if the afterlife is selective and thus something we merit through our efforts at moral self-improvement or our ability to believe in certain doctrinal formulations can animals be preemptively excluded from the future that God has prepared for what God loves.

If there is resurrection, it is an act of love and power that need not be limited to humans alone. If humans arise at the end time, there is no reason to think that animals do not also. James Herriot expresses this sentiment in his reply to an elderly woman who had been told that animals have no souls and thus was worried about the destiny of her pets: "If having a soul means being able to feel love and loyalty and gratitude, then animals are better off than a lot of humans." When pressed by the woman, he finally says all that can be said: "Wherever you are going, they are going too" (1987: 54–55).[15] Both animals and humans share the same fate and draw the same breath. "All go to the same place" (Ecclesiastes 3:19–21, NEB).

Significantly, the book of Revelation shows the animals joining in the heavenly chorus gathered round the throne of God (4:6–11; see also Ezekiel 1:5, 10). Four animals, which look like a lion, an ox, an eagle, and a human, are singing the praises of God. These animals could represent the restoration of the animal world in the Kingdom of God since they include wild and tame animals, birds, and humans, but biblical interpreters usually read the text as a symbol of human, not animal, reality. Bishop Irenaeus of Lyons established this hermeneutical tradition when he argued that the four animals are symbols of the four principal covenants given to the human race or the four dispensations of the Son of God. For Irenaeus, in fact, they are actually men disguised as animals. They are none other than the four evangelists, Matthew, Mark, Luke, and John (Irenacus, 1950: 428–29; see also Hyland, 1988: 59). Theology has followed this tradition by working against the literal language in order to make the animals symbolic and absent. The King James Version names these animals with the pejorative beasts, even though the Greek word, *zoon*, clearly means animal (as opposed to *therion*, which is the term used for the beast of the apocalypse). Other translations call these animals "living creatures," an attempt to use a vague phrase that also obscures the original meaning.

To be fair to Irenaeus himself, I should note that his eschatology is comprehensive, graphic, and inclusive. The whole creation is to be renewed in the end time. Discussing the passage in Isaiah about the lion and the lamb, Irenaeus warns against a metaphorical interpretation. "I am quite aware that some persons endeavor to refer these words to the case of savage men. . . . Nevertheless, in the resurrection of the just the words shall also apply to those animals mentioned. For God is rich in all things. And it is right that when the creation is restored, all the animals should obey and be in subjection to man, and revert to the food originally given by God (for they have been originally subjected in obedience to Adam), that is, the production of the earth" (1950: 563). Although Irenaeus places humanity in the center of the afterlife, he clearly sees a place there for animals (living on a vegetarian diet) as well. They will be more dependent on humans than ever before, but they also will not struggle against each other. Their relationship to us will define and enhance who they are, just as, by implication, our relationship to them will complete our own resurrected humanity. It is almost as if Irenaeus could not imagine an afterlife without the pleasure of human-animal interaction. It is common to dismiss such depictions of the afterlife as literalistic and crude (as if the presence of animals in a vision makes it less spiritual, an assumption that opposes spirituality to materiality), but what some see as a limit to Irenaeus's imagination also can be seen as its furthest extension, in the direction of God's own caring and loving.

The problem of the eschaton returns us to my first chapter, where I discussed the rich panorama of animal concern in the Hebrew scriptures. For most Christian theologians, as R. Kendall Soulen (1996) points out, the consummation of creation is represented as a return to Adam and Eve. The end will be like the very beginning, and in the beginning is humanity standing in the image of God. This shortcut on the road to restoring God's plans bypasses the Hebrew scriptures, and thus it completely dismisses the history of Israel as a relevant source for reflecting on the end of history. The price for this forgetfulness is what Soulen calls "soteriological foreshortening" (52). "Because Christian theologians coordinated God's work as Consummator with Adam and the image of God, they were perhaps too ready to conceive God's consummating work in protological and individualistic terms" (51). Redemption becomes interpreted in quasi-gnostic terms as an escape from nature and history. By correlating a theology of consummation with the very concrete and practical concerns of God's covenant with Israel, Christianity can make room for God's love for the whole earth, including the love of animals. Reflected in that image of God in which Adam and Eve are created is a relationship with animals that is elaborated in Israel's covenant with God, and only when that reflection becomes reality will the old age come to pass.

Epilogue: God's Nature as the Future of the World

In sum, nature is not what it was meant to be. "Whoever believes in nature," William Blake wrote, "disbelieves in God" (quoted in Cartmill, 1993: 123). Yet Christianity does not teach nostalgia; it does not ask us to look to the past as a golden age to be celebrated and copied. Instead, Christianity looks to the future and embeds human hopes in the context of the world as a whole. As John Stuart Mill wrote in his posthumously published essay "Nature," "The order of nature, in so far as unmodified by man, is such as no being, whose attributes are justice and benevolence, would have made, with the intention that his rational creatures should follow it as an example. If made wholly by such a Being, and not partly by beings of very different qualities, it could only be as a designedly imperfect work, which man, in his limited sphere, is to exercise justice and benevolence in amending" (1970: 25). It is no accident that Jews and Christians traditionally depict heaven as a garden, not a wild jungle, where all creatures live without being sacrificed to each other or for a cause. Those creatures who share with us the capacity to feel and relate also anticipate in their needs and desires the eternal Sabbath that will consummate the struggles of creation. Violence is not an original and necessary component of nature, so animals can be transformed and yet still flourish. Today we are less optimistic than Mill about how much we can change nature, but God's power is not limited, and we should work toward the horizon of peace that God provides. The nature of God defines what is natural—and thus what is worth preserving—in the world of nature. Let me conclude by offering some practical and concrete guidelines that are consequences of my attempt to rethink a theology of love for the animals.

We should not infer moral principles from nature. Saying that nature is good does not mean that nature is harmless. Even the Roman Catholic tradition of natural law appeals not to a description of what is but to a concept of what God intends. For Thomas Aquinas, natural law is appointed by reason and is, in fact, our rational participation in God's eternal law, which is nothing other than God's own nature. The only thing that is really natural, then, the only thing that is good in itself, is God. Everything else is good and right only to the extent that it participates in God's nature, a relationship that is partial now but will be complete someday. Nature, then, is a word that should signify the web of relations that includes God, humans, animals, and the earth.[1] Nature is something we are working toward, not something we find. It is a constructed concept, which means that we have to decide how we want to construct it.

We should not try to protect nature from ourselves as if nature's ultimate value is to be self-contained and isolated. We cannot, in the end, protect nature from ourselves because the earth is shrinking as human influence and the human population continue to spread and grow. But there are also theological reasons why nature and humanity belong together. Taking a walk in the woods or going camping can help us feel freed from everyday worries and the artificiality of much of our lives, but it is also important to remember that Christians are called to live in community, not away from it. The Spirit creates relationships of mutuality and harmony, thus pressuring the whole world toward a communion of love and peace. This does not mean that we have the right to exploit nature. On the contrary, we need to manage nature in order to create habitats for animals who cannot compete with growing human needs. Setting aside wild areas for the preservation of species demonstrates, of course, the fact that all land is subject to human management and cultivation. Management programs put into practice the Christian idea that nature too needs conversion, a bending not to human but to the divine will.

Not only does all land stand under human responsibility, but so do all animals. Because they idealize wild animals and hate to see them brought under human jurisdiction, many animal rights activists and environmentalists are against zoos. They see them as an imposition on animals, a kind of garden of animals, but zoos can also be an emblem of the coexistence of humans and animals, as well as a sign that animals do not need to exercise their predatory skills in order to live a full life.[2] Zoos should not become a substitute for the wild, but they can be a place where wild animals are permitted to flourish under human care. And with the continuing decline of the wild, zoos will become increasingly important in the future. Many zoos have become genetic arks and repositories of endangered species, fulfilling the Jewish and Christian theme that humans should save the animals. At their best, then, zoos educate us in the mutual dependency of humans and animals.

We should not encourage or enhance the violence in nature. Reintroducing predatory animals into areas where they have been eliminated might seem like a way of redeeming past acts of human cruelty, but it is also a way of increasing violence in nature. I am not suggesting that we kill all of the wolves, but there is no reason to engineer the repopulation of wolves just because the wolf is violent.[3] Wolves and other predatory animals are not needed to thin out the herds of their victims when there are other, more humane ways of controlling animal populations, and more research needs to be done on those alternatives.[4] The very fact that we have to capture and transport the wolves from one place to another and keep track of them to insure their survival demonstrates that even the wildest creatures are now under our providential care. Wolves, too, are our pets, whether we admit it or not. Perhaps St. Francis understood the wolf best when he made the sign of the cross over the wild wolf of Gubbio, which caused the wolf to confess, repent, and change his ways, a story that illustrates the Christian belief that carnivorous animals are not as God intends them to be but one day will join the peaceable kingdom.

We should worry about individual animals. If God numbers the hairs on our head (Matthew 10:29), then surely God counts animals as individuals and not just as members of species. Saving a beached whale strikes many people as a sentimental gesture and a token stunt, especially when so many animals eat each other anyway. According to the perspective I have developed here, however, it is a real act of charity, a demonstration of the principle that God cares for individuals and not just species. All creatures who are lost or in pain deserve what effort and attention we can give them. Not a single sparrow falls to the ground without God's knowledge and compassion. Jesus came to heal the sick and save the lost, so that saving an animal from a natural or a humanmade disaster is a concrete anticipation of the divine plan to restore all of life to its original harmony.

Finally, the animals who deserve our care the most are those we have domesticated, who have lived with us and contributed so much to human survival and culture. It is right, I am suggesting, to bring animals into a relationship with us, but it is wrong to treat them as mere instruments for human advantage. As a preliminary step toward vegetarianism, we should work for humane farming legislation, but we should also hope for that day when no animal will be sacrificed for trivial human pleasures. This will obviously mean far fewer farm animals than we now have, but they should never be bred out of existence. For all their service to us, someday they should be raised as lessons for human-animal partnership and companionship, and they should be treated as the pets they are, animals who have chosen to cast their destiny with us and who thus depend on us for their very survival. With so many ingenious substitutes for animal protein now being developed and marketed, and with a growing human population that needs the enormous amount of land and other resources that are necessary for the raising of farm animals, it is not a utopian fantasy to begin imagining the end of factory farming as we now know it.

The traditional humane-society approach to animal welfare is often criticized for focusing too exclusively on pets as the objects of their protective care. I think something about that focus is good and right. Pets are the key to understanding not only the destiny of animals but also our responsibility toward them. The problems that plague the pet world—overbreeding, abandonment, mistreatment—remain the most urgent problems facing a theology of nature today. The animals that have most given themselves to us deserve our greatest moral efforts. It is too easy to worry about animal problems in other parts of the world instead of dealing with the very intractable animal problems on our own doorsteps. If the Genesis story is to have any meaning in our world today, we must work toward a vision of animal peacefulness that begins with those animals who are already so much a part of our world. After all, all animals will one day be like them, so we should start learning from them now, in anticipation of what is yet to come, which will be a better and greater community of all beings than anything we can now imagine.

Notes

Introduction

1. For a book on animal care that is full of autobiography and personal reflection, see Sobosan (1991).

2. Contrast Nozick's comment with this statement from Nietzsche: "We do not regard the animals as moral beings. But do you suppose the animals regard us as moral beings?—An animal which could speak said: 'Humanity is a prejudice of which we animals at least are free' " (1982: 162).

3. For a critique of animal rights that develops a Wittgensteinian point of view, see Leahy (1993). Language, for Leahy, is a necessary prerequisite for having interests that deserve respect and attention.

4. For a spirited defense of the indirect duties argument, see Carruthers (1992).

Chapter One

1. Tillich was a great practitioner of correlational theology, but in his theoretical formulations his account of it was flawed, implying as it did that culture exclusively defines the questions for theology to answer (1951: 3–8).

2. Animals are occasionally used as agents of God's will in the Bible, but this is depicted as part of the mystery of divine providence. They do not act on their own, and thus they do not display an independent power that can rival God's authority.

3. Unless otherwise noted, all scripture quotations are from the New Revised Standard

Version of the Bible, copyright 1989 by the Division of Christian Education of the National Council of the Churches of Christ in the U.S.A. For a few quotations, I have used the New English Bible (noted as NEB in the text).

4. Some rabbinic commentators suggest that this story shows that God might have originally intended for animals to be partners or even mates for humans, a thought that is not absurd, because "the Judean farmer and animal-tender surely spent many pleasant hours with his cattle" (Schochet, 1984: 163). This story should resonate deeply with all those who love their companion animals.

5. Elijah Judah Schochet's verdict is that the Bible treats animals as the property of humans, to be used properly, but used nonetheless: "True, man has specific obligations toward animals; he is not to abuse or mistreat them. But these obligations are relatively few, and they bespeak more accurately the relationship of a master toward his servant, or even an artisan toward his tool, than that of a living being toward his fellow living being, also fashioned by the hand of God" (1984: 4). The Bible, he argues, promotes a kind of speciesism: "Holiness implies conformity to specific classes and genres of being, and the responsibility of maintaining the integrity and purity of these classes" (70). He suggests that meat eating was not common in ancient Israel due to practical, not ethical reasons. However, even Schochet admits that "it can be argued that Scripture does not command the Israelite to eat meat, but rather permits this diet as a concession to lust. One can postulate the existence of an unfolding 'spiritual evolutionary process' that will someday attain the pristine scriptural ideal of vegetarianism. But such ideas lack mass appeal and fail to wield authority" (300).

6. The Egyptians loved and deified animals, which might have contributed to their demythologization by the Hebrews. There was a city of dogs in Egypt, Cynopolis, where dogs were venerated, specially fed, mummified, and buried in a famous cemetery.

7. According to Schochet, rabbinic literature is full of stories promoting animal care. Noah and Joseph alone are called *zadik,* that is, "one who practices charity," because they provided food for both humans and animals in time of famine and emergency (1984: 148). The Jewish philosopher and biblical commentator Nachmanidies held that people lived longer before the flood because they only ate meat after it (Schwartz, 1988: 3). In Deuteronomy 11:15, God provides food for the cattle before he provides for people, and Jewish law generalizes from this that a person should not eat before first providing for his or her animals. Philo thought Moses commanded kindness to all animals, but Maimonides argued that though God's providence extends to humans as individuals, God watches over animals only in their species groupings as a whole. This raises the question of why humans should be concerned with individual animals if God is not.

8. The fact that Peter sees on the divine sheet animals of every kind and variety symbolizes the unity of Jews and Christians; the ingathering of the scattered members of Israel has begun. The story of Peter's vision is also reminiscent of the story of Noah. Noah is told to gather together every kind of animal, clean and unclean. The covenant God establishes with Noah is universal, just as Peter is being taught a more universal outlook. Unfettered feeding is not meant to justify human craving for meat; instead, it is symbolic of the idea that the grace of God is for everybody, regardless of food customs

and taboos. The diet that includes all animals reflects the new law of love that includes both Jews and Gentiles. In terms of its historical veracity, by the way, this story about Peter is suspect because Jews were not forbidden to socialize with Gentiles, so Peter hardly needed this vision in order to visit and baptize the God-fearing Cornelius.

9. Indeed, note the way in which chapter 5 of Revelation plays on the lion/lamb image. The context is the crisis of the scroll with seven seals, which nobody can open. Revelation 5:5 says, "Do not weep. See, the Lion of the tribe of Judah, the Root of David, has conquered, so that he can open the scroll and its seven seals." But the very next verse switches to the image of the slaughtered lamb, not the powerful lion. One persuasive way to read this switch is as a movement from a theology of power to one of weakness and vulnerability. See, for example, Placher (1994: 8–9). God's identification with the animal that suffers can also be read as the broadening of the incarnation to include, and thus redeem, the suffering of all creatures, especially those who are victims.

10. Of course, we do not have all of the teachings of Jesus, so it is reasonable to assume that those teachings the Gospel writers thought were less relevant to their situation were not recorded and passed along. Needless to say, the Gospel writers were more concerned about the differentiation of Christianity from Judaism and the promotion of Christianity to the world of Gentiles than they were with the love of animals. Nevertheless, enough evidence remains to place Jesus firmly in the tradition of Jewish compassion for animals and celebration of the world as the gift of God. Being committed to Jesus means following his Spirit in directions that are not always made as explicit as we would like in the New Testament. I return to this topic in chapter 7.

11. There is a tradition in patristic commentary linking the wild animals with satan. The deserts were widely regarded as the home of demons. This same ambiguity is found in stories of the Desert Fathers, who tamed wild animals both as a sign of restoring nature to its original peace and as a sign of battling with and overcoming demonic temptation.

12. Paul's statement in 1 Cor. 8:13 is similar: "Therefore, if food is a cause of their [Christians with a weak conscience] falling, I will never eat meat, so that I may not cause one of them to fall."

13. As Marcel Detienne argues in *Dionysos Slain,* "To change one's diet is to throw into doubt the relationship between gods, men, and beasts upon which the whole politico-religious system of the [ancient Greek and Roman] city rests" (quoted in Spencer: 54).

14. For a selection of readings from the Christian tradition supporting animal care, see Andrew Linzey (1989). Also see Rosen, ch. 1.

15. Some scholars speculate that James was a Nazirite who took special vows that included abstaining from meat. If so, then it is possible that Jesus was also a Nazirite, which means that Jesus too did not eat meat. The *Clementine Homilies* portray St. Peter as a vegetarian and argue against animal sacrifices.

16. Augustine thought that even though "we can perceive by their cries that animals die in pain" (1986: 105), animals do not have a rational soul and therefore are not related to us by a common nature. Moreover, he argued that the killing of "lice, fleas and bugs" (108) demonstrates the hypocrisy of vegetarianism. Finally, he ridiculed the idea that eating is a spiritual act: "Are you not ashamed to believe that God is to be sought with the nose and palate?" (92). Of course, Augustine was very careful to distance

himself from his Manichean past, so that arguing against vegetarianism was one way he could prove his orthodoxy.

17. Peter Singer blames St. Francis's limitations on his lack of philosophical rigor: "While this kind of ecstatic universal love can be a wonderful source of compassion and goodness, the lack of rational reflection can also do much to counteract its beneficial consequences" (1990: 198). St. Francis, who emphasized the place of animals in representations of the Nativity scene, did think that animals could praise God and were intended to be in harmony with humans.

18. For a wonderful history of the struggle of these vegetarian Christians, a struggle all but unknown in the church today, see *History of the Philadelphia Bible-Christian Church*.

19. Interestingly, the authors confess that one of them is a vegetarian but the other is not, which raises questions about their approach to the animal liberation movement.

20. As Linzey puts it in his most recent book, *Animal Theology*, "Since God's nature is love, and since God loves creation, it follows that what is genuinely given and purposed by that love must acquire some right in relation to the Creator" (1994: 24). But rights mediate the relationship of creature to creature, not creature to God. We have no rights before God, even though we have obligations and responsibilities stemming from the divine generosity and grace. If animals are genuinely given by God then we must respond to that gift in an appropriate manner, so the question of whether rights language is the best way to preserve a relationship of grace is still open. Linzey sometimes quotes an intriguing passage from Dietrich Bonhoeffer's *Ethics* (1978: 151) on this question, but in that passage Bonhoeffer is not referring to animals.

21. As Linzey indicates, much theological criticism of rights language is hypocritical. "It does seem somewhat disingenuous for Christians to speak so solidly for human rights and then query the appropriateness of rights language when it comes to animals" (1987: 72).

22. "To devise a moral theory that does not allow even for the possibility of conflict between one party and another is simply to deny that one or either party has moral standing" (Linzey, 1987: 90).

23. For Linzey's most explicit discussion of the emotions, see Linzey and Regan (1988b).

24. As Charles Pinches argues, "If I begin by convincing myself that morality only involves how I treat others' interests (human *or* nonhuman) and thereby come to understand those interests as entirely distinct from my own, then not only have I severed my own happiness or well-being logically from others, I have shut off the path to my moral education or transformation such that I might learn to become a person who is properly affected by the plight of my fellow creatures, human and nonhuman alike" (1993: 191–92).

25. I will work within and develop the generosity paradigm throughout my book, but I will also shift Linzey's emphasis from the sacrificial aspects of service to the mutuality of affection and love.

26. Rights language is thus a poor substitute for the theology of grace. "Rights language cannot capture the Christian vision of living in response to the grace of God. The relationship out of which rights language develops suggests that we humans *deserve* consideration from God for what we are or do. Rather, Christians affirm that our value comes as a gift from God; any graciousness we might have is the result of God's creating goodness. Thus rights language can be seen, at best, as the political minimum owed by

some *persons* to other *persons* in voluntary contractual relationships—the very lowest secular common denominator of gracious love" (Jung, 1993: 57).

Chapter Two

1. Hartshorne supports animal rights on the basis that the value of any life consists "*entirely* in the contribution it makes to the divine life" (1979: 50), and he concludes that "complete vegetarianism need not be and probably is not the most appropriate solution" (58).

2. Notice Cobb's interpretation of Noah and the flood: "God does not seem to be disturbed about the drowning of most of the members of all the species, innocent though they are of the crimes that brought about the flood. It is the species that matter. Only with human beings, we who are created in the image of God, does God call us individually by name and care for us personally" (Cobb, 1993: 173). Of course, many humans also died in the flood, so that by this logic God cares for animal species (not animal individuals) and human individuals (not the human species as a whole).

3. See Stephen Budiansky's informative work on domestication.

4. Leopold defends sport hunting as a basic human instinct and an inalienable right that is congruent with a holistic interpretation of nature. See the critique by Kheel (1985).

5. McDaniel (1990: 71) does favorably discuss pets, but he is even more drawn to wild animals because they demonstrate the limitations of human knowing and doing.

6. For a critique of what he calls ecological pantheism, see Clark (1993).

7. We do not eat each other (cannibalism has never been documented as an ordinary practice, although many cultures are quick to call their enemies cannibals), pets (as honorary humans, it would be too much like an act of cannibalism to eat them), primates (who look too much like us), carnivorous animals (which we hunt and kill, perhaps because we want the prerogative of eating animals for ourselves alone, but surprisingly avoid eating for the most part, perhaps because we eat only those animals we can completely dominate), or rodents (who, like carnivorous animals, escape our control).

8. "Domestic institutions depoliticize certain matters by personalizing and/or familiarizing them; they cast these as private-domestic or personal-familial matters in contradistinction to public, political matters" (Fraser, 1989: 168). Feminism has long politicized the personal and private, and such strategies should apply to diet as well.

9. Contractarian theories can be expanded to include domesticated animals, but only as an indirect benefit of the primary agreement between humans. "That dogs are granted a higher moral status than pigs would presumably be partly because dogs enter into a limited sort of reciprocal arrangement with us, and partly just because those who are full members of the moral club choose to grant dogs a higher status" (Johnson, 1991: 56). Also note Bernard Rollin's suggestion that "one may choose to see the human relationship to the dog as involving something like a social contract, in which the animals gave up their free, wild, pack nature to live in human society in return for care, leadership, and food, which people 'agreed' to provide in return for the dog's role as a sentinel, guardian, hunting companion and friend" (1992: 216–17). What feminists ar-

gue is that the nature of contractarianism needs to be changed; mutuality takes many more forms than just explicit agreement based on the rational consideration of self-interests.

10. Ironically, the acceptance of inconsistency can enable feminists to leave animals completely out of their deliberations. Janet Biehl has criticized inconsistency in feminist theory: "Ecofeminists who even acknowledge the existence of serious contradictions tend to pride themselves on the contradictions in their works as a healthy sign of 'diversity'— presumably in contrast to 'dogmatic,' fairly consistent, and presumably 'male' or 'masculine' theories" (1991: 3). Greta Gaard agrees, at least concerning one issue: "And in regard to vegetarianism, she is right: in the three anthologies published at the time of this writing, ecofeminism has failed to locate animals as central to any discussion of ethics involving women and nature" (1993: 6). More recent texts in ecofeminism have corrected this omission. Indeed, many feminists now argue that the oppression of women cannot be understood fully except in continuity with the treatment and representation of animals.

11. "Now humans violated animals by making them their slaves. In taking them in and feeding them, humans first made friends with animals and then killed them. When they began manipulating the reproduction of animals, they were even more personally involved in practices which led to cruelty, guilt, and subsequent numbness. The keeping of animals would seem to have set a model for the enslavement of humans, in particular the large-scale exploitation of women captives for breeding and labor, which is a salient feature of the developing civilizations" (Fisher, 1979: 197).

12. As Lori Gruen suggests, "The emotional force of kinship or closeness to another is a crucial element in thinking about moral deliberations. To ignore the reality of this influence in favor of some abstraction such as absolute equality may be not only impossible, but undesirable" (1993: 79).

13. For the best and most recent argument that candidates for moral consideration cannot be limited to rational adult humans (the full-personhood view) because such limitations would exclude not only marginal human beings but also animals, see Pluhar (1995).

14. Spinoza connects compassion for animals to "empty superstition and womanish tenderness" *(Ethics,* pt. IV, Prop. 37, note 1). For this citation and much more useful information, see Passmore (1975). Even works sympathetic to the animal rights movement frequently distance themselves from the direct expression of animal love because it too easily leads to fanaticism. See, for example, Preece and Chamberlain (1993: 1–2).

15. "This book is not about pets," Singer smugly asserts. "It is not likely to be comfortable reading for those who think that love for animals involves no more than stroking a cat or feeding the birds in the garden. It is intended rather for people who are concerned about ending oppression and exploitation wherever they occur, and in seeing that the basic moral principle of equal consideration of interests is not arbitrarily restricted to members of our own species" (1990: ii). My criticism of Singer is influenced by Josephine Donovan. See Regan (1985: 25–26) for his defense of his own hyperrationality.

16. For an exception to the systematic approach to the philosophy of animal liberation, see Clark (1984). This book is lesser known than the works of Singer and Regan,

perhaps because it does not rely on a single moral system to make its points. Clark uses an abrupt and uncompromising tone, mixing polemic, prophecy, poetry, and outright rage. He does not trade away his passion for respectability: "I am a committed crank and zoophile, and my hope is to convert my audience" (3). He aggressively takes the offensive against his would-be attackers: "If you think I exaggerate the wrong, you must either be ignorant or at odds with my principles. Your ignorance you must correct yourself, and cloak the truth no longer with sentiment and fantasies of cruel necessity" (11). Although I have learned much from Clark and appreciate his intensely personal style, I prefer to begin with neither a discourse on method nor an anarchic scattering of pleas and arguments; rather, I want to focus on a particular relationship and find therein the resources for a revolution in moral sensibility and intellectual perception.

17. I do not mean to imply that women, as a whole, are more caring than men. For a critique of essentialism on these issues, see Fuss (1989).

Chapter Three

1. In an interesting survey of attempts to establish animal intelligence, Douglas Keith Candland concludes that we must believe in animal minds, but we know other minds only on the basis of our own: "When my dog barks at me, do I not attribute to the dog some purpose reflected in my reflecting about the contents of the dog-mind? In this way, the mind of my dog is inextricably bound to my mind, for I have no way to create its mind other than by applying the categories and concepts of my own" (1993: 369).

2. Indeed, her entire idea about a pointless object that nevertheless exercises human faculties is drawn from Kant's aesthetics. Looking at art as the realm of free play, which liberates reason from the demands of explanation and understanding, is a longstanding paradigm within aesthetics. Freud said it well: "Beauty has no obvious use; nor is there any clear cultural necessity for it. Yet civilization could not do without it" (1961: 29).

3. For a similar reading of the animal rights movement, see Jasper and Nelkin (1992). Also see the story of the *embourgeoisement* of pets in nineteenth century Paris in Kete (1994).

4. For the classic account of animal trials, see Evans (1904).

5. Plutarch may have been the first to advocate vegetarianism on the grounds of universal benevolence rather than transmigration or asceticism. See the informative work of Dombrowski (1984). For the Neoplatonists like Porphyry, purity was the chief concern: "To eat meat only because it tastes good is to delay our return to our 'home,' the road to which is paved with reason and restraint rather than with the Bacchic fury needed to slaughter animals. The goal is to transmute body into soul, not the other way around" (Dombrowski, 1984: 111). Frugality in eating is a mirror of the simplicity of the soul. For Dombrowski, the distinctive character of Greek vegetarianism is that it occurs in the context of virtue or excellence (*areté*); it is part of the individual's striving to become the best human being he or she can become.

6. Note that Ritvo does not see medieval animal trials in a purely Durkheimian perspective: "As animals were released from the burden of guilt for witchcraft, homicide, sodomy, and other crimes, a sense of independence and power that had been implicit

in the ability to intentionally transgress was also withdrawn" (1987: 2). James Turner argues that blood sports were criminalized because they did not fit into lifestyle patterns demanded by industrialization: because the conclusion of blood sports "depended on the endurance of the animals, they could go on for hours and could not be ended at the stroke of the clock. Since they went hand in hand with gambling and drinking, they promoted prodigality instead of thrift, irregularity instead of sobriety and orderliness" (1980: 25).

7. According to Lansbury, "At this time [late nineteenth-century England] popular opinion held that the workers were inherently deficient in all feelings of compassion towards animals because they were so like animals themselves. Therefore it was the duty of all enlightened people to train and discipline them as though they were dogs that had never known a collar or a command" (1985: 39). Moreover "The belief that compassion for animals was a manifestation of sexual frustration was long held to be a medical fact, and like a great many other convictions of similar bias it lacked both logic and sense" (83). "Women saw themselves as horses being flogged and beaten, and many saw their own condition hideously and accurately embodied in the figure of an animal bound to a table by straps with the vivisector's knife at work on its flesh" (84).

8. Interestingly, one of the first writers to clearly defend the intelligence of animals was a woman, Margaret Cavendish, whose essays in the 1650s and 1660s connected meat cooking with military battles. It is also interesting that Thomas Taylor connected women's and animal rights, arguing that if women are given rights then even animals will eventually receive them. His *A Vindication of the Rights of Brutes* (1792), which draws heavily from Porphyry's *De abstinentia,* is an ironic reply to Mary Wollstonecraft's *A Vindication of the Rights of Woman.*

9. See chapter 2 of Adams (1994) and note this provocative comment: "Essentially animal experimentation is to 'scientific knowledge' what pornography is to literary culture, and each is protected by this relationship" (46). Andreas-Holger Maehle and Ulrich Tröhler tell the story of how Galen of Pergamon (c. 130–201), physician to the Roman emperor Marcus Aurelius, recommended, for research that involved exposure of the brain, pigs or goats rather than apes, because "you avoid seeing the unpleasant expression of the ape when it is being vivisected" (1987: 15).

10. William Harrison, in his commentary in *Holinshed's Chronicles of England, Scotland, and Ireland,* quoted in Serpell (1988: 36).

11. According to Thomas, this was a slow process. "The Eastern view of dogs as filthy scavengers had been transmitted via the Bible to medieval England and was still widely current in the sixteenth century" (1983: 105). Nonetheless, medieval tombs showing a human figure with hounds at the feet indicate a growing appreciation for the symbolic value of the dog's loyalty, and a French greyhound, St. Guinefort, became a saint in the thirteenth century after, so the story goes, saving a child from a snake and being unjustly killed. The Stuarts in England represent a real turning point; they were obsessed with dogs, and the aristocracy increasingly took dogkeeping to be a sign of being a gentleman. English law first recognized dogs as property in 1588. Dogkeeping could not be established fully as an institution until three characteristics could develop: first, dogs were allowed into the house (and indeed, in England often went to church); second, dogs were given individual, personalized, human names; and third, dogs were not eaten.

12. "The standards they developed suggest that what they valued was arbitrariness— the ability to produce animals with surprising or unnatural characteristics. Often the rarest traits, meaning those that were furthest from a strain's inherent inclinations and so offered the strongest evidence of the breeder's influence, provoked the greatest admiration" (Ritvo, 1988: 24).

13. For a leftist and functionalist critique of petkeeping, see the fascinating essay by Marc Shell. Shell at once marginalizes and magnifies petkeeping practices: "Pethood is itself a relatively kindly and unthreatening institution" (1986: 142). Nevertheless, by representing an idealized interconnection of kin and kind, pets inhibit reflection on the cross-cultural interhuman reality. "In this way pethood helps to conceal even from would-be kindly human beings the brutally inhumane reality of the doctrine of universal (human) brotherhood" (142). Those influenced by Marx traditionally are not sympathetic to attempts to reenchant humanity's relationship to nature and animals. For Marx, one of the few good things that capitalism accomplished was the end of the deification of nature (see Marx, 1971: 94–95).

14. See Leach for a survey of these myths. "If any one outstanding thing emerges from this survey, it is the so-called 'savages' ' awareness of the ancient intelligence of the dog, his sense of unity with the dog, and recognition of the mystery of his spirit. 'It is true that whenever a person loves a dog he derives great power from it,' said one old Seneca chief. This is something the modern world seems to have lost, except on the part of a rare individual here and there" (1961: xi). Among the ancient peoples, the Zoroastrians probably had the highest esteem for dogs, which they associated with their god Ahura-Mazda. They considered it a crime to fail to feed dogs, to mistreat them, or to kill them.

15. When I have heard this statement quoted, the reference to children is frequently (and significantly) deleted.

16. Freud (1989: 157–64) is interested in animals only in relation to phobias and dreams. In that tradition, Leonard J. Simon writes, "they do indeed add something of their own. But the personality and behavior of the pet (and the character of the inkblot) are ambiguous and malleable enough to provide a fertile field on which the pet owner can project his own inner life. What he creates in this way is not his external image or his conscious desire but the image of his unconscious needs" (1984: 231). Simon assumes that pets make no demands on us of their own, a very questionable assumption.

17. Dekkers argues that the taboo against animal love makes it possible because we know that such love is crossing limits and is, therefore, dangerous and exciting. See the excellent review by Doniger (1994: 3–6). What Dekkers does not seriously investigate is the way in which the taboo against bestiality has been used to scapegoat the defenseless (many of those who were executed as witches in the Middle Ages were elderly women who tended cats and other pets) and to provide a check against fondness and affection for animals.

18. For a comprehensive bibliography on the therapeutic value of pets, see Karen Miller Allen (1985).

19. "Men benefit most because they are more sensitive to the loss of companionship than women and have greater need of an animal to express affection, especially through

touch. Men touch people less frequently than women, but they touch animals as frequently or more frequently than women" (Beck and Katcher, 1983a: 25).

Chapter Four

1. See Jacques Derrida (1995a: 255–87) for his identification of sacrificial ideology with any and every humanism, as well as his connection between meat eating and the metaphysical construction of subjectivity.

2. Fiddes continues, "The fact that most of us make little mention of the domination inherent in rearing animals for slaughter does not indicate that it is irrelevant. On the contrary, that which remains unsaid about meat conveys an added dimension of meaning which is particularly potent" (1991: 44). "Paradoxically, this obscurity preserves and perpetuates the influence of these implicit meanings since, not being recognized, they can scarcely be challenged" (44).

3. "To the child, there is no clear line separating objects from living things; and whatever has life has life very much like our own. If we do not understand what rocks and trees and animals have to tell us, the reason is that we are not sufficiently attuned to them. To the child trying to understand the world, it seems reasonable to expect answers from those objects which arouse his curiosity. And since the child is self-centered, he expects the animal to talk about the things which are really significant to him, as animals do in fairy tales, and as the child himself talks to his real or toy animals. A child is convinced that the animal understands and feels with him, even though it does not show it openly" (Bettelheim, 1977: 46).

4. "The notion that talking-animal narratives are not really about animals—that the worthwhile ones, at least, must surely be about something more important than mere animals—is quite consistent with the far wider cultural trivialization and marginalization of animals" (Steve Baker, 1993: 138).

5. In actuality, the range and quality of dog representations in Western art is really remarkable, as seen in Robert Rosenblum (1988).

6. According to Veblen, the dog is the closest thing the middle and lower classes can have to a servant: "The dog has advantages in the way of uselessness as well as special gifts of temperament. . . . He is the filthiest of the domestic animals in his person and the nastiest in his habits. For this he makes up in a servile, fawning attitude towards his master, and a readiness to inflict damage and discomfort on all else. The dog, then, commends himself to our favor by affording play to our propensity for mastery, and as he is also an item of expense, and commonly serves no industrial purpose, he holds a well-assured place in men's regard as a thing of good repute" (1979: 141). Veblen can make such charges only from the perspective of a totalizing utilitarianism; in his ideal society, only the useful would be true. His indictment of "surplus value" ironically perpetuates the most distinctive traits of capitalism.

7. Baudrillard's early work analyzes consumption as the appropriation and manipulation of sign values rather than the use or enjoyment of the actual objects behind the signs. Baudrillard draws from Veblen but argues against the reign of utility that Veblen

himself perpetuates: "Use value is the expression of a whole metaphysic: that of utility. It registers itself as a kind of *moral law* at the heart of the object—and it is inscribed there as the finality of the 'need' of the subject" (1981: 133).

8. Hearne also downplays some of the negative aspects of dog training and breeding. Ritvo (1987) suggests that breeding was originally a continuation of medieval attempts to impose classificatory schemes onto nature: "The institutions that defined the dog fancy projected an obsessively detailed vision of a stratified order which sorted animals and, by implication, people into snug and appropriate niches" (93). Moreover, "The juxtaposition of arbitrarily established criteria (the major purpose of which was to make judgment possible) with swiftly changing fashions not only in favorite breeds but in preferred types within those breeds symbolized a society where status could reflect individual accomplishments and was, as a result, evanescent, lacking in foundation, and in constant need of reaffirmation. As most dog fanciers were, in this sense, self-created, so their exploitation of the physical malleability of their animals was extremely self-referential. Its goal was to celebrate their desire and ability to manipulate, rather than to produce animals that could be measured by such extrinsic standards as utility, beauty, or vigor. Thus it was an index of their paradoxical willingness aggressively to reconceive and refashion the social order in which they coveted a stable place" (115).

9. "The idea that dogs want to please us leaves us free to believe that our pleasure is worth working for, and that dogs are far too deeply in the grip of adoration ever to have a critical thought about our intellectual or physical failures of grace" (Hearne, 1994: 188).

10. "The language is invocative; it exists before the divorce between the literal and the metaphorical" (Hearne, 1994: 193).

11. "Talk of conditioned responses is helpful in understanding some of a trained animal's development, just as it is helpful in understanding some of a dancer's or a poet's or an actor's development, but the performances of the greatest animals make much more sense if they are understood as rudimentary progressions of at least one primeval artistic impulse, the impulse to play with meaning" (Hearne, 1994: 186).

12. Coral Lansbury criticizes the moralization of animals in much nineteenth- and early twentieth-century fiction: "What can be argued is that from the middle of the nineteenth century, animals were sacrificed to fiction before they were sacrificed to science" (1985: 180). "Animal stories proliferated as the actual world of animals receded to reveal a landscape of fictional creatures who existed only to provide a moral message for children" (183). Stories that try too quickly to make a moral point leave little room for animal otherness. Notice, for example, Thomas Mann's ideological description of dog obedience in his otherwise moving tale "A Man and His Dog": "It is a deep-lying patriarchal instinct in the dog which leads him—at least in the more manly, outdoor breeds—to recognize and honor in the man of the house and head of the family his absolute master and overlord, protector of the hearth; and to find in the relation of vassalage to him the basis and value of his own existence, whereas his attitude towards the rest of the family is much more independent" (1954: 229–30). Mann does have a wonderful comment about how dogs make figurative language literal: "Animals are more primitive and less inhibited in giving expression to their mental state—there is a sense in which one might say they are more human: descriptive phrases which to us have

become mere metaphor still fit them literally, we get a fresh and diverting sense of their meaning when we see it embodied before our eyes" (276).

13. In a similar fashion, Barbara Noske (1989) advocates an anthropology of animals based on empathic identification, an imaginative attempt to discover the world of the animal by learning through observing and imitating the language of the animal and, by implication, abandoning human language.

14. For this contrast, compare the rather moralistic stories in Roger Caras (1987) with the more oblique, even obscure portraits of the otherness of dogs in Jeanne Schinto (1990).

15. See Ackerley's *My Father and Myself* (1968: 216–19), which is dedicated to Tulip, for the full context of Ackerley's relationship to his dog. Also see his wonderful portrait of the dog Evie in *We Think the World of You* (1960).

16. Note too the enigmatic opening line of Rainer Maria Rilke's Eighth Elegy of the *Duino Elegies:* "With all its eyes the animal looks into the open" (Mit allen Augen sieht die Kreatur das Offene).

17. Of course, the distance of cats can also be praised as a way of forcing humans to respect their integrity. As Vicki Hearne comments, "Cats, unlike horses and dogs, are more likely in domestic situations (hanging around the house) to force the dimmest of us temporarily at least to abandon our epistemological heavy-handedness" (1986: 240).

18. I do not mean to say that all dog breeds are healthy and right; some dogs have suffered much due to unwarranted distortions of their physical features. Nevertheless, breeding at its best demonstrates not so much intervention but the intermingling of human hopes and desires with the world of the dog.

19. Dogs were persecuted because their closeness to humans allowed them to function as scapegoats; as James Turner notes, "Cruelty implies a desire to inflict pain and thus presupposes an empathetic appreciation of the suffering of the object of cruelty" (1980: 2). For more on cruelty toward dogs, especially in nineteenth-century New York City, see Carson (1972).

20. Turner echoes the easy criticism that kindness to animals is a substitute for kindness to other human beings: "Kindness to animals profaned no social taboos and upset no economic applecarts, either in the theoretical systems of political economists or in the harsh daily encounter of capital and labor. When other channels were blocked, the rising tide of sympathy almost inevitably flowed to animals, especially now that they had drawn concern for other reasons" (1980: 37). Only if our emotions are limited, that is, only if they constitute a quantifiable entity that is in short supply relative to demand, can the argument be made that love for dogs is a substitute for love for other human beings. Certainly, some dog lovers operate out of such an economy, but I am suggesting that dog love can also create an economy of abundance, where emotions are severed from the scenario of scarcity. In any case, the question of dogs is ultimately one of theological significance. With a dog, one is never alone, and in this sense dogs serve a Christological—even more than therapeutic—function in North American culture.

21. Clearly, I am not defending here the pet industry, which frequently markets pets as easy supplements to the rigor of daily life, with the result that pets are often used

and abused (frequently through abandonment), contributing significantly to animal suffering in this country.

22. "Perhaps it [petkeeping] is a sign of the desperate strength of the human loyalty to things larger than man, a silent thrust toward recovery of balance in a world overwhelmed with human weight and the noise of self-praise and self-denunciation" (Shepard, 1978: 206). "Even pets, strange as it may seem, have played their part in its [the reign of anthropocentrism] downfall. For when we elevate companion animals to the status of persons, when we empathize with them and acknowledge their resemblance to ourselves, it eventually becomes clear that the notion of human ascendancy is a phantom: a dangerous, egotistical myth that currently threatens our survival" (Serpell, 1986: 187).

23. In a discussion of Baudelaire's "Les bons chiens" (The good dogs), Jacques Derrida comments: "The demand of the good dogs is essential because they demand that one *give* to them, to be sure, and that one give what one *has*, but that one give by *taking* them, by taking what they *are* and by taking them such as they *are*" (1991: 144). Dogs put us on trial by giving us an obligation, if we but see it; our gratitude, in the form of taking this gift as it is, that is, the dog itself, acquits us of the guilt of this debt.

24. Yet such charity should lead to legislative improvements for the status of pets. As Bernard Rollin writes, buying a pet should be more like adopting a child: "Pet ownership should be seen as a privilege, not a right. The pet owner must be prepared to follow certain rules. Violations of these rules should be punished by meaningful penalties" (1992: 231).

25. For an imaginative reconstruction of the first entrance of the dog into the human circle that emphasizes risk and generosity on both sides, see Lorenz (1964).

26. It is interesting, though, that Hegel's master-slave dialectic can perhaps illuminate the human-dog relationship. Hegel showed how the master ends up a slave to a dependence on domination, while the slave, forced to resort to cunning, grows in strength and power. Who is to say who has triumphed in the domestication of pets—humans or dogs?

Chapter Five

1. Every gift relationship creates an ethical bond, since what is given urges a response and thus a responsibility. The gift relationship also limits the ethics of responsibility to a particular exchange that tends to ignore more abstract obligations like the good of the public or the equal distribution of goods. As Jacques Derrida writes in an analysis of this problem, "How would you ever justify the fact that you sacrifice all the cats in the world to the cat you feed at home every morning for years, whereas other cats die of hunger at every instant?" (1995b: 71). For a nuanced analysis of sympathy and animals, see Smith (1993).

2. Similar experiments have been performed in modern times to "prove" the importance of physical contact and comfort. Harry F. Harlow, whose work is much praised in the scientific literature, raised monkeys in complete isolation in order to demonstrate

the consequences of maternal deprivation. Other scientists have followed his lead by inducing helplessness in dogs in order to study the psychology of terror and hopelessness.

3. Alvin Plantinga makes a similar argument when he ascribes natural evil to "the activity of beings that are free and rational but nonhuman" (1990: 108).

4. "The animal does not calculate an actuarial cost/benefit scheme on the basis of which he finds whether or not he is getting a fair deal. He simply trusts the people he has grown up to know. At every step he has an expectation that those people will be friendly and will not attack. Unilateral termination of the relationship by the human participants on the grounds that the animal has received all the benefit he is able to 'pay' for is essentially a betrayal. In a pact which was essentially one of mutual trust, non-aggression, and helpfulness, the animal partner has not reneged, it is simply that his means are not what they were. But what the animal 'agreed' to was the formation of a relationship, not a financial bargain. He has fulfilled the 'contract' and will continue to do so. If the relationship were between unequal humans I do not think we should hesitate to say that the cleverer partner has cheated and violated the less intelligent partner's right to have the terms of his contract honored" (Rodd, 1990: 243). In contrast to John Rawls, Rodd suggests we imagine that the original and hypothetical members of the moral contract "do not know whether they will have strong attachments to any moral patient in the real world. If this is the case, it will be in their interests to safeguard the interests of moral patients to avoid suffering emotional distress by mistreatment of moral patients to whom they are attached" (242).

5. Indeed, the image of the divine shepherd and human sheep is employed very differently in Hinduism, a difference that should make Christians pause in their use of this metaphor. In Hinduism, according to Wendy Doniger, the metaphor emphasizes the aggressive side of the divine. "Thus, human men and women are indeed God's sheep, his sacrificial sheep. God keeps his flocks, all right, and watches over them—to make sure that they don't get away from him, so that he can butcher and eat them" (1987: 175). For Hindus, the image of the cowherd (who is always vegetarian) is more gentle and innocent than the image of the shepherd (who is not vegetarian). The cow (supposedly) willingly and generously gives her milk (perhaps in return for not being eaten), and thus the relationship between cowherd and cow is a more appropriate analogy for the relationship between God and humans. In Christian myth, Doniger points out, God is both shepherd and slaughtered lamb. Christ "himself is not a lamb; he comes to replace the lamb precisely so that the lamb—symbolic of all that is vulnerable and pure—will no longer be killed" (180).

6. According to Hegel, if Schleiermacher is right that feeling is the basic determination of human being and the feeling of absolute dependence the basic experience of religion, then "the dog is the best Christian, for it has this most strongly. . . . The dog also has feelings of redemption when its hunger is appeased by a bone" (quoted in Barth [1982: 186]).

7. Hardy quotes from Francis Bacon's *Essays Civil and Moral:* "They that deny a God destroy man's nobility; for certainly man is of kin to the beasts by his body; and, if he be not of kin to God by his spirit, he is a base and ignoble creature. It destroys likewise magnanimity, and the raising of human nature; for take an example of a dog, and mark

what a generosity and courage he will put on when he finds himself maintained by a man, who to him is instead of a God, or *melior natura;* which courage is manifestly such as that creature, without that confidence of a better nature than his own, could never attain" (1975: 155).

8. Augustine makes the argument that knowing and loving are interconnected in his *On the Trinity* (1963: Book 9).

9. For a survey of cultures that eat dogs, even when they encourage affection for them (just as Westerners can be affectionate toward farm animals that they nonetheless eat), see Simoons (1961: chap. 8).

10. There is another image, beautifully captured by Louise Glück in her poem "The Gift," of her young son, standing at the screen door, calling out for dogs, any dog. Sometimes, by sheer coincidence, a dog actually does come to the door. "May he believe this is not an accident?" she asks the Lord. "At the screen welcoming each beast in love's name, Your emissary" (Duemer and Simmerman, 1996: 92). Maybe we must be like children to realize that God does send us the dogs we happen upon in our lives, answering our desire to call forth love.

Chapter Six

1. For a critique of Barth's general interpretation of grace as gift, see Webb (1996b).

2. "I believe in Jesus Christ, God's Son our Lord, in order to perceive that God the Almighty, the Father, is the Creator of heaven and earth. If I did not believe the former, I could not perceive and understand the latter" (Barth, 1958: 29). I should note that I am not arguing that Christocentrism necessarily excludes concern for animals. On the contrary, I am arguing that the vision of the suffering of God is necessary for our identification with the suffering of animals.

3. Barth views animals as analogies. "Only analogically can we bring [animal life] under the concept of respect for life. . . . If we try to bring animal and vegetable life too close to human, or even class them together, we can hardly avoid the danger of regarding and treating human life, even when we really want to help, from the aspect of the animal and vegetable, and therefore in a way which is not really apposite" (1961: 350).

4. Barth argues that the animals were given to man to name not for friendship but for contrast, in order to make Adam more eager for his true companion, Eve. "What if he had been content with the company of an animal for the lack of anything better?" (1958: 293). Although Barth is right that the completion of humanity lies in human-human relationships, he is wrong to suggest that people cannot be friends to both animals and each other at the same time. He also misses the poignancy of the Genesis story, that Adam really does seek partnership with the animals in his initial loneliness.

5. For Walter Burkert, hunting involved such a tremendous revolution—in terms of gender differentiation, tools, and social organization—that a cultural form was necessary to navigate this transition. Moreover, the release of dangerous aggression led to fears and guilt that had to be redirected and dramatized. "Christianity," he argues, "is here no more than a transparent cover for the ancient form that underlies it, that is to say,

for the sacred act of blood-sacrifice" (1983: 9). From a different perspective, Sallie Abbott (1990) argues that hunting breaks the basic bond of kinship that humans share with animals; thus, the spilling of blood needs to be ritualized and propitiated. For a critique of theories of human development based on hunting, see Cartmill (1993).

6. Even today, access to the places where animals are raised and killed is strictly controlled and limited. For an artistic record of visits to various slaughterhouses, see Sue Coe (1985).

7. "It is indeed odd that the most carnivorous nations of the modern world are most outraged by blood sacrifice—the blood of the shambles, of the abattoir, being unseen, does not affect them" (Ashby, 1988: 53).

8. Also note the following: "In sacrifice, the death of the animal or the burning of the loaf is incidental to the action itself: it is part of a wider and deeper action" (Ashby, 1988: 118).

9. Hinduism also has myths and stories that express misgivings about killing animals and thus advocate vegetable substitutes for bloody sacrifices, so that eventually animal sacrifices were discontinued in Hindu temples. See Doniger (1988: chap. 4).

10. It is possible to read even these stories as indications of Jesus' indifference to the Temple cult. Lloyd Gaston (1970: 90–192) argues that opposition to the Temple cult was traditionally connected to an opposing conception of the purity of that cult and that Jesus was indifferent (rather than opposed) to all cultic matters.

11. Commenting on Mark 2:1–12, James D. G. Dunn has argued that Jesus "pronounced the man's sins forgiven *outside the cult and without any reference* (even by implication) *to the cult*. It was not so much that he usurped the role of God in announcing sins forgiven. It was rather that he usurped the role of God *which God had assigned to priest and cult*. God could forgive sins no doubt when and as he chose. But man could only promise and pronounce the forgiveness of sins when he operated within the terms and structures provided by God—the Temple, priesthood and sacrifice. In that sense, as usurping the prerogative of God in disregard for the terms laid down by God, what Jesus said and did could be counted as a kind of blasphemy" (1991: 46).

12. The only such interpretation of the Temple confrontation that I can find is in J. R. Hyland (1988). Commentators usually downplay what a messy process the killing of animals must have been in the Temple: "The stench of blood and of roasting flesh can hardly have been drowned by the smoke of incense; nor can the cries of traders, or the uplifted voices of priests and pilgrims at prayer, have drowned the screeching of the beasts as they had their throats cut, and their blood scattered in the time-honoured manner" (Wilson, 1992: 174).

13. As Ched Myers argues, "Jesus attacks the temple institutions because of the way they exploit the poor" (1992: 299). Myers argues that Jesus called for an end to the entire cultic system on the basis of solidarity with the poor and the exploited. During the time of Jesus, the Temple did function as a tax-collection agency for Rome, a foreign power, making the priests seem to some to be collaborators. See also Horsley (1987).

14. For Chilton, the issue at stake in the cleansing of the Temple was the purity of the animals. "Jesus' occupation of the Temple was directed against animals that did not genuinely belong, in his estimation, to those who were to offer them, because they were

procured by means of a purely financial transaction in the Temple" (1992: 128). If you offer an animal, it should be your own, something you really give away (perhaps this is the origin of the custom of laying hands on the animal) and not something that can be trafficked in an impersonal and mass basis. Jesus, in other words, was working against the commodification of animals. Chilton also suggests that by the time of the Last Supper, that is, after the failure of the Temple cleansing, Jesus turned against the impure sacrifices of the Temple and made the claim that God preferred instead the simplicity of a pure meal. "Eschatological purity had become more important than place, and the authorities of the Temple could never accept any such inversion of their own ideological priorities" (154).

15. "He seems to have thought that those who followed him belonged to God's elect, even though they did not do what the Bible itself requires. . . . Although he did not oppose the law, he did indicate that what was most important was accepting him and following him. This could eventually lead to the view that the law was unnecessary, but it appears that Jesus himself did not draw this conclusion, nor does this seem to have been an accusation against him" (Sanders, 1993: 235–36).

16. Scholars frequently infer from Acts 2:46 that the early Christians sacrificed at the Temple, but the passage does not say that they engaged in Temple worship. "A careful reading of Lucan portrayals in the early chapters of Acts indicates that when Jesus' followers are praying or 'breaking bread' they are not in the Temple at all, and when they are in the Temple area they are there to preach about Jesus, to do healings and exorcisms, and generally to build their movement (Acts 3:1–11; 5:12–16). As the principal public meeting place in Jerusalem, the Temple courtyard was the obvious place for such activities" (Horsley, 1994: 131). Horsley argues that it was the priests, not the Pharisees, who were the enemies of both Jesus and the early Christians.

17. In chapter 7 I will argue that the spiritualization of Christian eschatology can be taken too far, especially when it thereby imagines the afterlife as home to only human, and not animal, reality.

18. For a collection of essays that stresses the importance of sacrifice in early Christian theology and the continuity of sacrificial thought throughout Christian theology, see Sykes (1991). Even Sykes, however, acknowledges in his essay that "the New Testament evidence, it will be universally admitted, does not immediately suggest that the idea of sacrifice is the prime category for the interpretation of the death of Christ" (287).

19. In Girard's early work, sacrifice does not involve the divine; it is a purely psychosocial phenomenon for the purpose of controlling and justifying violence. He believes that as people increasingly come to realize that sacrificial victims are actually scapegoats, the drive to sacrifice others will diminish and eventually disappear. His program is liberal in the sense that he thinks a better understanding of sacrifice will alter its role in our culture. In his later work (see the most recent essays gathered in Girard, 1996) it becomes increasingly clear that Girard defends the more traditional Christian position that God really participates in the life and death of Jesus Christ. Jesus not only is a victim but also willingly gives of himself, as an offering, in order to identify with suffering. Desire that is not bound by negative mimesis, that is, desire that seeks after God, is born of grace.

20. " 'Christianity' only defends its own victims. Once victorious, it becomes, in turn, a tyrannical oppressor and persecutor. As for Christianity's own acts of violence, it bears witness to the same blindness as its own persecutors" (Girard, 1986: 201).

21. Girard even thinks that animals were domesticated for the purposes of sacrifice, not for economic reasons or the needs of companionship (1987: 68–71). For a survey of ancient practices of transferring guilt, sin, or disease onto animals, see Frazer (1922: 624–28).

Chapter Seven

1. Passover was the central Jewish feast that continued after the destruction of the Temple, so distinguishing Christian ritual from the Passover became a primary task of the early church. The theological investment in linking the Last Supper with the Passover (in order to argue that it replaces the Passover) is so great that it is impossible to know for certain the actual historical relationship. I am more interested in the theology of the eucharist than in the detailed questions of historical probability.

2. For a vegetarian Seder ceremony, see Kalechofsky (1985).

3. Some have argued that the Gospel depiction of Jesus eating fish is meant symbolically, not literally, since the Greek term for fish is an ancient symbol for Christ and Christianity. Moreover, both examples of Jesus eating fish (John 21:13 and Luke 24:42–43) are postresurrection, and they might have been invented to combat those who denied the reality of Jesus' bodily resurrection. See Holmes-Gore (1971: chap. 7). It is also interesting that the miracle of the great fish catch told in John 21:6 and Luke 5:4 is very similar to a story told about Pythagoras (see Gorman, 1979: 109), except that Pythagoras told the fishermen to let the fish go (and he paid them the price the fish would have brought in the market).

4. Although the Ebionites were a small group, the fact that they practiced vegetarianism shows that early in Christian history the possibility existed that Christians could combine two premises—the death of Jesus as the end of animal sacrifices and the Hebraic insistence that animals can only be killed in a ritualized manner—to obtain the conclusion that vegetarianism is mandatory for followers of Jesus.

5. There are also stories about talking dogs in the early church, as in the Acts of Peter (see Hennecke: 291). For an account of cynocephalic literature and a discussion of early Christian myths about dog-men who lose their monstrous features upon conversion to the faith, see David Gordon White (1991).

6. Notice, though, how the imagery of meat still creeps, naturally and unnoticed, into the language of Davies. In lamenting the often neglected role of the eucharist in the worship service, he writes about "Protestants who in the recent past seemed to regard the Eucharist as mere angel cake for the pious who had already received a meal of sirloin steak in the sermon" (1993: 129).

7. A beggar objects to the meat, which prompts Zarathustra to talk about strength, war, and festivals. Meat is not incidental to the aggressive persona Nietzsche creates for Zarathustra, a set of values in direct opposition to (the by implication vegetarian) Jesus.

8. Note, though, this interesting remark: "However, God was not and is not bound to

choose and to decide Himself for man alone and to show His loving-kindness to him alone. The thought of any insignificant being outside the human cosmos being far more worthy of divine attention than man is deeply edifying and should not be lightly dismissed" (Barth, 1978: 73).

9. I am not making the heretical suggestion that in the incarnation God merely adopts a material form. Traditional theology maintains that Jesus Christ is both fully human and fully divine, not just a divine being disguised in a physical uniform. Nevertheless, the idea that the second person of the Trinity is fully human suggests to me that God intimately shares the plight of suffering, self-aware, and feeling flesh, that God affirms all embodiment, regardless of intellectual development or rational capacities.

10. For an approach to this topic that is both moving and playful, see the beautiful tribute to the spiritual reconciliation of an artist with his deceased dog by George Rodrigue. "And as I was to Blue Dog, so was I to God, saved only by accepting his grace. We love by being loved" (1994).

11. The Bible extends moral responsibility to animals, as when, during God's revelation to Moses, animals and humans were both threatened with punishment if they touched the mountain (Exodus 19:13). The Bible also demands the death penalty for an ox that gores a man or woman to death (Exodus 21:28).

12. Ward admits that the afterlife will not erase earthly pain. "One must remember that the Christian belief is that there is an existence after earthly life which is so glorious that it makes earthly suffering pall in comparison; and that such eternal life is internally related to the acts and sufferings of worldly life, so that they contribute to, and are essential parts of, the sort of glory which is to come. The Christian paradigm here is the resurrection body of Jesus, which is glorious beyond description, but which still bears the wounds of the cross. So the sufferings of this life are not just obliterated; they are transfigured by joy, but always remain as contributory factors to make us the sort of individual beings we are eternally" (1974: 223).

13. As Keith Ward notes, "Immortality, for animals as well as humans, is a necessary condition of any acceptable theodicy; that necessity, together with the other arguments for God, is one of the main reasons for believing in immortality" (1982: 202).

14. Heidegger also thought that since animals cannot experience death as death, they merely perish; in a way, they do not properly die.

15. Herriot can describe the meat he eats with the same graceful prose with which he describes the animals he saves and loves, and thus he is a good example of the ambiguity of and limits to compassion for animals. Throughout his work, though, there is a recognition of "the mutually depending, trusting and loving association between man and animal" (1987: 272).

Epilogue

1. For good discussions of the various contested meanings of nature, see Dizard (1994) and Soper (1995).

2. "Captive animals often live longer than wild ones; for many animals it must be true that only with man's protection have they any chance of (as we say) old age"

(Bostock, 1993: 64). Moreover, "We are in some degree conferring on our captive animals the protection from violent death and from disease which civilization has (to some extent) conferred on ourselves" (66).

3. Tom Regan (1983: 285) argues that all animals have the right to be protected from harm, but he then argues that since the wolf is not a moral agent, it cannot violate the sheep's right not to suffer a painful and violent death. Therefore, he concludes, we need not worry about the sheep. Even if the wolf is not a moral agent, however, it does not follow that we should not intervene to protect the sheep. The wolf is not responsible for violating the rights of sheep, but the rights of sheep are still violated, just as the rights of a person would be violated if attacked by a (morally innocent) wolf. We have a duty to protect the rights of animals, even if they are violated by other animals who have no similar responsibility.

4. For a critique of hunting as a form of wildlife management, see Ron Baker (1985).

Bibliography

Abbott, Sallie (1990). "The Origins of God in the Blood of the Lamb." In *Reweaving the World: The Emergence of Ecofeminism*, ed. Irene Diamond and Gloria Feman Orenstein. San Francisco: Sierra Club Books.

Ackerley, J. R. (1960). *We Think the World of You*. London: Bodley Head.

———— (1965). *My Dog Tulip*. New York: Poseidon Press.

———— (1968). *My Father and Myself*. San Diego: Harcourt Brace Jovanovich.

Adams, Carol J. (1990). *The Sexual Politics of Meat:, A Feminist-Vegetarian Critical Theory*. New York: Continuum.

————(1993). "Feeding on Grace: Institutional Violence, Christianity, and Vegetarianism." In *Good News for Animals?*, ed. Charles Pinches and Jay B. McDaniel. Maryknoll, N.Y.: Orbis Books.

———— (1994). *Neither Man nor Beast: Feminism and the Defense of Animals*. New York: Continuum.

Adams, Carol J., and Josephine Donovan, eds. (1995). *Animals and Women: Feminist Theoretical Explorations*. Durham: Duke University Press.

———— (1996). *Beyond Animal Rights: A Feminist Caring Ethic for the Treatment of Animals*. New York: Continuum.

Adams, Carol J., and Marjorie Procter-Smith (1993). "Table Life or 'Taking on Life'?: Table Talk and Animals." In *Ecofeminism and the Sacred*, ed. Carol J. Adams. New York: Continuum.

Adams, Richard (1977). *The Plague Dogs*. New York: Fawcett Crest.

Alcott, William A. (1838). *Vegetable Diet: As Sanctioned by Medical Men and by Experience in All Ages*. Boston: March, Capen & Lyon.

Allen, Karen Miller (1985). *The Human-Animal Bond: An Annotated Bibliography*. Metuchen, N.J.: Scarecrow Press.

Allen, Mary (1983). *Animals in American Literature.* Urbana: University of Illinois Press.

Ambrose (1961). *The Fathers of the Church.* Trans. John J. Savage. New York: Fathers of the Church.

Aquinas, St. Thomas (1948). *Summa Theologica.* Vol. 3. New York: Benziger Brothers.

Ashby, Godfrey (1988). *Sacrifice: Its Nature and Purpose.* London: SCM Press.

Athanasius (1980). *The Life of Antony.* Trans. Robert C. Gregg. New York: Paulist Press.

Augustine (1963). *On the Trinity.* Trans. Stephen McKenna. Washington, D.C.: Catholic University of America Press.

———— (1984). *City of God.* New York: Penguin Books.

———— (1986). *The Catholic and Manichaean Ways of Life.* Trans. Donald A. Gallagher and Idella J. Gallagher. Washington, D.C.: Catholic University of America Press.

Baker, Ron (1985). *The American Hunting Myth.* New York: Vantage Press.

Baker, Steve (1993). *Picturing the Beast: Animals, Identity, and Representation.* Manchester, N.Y.: Manchester University Press.

Balasuriya, Tissa (1979). *The Eucharist and Human Liberation.* Maryknoll, N.Y.: Orbis Books.

Barth, Karl (1958). *Church Dogmatics,* III/1. Ed. G. W. Bromiley and T. F. Torrance. Edinburgh: T. & T. Clark.

———— (1961). *Church Dogmatics,* III/4. Ed. G. W. Bromiley and T. F. Torrance. Edinburgh: T. & T. Clark.

———— (1978). *The Humanity of God.* Trans. John Newton Thomas and Thomas Wieser. Atlanta: John Knox Press.

———— (1982). *The Theology of Schleiermacher.* Ed. Dietrich Ritschl, trans. Geoffrey W. Bromiley. Grand Rapids: Eerdmans.

Barzun, Jacques (1983). *A Stroll with William James.* Chicago: University of Chicago Press.

Baudrillard, Jean (1981). *For a Critique of the Political Economy of the Sign.* Trans. Charles Levin. St. Louis: Telos Press.

Bazell, Dianne M. (1997). "Strife among the Table-Fellows: Conflicting Attitudes of Early and Medieval Christians toward the Eating of Meat." *Journal of the American Academy of Religion* 65:73–99.

Beck, Alan M., and Aaron Honori Katcher, eds. (1983a). *Between Pets and People.* New York: G. P. Putnam's Sons.

———— (1983b). *New Perspectives on Our Lives with Companion Animals.* Philadelphia: University of Pennsylvania Press.

———— (1988). "Health and Caring for Living Things." In *Animals and People Sharing the World,* ed. Andrew N. Rowan. Hanover, North.: University Press of New England.

Benhabib, Seyla (1987). "The Generalized and the Concrete Other." In *Feminism as Critique: On the Politics of Gender,* ed. Seyla Benhabib and Drucilla Cornell. Minneapolis: Univeristy of Minnesota Press.

Berger, John (1980). *About Looking.* New York: Pantheon Books.

Berman, Louis A. (1982). *Vegetarianism and the Jewish Tradition.* New York: Ktav.

———— (1992). "The Dietary Laws as Atonement for Flesh-Eating." In *Judaism and Animal Rights,* ed. Robert Kalechofsky, Marblehead. Mass.: Micah Publications.

Bettelheim, Bruno (1977). *The Uses of Enchantment: The Meaning and Importance of Fairy Tales.* New York: Vintage Books.

Biehl, Janet (1991). *Rethinking Ecofeminist Politics.* Boston: South End Press.

Birch, Charles, and John Cobb (1981). *The Liberation of Life: From the Cell to the Community.* New York: Cambridge University Press.

Bokser, Ben Zion, trans. (1989). *The Talmud: Selected Writings.* New York: Paulist Press.

Bonhoeffer, Dietrich (1978). *Ethics.* Ed. Eberhard Bethge. New York: Macmillan.

Bostock, Stephen (1993). *Zoos and Animal Rights.* New York: Routledge.

Bratton, Susan Power (1988). "The Original Desert Solitaire: Early Christian Monasticism and Wilderness." *Environmental Ethics* 10:31–53.

Brock, Rita Nakashima (1988). *Journeys by Heart: A Christology of Erotic Power.* New York: Crossroad.

Buber, Martin (1970). *I and Thou.* Trans. Walter Kaufmann. New York: Charles Scribner's Sons.

Budiansky, Stephen (1992). *The Covenant of the Wild: Why Animals Chose Domestication.* New York: William Morrow.

Bull, Malcom, and Keith Lockhart (1989). *Seeking a Sanctuary: Seventh-Day Adventism and the American Dream.* San Francisco: Harper & Row.

Burkert, Walter (1983). *Homo Necans: The Anthropology of Ancient Greek Sacrificial Ritual and Myth.* Trans. Peter Bing. Berkeley: University of California Press.

Bynum, Caroline Walker (1987). *Holy Feast and Holy Fast: The Religious Significance of Food to Medieval Women.* Berkeley: University of California Press.

Candland, Douglas Keith (1993). *Feral Children and Clever Animals.* New York: Oxford University Press.

Caras, Roger, ed. (1987). *Treasury of Great Dog Stories.* London: Robson Books.

Carruthers, Peter (1992). *The Animals Issue.* Cambridge: Cambridge University Press.

Carson, Gerald (1957). *The Cornflake Crusade.* New York: Rinehart & Co.

——— (1972). *Men, Beasts, and Gods.* New York: Charles Scribner's Sons.

Cartmill, Matt (1993). *A View to a Death in the Morning: Hunting and Nature through History.* Cambridge: Harvard University Press.

Chilton, Bruce (1992). *The Temple of Jesus: His Sacrificial Program within a Cultural History of Sacrifice.* University Park: Pennsylvania State University Press.

Clark, Stephen R. L. (1984). *The Moral Status of Animals.* Oxford: Oxford University Press.

——— (1993). *How to Think about the Earth.* New York: Mowbray.

Coats, C. David (1991). *Old MacDonald's Factory Farm.* New York: Continuum.

Cobb, John (1993). "Economics for Animals as Well as People." In *Good News for Animals?,* ed. Charles Pinches and Jay B. McDaniel. Maryknoll, N.Y.: Orbis Books.

Coe, Sue (1995). *Dead Meat.* New York: Four Walls Eight Windows.

Cohen, Noah J. (1976). *Tsa'ar Ba'ale Hayim: The Prevention of Cruelty to Animals.* Jerusalem: Feldheim Publishers.

Comstock, Gary L. (1993). "Pigs and Piety: A Theocentric Perspective on Food Animals." In *Good News for Animals?,* ed. Charles Pinches and Jay B. McDaniel. Maryknoll, N.Y.: Orbis Books.

Cox, Harvey (1970). *The Feast of Fools.* Cambridge: Harvard University Press.

Curtin, Deane (1991). "Toward an Ecological Ethic of Care." *Hypatia* 6:60–74.

Daly, Robert (1978). *The Origins of the Christian Doctrine of Sacrifice.* Philadelphia: Fortress Press.

Darwin, Charles (n.d.). *The Descent of Man.* New York: Modern Library.

Davies, Horton (1993). *Bread of Life and Cup of Joy.* Grand Rapids: Eerdmans.

Dekkers, Midas (1994). *Dearest Pet: On Bestiality.* Trans. Paul Vincent. London: Verso.

Derrida, Jacques (1991). *Given Time: 1. Counterfeit Money.* Trans. Peggy Kamuf. Chicago: University of Chicago Press.

———— (1995a). " 'Eating Well,' or the Calculation of the Subject." In *Points . . . : Interviews, 1974–1994,* ed. Elisabeth Weber, trans. Peter Connor and Avital Ronell. Stanford: Stanford University Press.

———— (1995b). *The Gift of Death.* Trans. David Wills. Chicago: University of Chicago Press.

Detienne, Marcel, and Jean-Paul Vernant, eds. (1989). *The Cuisine of Sacrifice among the Greeks.* Trans. Paula Wissing. Chicago: University of Chicago Press.

Dickinson, Emily (1958). *Selected Letters.* Ed. Thomas H. Johnson. Cambridge: Harvard University Press.

Dillard, Annie (1982). *Living by Fiction.* New York: Harper & Row.

Dizard, Jan E. (1994). *Going Wild: Hunting, Animal Rights, and the Contested Meaning of Nature.* Amherst: University of Massachusetts Press.

Dombrowksi, Daniel A. (1984). *The Philosophy of Vegetarianism.* Amherst: University of Massachusetts Press.

———— (1988). *Hartshorne and the Metaphysics of Animal Rights.* Albany: SUNY Press.

Doniger, Wendy (1987). "The Good and Evil Shepherd." In *Gilgul: Essays on Transformation, Revolution, and Permanence in the History of Religions,* ed. S. Shaked, D. Shulman, and G. G. Stroumsa. Leiden: E. J. Brill.

———— (1988). *Other Peoples' Myths.* New York: Macmillan.

———— (1994). "Calf and Other Loves." *London Review of Books,* Aug. 4, 3–6.

Donovan, Josephine (1990). "Animal Rights and Feminist Theory." *Signs* 15:350–75.

Dostoevsky, Fyodor (1957). *The Brothers Karamazov.* Trans. Constance Garnett. New York: New American Library.

Duemer, Joseph, and Jim Simmerman, eds. (1996). *Dog Music: Poetry about Dogs.* New York: St. Martin's Press.

Dunn, James D. G. (1991). *The Partings of the Ways.* Philadelphia: Trinity Press International.

Elliott, J. K. (1993). *The Apocryphal New Testament.* Oxford: Clarendon Press.

Eusebius (1965). *The History of the Church.* Trans. G. A. Williamson. New York: Penguin Books.

Evans, M. P. (1904). *Criminal Prosecution and Capital Punishment of Animals.* London: William Heinemann.

Feeley-Harnik, Gillian (1994). *The Lord's Table: The Meaning of Food in Early Judaism and Christianity.* Washington, D.C.: Smithsonian Institution Press.

Ferrier, Todd J. (1926). *On Behalf of the Creatures.* London: Order of the Cross.

Fiddes, Nick (1991). *Meat: A Natural Symbol.* London: Routledge.

Fisher, Elizabeth (1979). *Woman's Creation.* New York: McGraw-Hill.

Fraser, Nancy (1989). *Unruly Practices: Power, Discourse, and Gender in Contemporary Social Theory.* Minneapolis: University of Minnesota Press.

Frazer, James George (1922). *The Golden Bough.* New York: Collier Books.

Freud, Sigmund (1961). *Civilization and Its Discontents.* Trans. James Strachey. New York: W. W. Norton.

——— (1989). *Totem and Taboo.* Trans. James Strachey. New York: W. W. Norton.

Frost, Robert (1995). *Collected Poems, Prose, and Plays.* Ed. Richard Poirier and Mark Richardson. New York: The Library of America.

Fuss, Diana (1989). *Essentially Speaking: Feminism, Nature, and Difference.* New York: Routledge.

Gaard, Greta (1993). "Living Interconnections with Animals and Nature." In *Ecofeminism: Women, Animals, Nature,* ed. Greta Gaard. Philadelphia: Temple University Press.

Garber, Marjorie (1996). *Dog Love.* New York: Simon & Schuster.

Gaston, Lloyd (1970). *No Stone on Another.* Leiden: E. J. Brill.

Girard, René (1977). *Violence and the Sacred.* Trans. Patrick Gregory. Baltimore: Johns Hopkins University Press.

——— (1986). *The Scapegoat.* Trans. Yvonne Freccero. Baltimore: Johns Hopkins University Press.

——— (1987). *Things Hidden since the Foundation of the World.* Trans. Stephen Bann and Michael Metteer. Stanford: Stanford University Press.

——— (1996). *The Girard Reader.* Ed. James Williams. New York: Crossroad.

Gorman, Peter (1979). *Pythagoras: A Life.* London: Routledge & Kegan Paul.

Gorringe, Timothy (1996). *God's Just Vengeance.* Cambridge: Cambridge University Press.

Gottfried, Robert R. (1995). *Economics, Ecology, and the Roots of Western Faith: Perspectives from the Garden.* Lanham, Md: Roman & Littlefield.

Grassi, Joseph (1985). *Broken Bread and Broken Bodies: The Lord's Supper and World Hunger.* Maryknoll, N.Y.: Orbis Books.

Green, Arthur (1992). *Seek My Face, Speak My Name: A Contemporary Jewish Theology.* Northvale, N.J.: Jason Aronson.

Grimm, Veronika E. (1996). *From Feasting to Fasting: The Evolution of a Sin.* New York: Routledge.

Gruen, Lori (1993). "Dismantling Oppression." In *Ecofeminism, Women, Animals, Nature,* ed. Greta Gaard. Philadelphia: Temple University Press.

Gustafson, James (1981). *Ethics from a Theocentric Perspective,* vol. 1, *Theology and Ethics.* Chicago: University of Chicago Press.

Haran, Menahem (1978). *Temples and Temple-Service in Ancient Israel.* Oxford: Clarendon Press.

Hardy, Alister (1975). *The Biology of God.* New York: Taplinger.

Harrison, Beverly (1985). *Making the Connections: Essays in Feminist Social Ethics.* Ed. Carol S. Robb. Boston: Beacon Press.

Hartshorne, Charles (1979). "The Rights of the Subhuman World." *Environmental Ethics* 1:49–60.

Hauerwas, Stanley, and John Berkman (1993). "A Trinitarian Theology of the 'Chief

End of All Flesh.' " In *Good News for Animals?*, ed. Charles Pinches and Jay B. McDaniels Maryknoll, N.Y.: Orbis Books.

Hearne, Vicki (1986). *Adam's Task: Calling Animals by Name.* New York: Knopf.

——— (1992). *Bandit: Dossier of a Dangerous Dog.* New York: HarperPerennial.

——— (1994). *Animal Happiness.* San Francisco: HarperCollins.

Heidegger, Martin (1959). *An Introduction to Metaphysics.* Trans. Ralph Manheim. New Haven: Yale University Press.

Heiman, Marcel (1956). "The Relationship between Man and Dog." *Psychoanalytic Quarterly* 25:568–585.

Hennecke, Edgar (1965). *New Testament Apocrypha,* vol. 2. Philadelphia: Westminster Press.

Herriot, James (1987). "The Card over the Bed." In *James Herriot's Dog Stories.* New York: St. Martin's Press.

Hick, John (1977). *Evil and the God of Love.* Rev. ed. San Francisco: Harper & Row.

History of the Philadelphia Bible-Christian Church (1922). Philadelphia: J. B. Lippincott.

Hoffman, Joseph, trans. (1987). *Celsus on the True Doctrine.* New York: Oxford University Press.

Holmes-Gore, V. A. (1971). *These We Have Not Loved.* Ashingdon, Eng: C. W. Daniel.

Horsley, Richard A. (1987). *Jesus and the Spiral of Violence.* San Francisco: Harper & Row.

——— (1994). *Sociology and the Jesus Movement.* New York: Continuum.

Houston, Walter (1993). *Purity and Monotheism: Clean and Unclean Animals in Biblical Law.* Sheffield, Eng.: JSOT Press.

Hügel, Friedrich von (1923). *Essays and Addresses on the Philosophy of Religion: First Series.* New York: E. P. Dutton.

Hume, C. W. (1957). *The Status of Animals in the Christian Religion.* London: Universities Federation for Animal Welfare.

Hyland, J. R. (1988). *The Slaughter of Terrified Beasts.* Sarasota, Fla.: Viatoris Ministries.

Hyman, Stanley Edgar (1962). *The Tangled Web: Darwin, Marx, Frazer, and Freud as Imaginative Writers.* New York: Atheneum.

Irenaeus, (1950). *Against Heresies.* In *The Ante-Nicene Fathers,* vol. 1, ed. Alexander Roberts and James Donaldson. Grand Rapids: Eerdmans.

James, Montague Rhodes (1975). *The Apocryphal New Testament.* Oxford: Clarendon Press.

Jasper, James M., and Dorothy Nelkin (1992). *The Animal Rights Crusade: The Growth of a Moral Protest.* New York: Macmillan.

Jay, Nancy (1992). *Throughout Your Generations Forever: Sacrifice, Religion, and Paternity.* Chicago: University of Chicago Press.

Johnson, Lawrence E. (1991). *A Morally Deep World.* Cambridge: Cambridge University Press.

Julian of Norwich (1978). *Showings.* Trans. Edmund Colledge and James Walsh. New York: Paulist Press.

Jung, L. Shannon (1993). "Animals in Christian Perspective." In *Good News for Animals?*, ed. Charles Pinches and Jay B. McDaniel. Maryknoll, N.Y.: Orbis Books.

Kalechofsky, Roberta (1985). *Haggadah for the Liberated Lamb*. Marblehead, Masso: Micah Publications.

———, ed. (1992). *Judaism and Animal Rights: Classical and Contemporary Responses*. Marblehead, Masso: Micah Publications.

Käsemann, Ernst (1980). *Commentary on Romans*. Trans. Geoffrey W. Bromiley. Grand Rapids: William B. Eerdmans.

Keller, Catherine (1986). *From a Broken Web: Separation, Sexism, and Self*. Boston: Beacon Press.

Kempe, Margery (1989). *The Book of Margery Kempe*. Trans. Barry Windeatt. New York: Penguin Books.

Kete, Kathleen (1994). *The Beast in the Boudoir*. Berkeley: University of California Press.

Kheel, Marti (1985). "The Liberation of Nature: A Circular Affair." *Environmental Ethics* 7:135–149.

——— (1990). "Ecofeminism and Deep Ecology: Reflections on Identity and Difference." In *Reweaving the World: The Emergence of Ecofeminism*, ed. Irene Diamond and Gloria Feman Orenstein. San Francisco: Sierra Club Books.

Kook, Abraham Isaac (1978). *Abraham Isaac Kook: The Lights of Penitence, the Moral Principles, Lights of Holiness, Essays, Letters, and Poems*. Trans. Ben Zion Bokser. New York: Paulist Press.

Lansbury, Coral (1985). *The Old Brown Dog: Women, Workers, and Vivisection in Edwardian England*. Madison: University of Wisconsin Press.

Lawrence, Elizabeth A. (1989). "Neoteny in American Perceptions of Animals." In *Perceptions of Animals in American Culture*, ed. R. J. Hoage. Washington, D. C.: Smithsonian Institution Press.

Leach, Maria (1961). *God Had a Dog*. New Brunswick, N.J.: Rutgers University Press.

Leahy, Michael P. T. (1991). *Against Liberation: Putting Animals in Perspective*. New York: Routledge.

Le Guin, Ursula K. (1987). *Buffalo Gals and Other Animal Presences*. New York: Penguin.

Leopold, Aldo (1949). *A Sand County Almanac*. New York: Oxford University Press.

Lévi-Strauss, Claude (1969). *The Raw and the Cooked*. Trans. John and Doreen Weightman. New York: Harper & Row.

——— (1973). *Totemism*. Trans. Rodney Needham. Harmondsworth, Eng.: Penguin.

Lewis, C. S. (1962). *The Problem of Pain*. New York: Macmillan.

Linzey, Andrew (1986). "The Place of Animals in Creation." In *Animal Sacrifices: Religious Perspectives on the Use of Animals in Science*, ed. Tom Regan. Philadelphia: Temple University Press.

——— (1987). *Christianity and the Rights of Animals*. London: SPCK.

——— (1993). "Vampire's Dilemma, Animal Rights, and Parasitical Nature." In *Good News for Animals?*, ed. Charles Pinches and Jay B. McDaniel. Maryknoll, N.Y.: Orbis Books.

——— (1994). *Animal Theology*. Urbana: University of Illinois Press.

Linzey, Andrew, and Tom Regan, eds. (1988a). *Animals and Christianity: A Book of Readings.* New York: Crossroad.

——— (1988b). *Song of Creation: An Anthology of Poems in Praise of Animals.* Hants, U.K.: Marshall Morgan and Scott.

——— (1989). *Love the Animals: Meditations and Prayers.* New York: Crossroad.

Locke, John (1984). *Essay Concerning Human Understanding,* vol. 2. Oxford: Clarendon Press.

Lorenz, Konrad (1964). *Man Meets Dog.* Harmondsworth, Eng.: Penguin.

——— (1981). *The Foundations of Ethology.* New York: Simon and Schuster.

MacIntyre, Alasdair (1990). *Three Rival Versions of Moral Enquiry.* Notre Dame: University of Notre Dame Press.

Maehle, Andreas-Holger, and Ulrich Tröhler (1987). "Animal Experimentation from Antiquity to the End of the Eighteenth Century." In *Vivisection in Historical Perspective.* ed. Nicolaas A. Rupke. London: Croom Helm.

Mann, Thomas (1954). *Death in Venice and Seven Other Stories.* Trans. H. T. Lowe-Porter. New York: Vintage Books.

Marx, Karl (1971). *The Grundrisse.* Trans. David McLellan. New York: Harper.

Masri, Al-Hafiz B. A. (1987). *Islamic Concern for Animals.* Petersfield, Eng.: Athene Trust.

McCaig, Donald (1984). *Nop's Trials.* New York: Crown.

McDaniel, Jay B. (1989). *Of God and Pelicans: A Theology of Reverence for Life.* Louisville: Westminster/John Knox Press.

——— (1990). *Earth, Sky, Gods and Mortals.* Mystic, Conn.: Twenty-Third Publications.

——— (1993). "A God Who Loves and a Church That Does the Same," in *Good News for Animals?,* ed. Charles Pindres and Jay B. McDaniel. Maryknoll, N.Y.: Orbis Books.

McFague, Sallie (1987). *Models of God: Theology for an Ecological, Nuclear Age.* Philadelphia: Fortress Press.

——— (1993). *The Body of God: An Ecological Theology.* Minneapolis: Fortress Press.

McKelvey, R. J. (1969). *The New Temple: The Church in the New Testament.* London: Oxford University Press.

Meeks, Wayne (1986). *The Moral World of the First Christians.* Philadelphia: Westminster Press.

Midgley, Mary (1978). *Beast and Man.* Ithaca: Cornell University Press.

——— (1983). *Animals and Why They Matter.* Athens: University of Georgia Press.

Milbank, John (1990). *Theology and Social Theory: Beyond Secular Reason.* Oxford: Blackwell.

Mill, John Stuart (1970). *Three Essays on Religion.* New York: AMS Press.

Moltmann, Jürgen (1991). *God in Creation.* Trans. Margaret Kohl. New York: HarperCollins.

Money, John (1985). *The Destroying Angel: Sex, Fitness, and Food in the Legacy of Degeneracy Theory.* Buffalo, N.Y.: Prometheus Books.

Murray, Robert (1992). *The Cosmic Covenant.* London: Sheed and Ward.

Myers, Ched (1992). *Binding the Strong Man: A Political Reading of Mark's Story of Jesus.* Maryknoll, N.Y.: Orbis Books.

Nelson, Richard D. (1993). *Raising Up a Faithful Priest: Community and Priesthood in Biblical Theology.* Louisville: Westminster/John Knox Press.

Neville, Robert (1984). "Buddhism and Process Philosophy." In *Buddhism and American Thinkers,* ed. Kenneth K. Inada and Nolan P. Jacobson. Albany: SUNY Press.

Nietzsche, Friedrich (1968). *Thus Spoke Zarathustra.* In *The Portable Nietzsche,* trans. Walter Kaufmann. New York: Penguin.

——— (1982). *Daybreak.* Trans. R. J. Hollingdale. Cambridge: Cambridge University Press.

Noddings, Nel (1984). *Caring: A Feminist Approach to Ethics and Moral Education.* Berkeley: University of California Press.

Noske, Barbara (1989). *Humans and Other Animals: Beyond the Boundaries of Anthropology.* London: Pluto Press.

Nozick, Robert (1983). "About Mammals and People." *New York Times Book Review,* Nov. 27.

Nurbakhsh, Javad (1989). *Dogs from a Sufi Point of View.* Trans. Terry Graham. London: Khaniqahi-Nimatullahi Publications.

Nussbaum, Martha C. (1990). *Love's Knowledge: Essays on Philosophy and Literature.* New York: Oxford University Press.

Outler, Albert C. (1985). *The Works of John Wesley.* Vol. 2. Nashville: Abingdon.

Ozment, Steve (1992). *Protestants: The Birth of a Revolution.* New York: Doubleday.

Paglia, Camille (1991). *Sexual Personae.* New York: Random House.

Passmore, John (1975). "The Treatment of Animals." *Journal of the History of Ideas* 36:195–218.

Pinches, Charles (1993). "Each According to Its Kind: A Defense of Theological Speciesism." In *Good News for Animals?,* ed. Charles Pinches and Jay B. McDaniel. Maryknoll, N.Y.: Orbis Books.

Placher, William C. (1994). *Narratives of a Vulnerable God.* Louisville: Westminster/John Knox Press.

Plantinga, Alvin (1990). "God, Evil, and the Metaphysics of Freedom." In *The Problem of Evil,* ed. Marilyn McCord Adams and Robert Merrihew Adams. New York: Oxford University Press.

Plaskow, Judith (1980). *Sex, Sin, and Grace.* Lanham: University Press of America.

Plato (1985). *The Republic.* Trans. Richard W. Sterling and William C. Scott. New York: Norton.

Pluhar, Evelyn B. (1995). *Beyond Prejudice: The Moral Significance of Human and Nonhuman Animals.* Durham: Duke University Press.

Plumwood, Val (1991). "Nature, Self, and Gender: Feminism, Environmental Philosophy, and the Critique of Rationalism." *Hypatia* 6.

Preece, Rod, and Lorna Chamberlain (1993). *Animal Welfare and Human Values.* Waterloo, Ont.: Wilfrid Laurier University Press.

Prest, John (1981). *The Garden of Eden: The Botanic Garden and the Re-Creation of Paradise.* New Haven: Yale University Press.

Primavesi, Anne (1991). *From Apocalypse to Genesis.* Minneapolis: Fortress Press.

Rachels, James (1990). *Created from Animals: The Moral Implications of Darwinism.* Oxford: Oxford University Press.

Rawls, John (1971). *A Theory of Justice.* Cambridge: Harvard University Press.

Regan, Tom (1983). *The Case for Animal Rights.* Berkeley: University of California Press.

———— (1985). "The Case for Animal Rights." In *In Defense of Animals,* ed. Peter Singer. New York: Harper & Row.

———— (1991). *The Thee Generation.* Philadelphia: Temple University Press.

———— (1993). "Christianity and the Oppression of Animals," In *Good News for Animals?,* ed. Charles Pinches and Jay B. McDaniel. Maryknoll, N.Y.: Orbis Books.

Rimbach, James A. (1982). "The Judeo-Christian Tradition and the Human/Animal Bond." *International Journal of Studies in Animal Problems* 3:198–207.

Ritvo, Harriet (1987). *The Animal Estate: The English and Other Creatures in the Victorian Age.* Cambridge: Harvard University Press.

———— (1988). "The Emergence of Modern Pet-Keeping." In *Animals and People Sharing the World,* ed. Andrew N. Rowan. Hanover, N.H.: University Press of New England.

Roberts, Alexander, and James Donaldson, eds. (1950). *The Ante-Nicene Fathers,* vol. 1. Grand Rapids: Eerdmans.

———— (1962). *The Ante-Nicene Fathers,* vol. 2. Grand Rapids: Eerdmans.

———— (1956). *The Ante-Nicene Fathers,* vol. 4. Grand Rapids: Eerdmans.

Rodd, Rosemary (1990). *Biology, Ethics, and Animals.* Oxford: Clarendon Press.

Rodrigue, George, and Lawrence S. Freundlich (1994). *Blue Dog.* New York: Viking Studio Books.

Rollin, Bernard (1992). *Animal Rights and Human Morality.* Rev. ed. Buffalo, New York: Prometheus Books.

Rosen, Steven (1987). *Food for the Spirit: Vegetarianism and the World Religions.* New York: Bala Books.

Rosenblum, Robert (1988). *The Dog in Art from Rococo to Post-Modernism.* New York: Harry N. Abrams.

Ruether, Rosemary Radford (1992), *Gaia and God.* San Francisco: Harper.

Ryder, Richard D. (1989). *Animal Revolution: Changing Attitudes towards Speciesism.* Oxford: Basil Blackwell.

Sanders, E. P. (1985). *Jesus and Judaism.* Philadelphia: Fortress Press.

———— (1993). *The Historical Figure of Jesus.* New York: Penguin.

Santmire, H. Paul (1985). *The Travail of Nature.* Philadelphia: Fortress Press.

Sartre, Jean-Paul (1981). *The Words.* Trans. Bernard Frechtman. New York: Vintage Books.

Scarry, Elaine (1985). *The Body in Pain: The Making and Unmaking of the World.* New York: Oxford University Press.

Schinto, Jeanne, ed. (1990). *The Literary Dog.* New York: Atlantic Monthly Press.

Schneemelcher, Wilhelm, ed. (1991). *New Testament Apocrypha,* vol. 1. Louisville: Westminster/John Knox Press.

Schochet, Elijah Judah (1984). *Animal Life in Jewish Tradition.* New York: Ktav.

Schwartz, Richard H. (1988). *Judaism and Vegetarianism.* Marblehead, Masso: Micah Publications.

Serpell, James (1986). *In the Company of Animals.* Oxford: Basil Blackwell.

———— (1988). "Pet-Keeping in Non-Western Societies." In *Animals and People Sharing the World,* ed. Andrew N. Rowan. Hanover, N.H.: University Press of New England.

Shell, Marc (1986). "The Family Pet." *Representations* 15:121–153.

Shepard, Paul (1978). *Thinking Animals.* New York: Viking Press.

———— (1996). *The Others: How Animals Made Us Human.* Washington, D.C.: Island Press.

Shwabe, Calvin W. (1984). "Drinking Cow's Milk: The Most Intense Man-Animal Bond." In *The Pet Connection,* ed. Robert K. Anderson et al. Minneapolis: University of Minnesota Center to Study Human-Animal Relationships.

Simon, Leonard J. (1984). "The Pet Trap: Negative Effects of Pet Ownership on Families and Individuals." In *The Pet Connection,* ed. Robert K. Anderson et al. Minneapolis: University of Minnesota Center to Study Human-Animal Relationships.

Simoons, Frederick J. (1961). *Eat Not This Flesh.* Madison: University of Wisconsin Press.

Singer, Isaac Bashevis (1989). "The Letter Writer." In *The Seance and Other Stories,* quoted in *The Extended Circle: A Commonplace Book of Animal Rights,* ed. Jon Wynne-Tyson. New York: Paragon House.

Singer, Peter (1990). *Animal Liberation.* Rev. ed. New York: Avon Books.

Slicer, Deborah (1991). "Your Daughter or Your Dog?: A Feminist Assessment of the Animal Research Issue." *Hypatia* 6: 108–24.

Smith, Steven G. (1993). "Sympathy, Scruple, and Piety: The Moral and Religious Valuation of Nonhumans." *Journal of Religious Ethics* 21:319–42.

Sobosan, Jeffrey G. (1991). *Bless the Beasts: A Spirituality of Animal Care.* New York: Crossroad.

Soper, Kate (1995). *What Is Nature?* Oxford: Blackwell.

Soulen, R. Kendall (1996). *The God of Israel and Christian Theology.* Minneapolis: Fortress Press.

Snyder, Gary (1990). *The Practice of the Wild.* Berkeley: North Point Press.

Spencer, Colin (1995). *The Heretic's Feast: A History of Vegetarianism.* Hanover, N.H.: University Press of New England.

Stein, Gertrude (1936). *The Geographical History of America; or, The Relation of Human Nature to the Human Mind.* New York: Random House.

Stephens, John Richard, ed. *The Dog Lover's Literary Companion.* Rochlin, Calif.: Prima.

Sterchi, Beat (1988). *Cow.* Trans. Michael Hofmann. New York: Pantheon Books.

Stull, Bradford T. (1994). *Religious Dialectics of Pain and Imagination.* Albany: SUNY Press.

Swinburne, Richard (1979). *The Existence of God.* Oxford: Clarendon Press.

Sykes, S. W., ed. (1991). *Sacrifice and Redemption.* Cambridge: Cambridge University Press.

Szasz, Kathleen (1968). *Petishism?: Pets and Their People in the Western World.* New York: Holt, Rinehart and Winston.

Tester, Keith (1991). *Animals and Society: The Humanity of Animal Rights.* New York: Routledge.

Thomas, Elizabeth Marshall (1993). *The Hidden Life of Dogs.* Boston: Houghton Mifflin.

———— (1996). *Certain Poor Shepherds.* New York: Simon & Schuster.

Thomas, Keith (1983). *Man and the Natural World.* New York: Pantheon Books.

Tillich, Paul (1951). *Systematic Theology,* vol. 1. Chicago: University of Chicago Press.

———— (1957). *Systematic Theology,* vol. 2. Chicago: University of Chicago Press.

Toperoff, Shlomo Pesach (1995). *The Animal Kingdom in Jewish Thought.* Northvale, N.J.: Jason Aronson.

Tracy, David (1987). *Plurality and Ambiguity.* San Francisco: Harper & Row.

Tronto, Joan (1993). *Moral Boundaries: A Political Argument for an Ethic of Care.* New York: Routledge.

Tuan, Yi-Fu (1984). *Dominance and Affection: The Making of Pets.* New Haven: Yale University Press.

Turner, James (1980). *Reckoning with the Beast.* Baltimore: Johns Hopkins University Press.

Underhill, Evelyn (1943). *The Letters of Evelyn Underhill.* Ed. Charles Williams. London: Longmans, Green.

Updike, John (1993). "Another Dog's Death." In *Collected Poems, 1953–1993.* New York: Knopf.

Veblen, Thorstein (1979). *The Theory of the Leisure Class.* New York: Penguin.

Waddell, Helen (1996). *Beasts and Saints.* Grand Rapids: William B. Eerdmans.

Ward, Keith (1974). *The Concept of God.* New York: St. Martin's Press.

———— (1982). *Rational Theology and the Creativity of God.* New York: Pilgrim Press.

Webb, Stephen H. (1991). *Re-Figuring Theology: The Rhetoric of Karl Barth.* Albany: SUNY Press.

———— (1993a). *Blessed Excess: Religion and the Hyperbolic Imagination.* Albany: SUNY Press.

———— (1993b). "A Hyperbolic Imagination: Theology and the Rhetoric of Excess." *Theology Today* 50:56–67.

———— (1994). "Nature's Spendthrift Economy: The Extravagance of God in Annie Dillard's *Pilgrim at Tinker Creek.*" In *Soundings* 77:429–51.

———— (1995a). "Pet Theories: A Theology for the Dogs." In *Soundings* 78:213–37.

———— (1995b). "The Rhetoric of and about Excess in William James's *The Varieties of Religious Experience.*" *Religion and Literature* 27:27–45.

———— (1996a). "Ecology vs. the Peaceable Kingdom: Toward a Better Theology of Nature." In *Soundings* 79:239–52.

———— (1996b). *The Gifting God: A Trinitarian Ethics of Excess.* Oxford: Oxford University Press.

White, David Gordon (1991). *Myths of the Dog-Man.* Chicago: University of Chicago Press.

White, T. H. (1968). *The White/Garnett Letters.* Ed. David Garnett. London: Jonathan Cape.

Wilken, Robert L. (1992). *The Land Called Holy: Palestine in Christian History and Thought.* New Haven: Yale University Press.

Williams, George H. (1962). *Wilderness and Paradise in Christian Thought.* New York: Harper & Brothers.

Wilson, A. N. (1992). *Jesus: A Life.* New York: W.W. Norton.

Wittgenstein, Ludwig (1978). *Philosophical Investigations.* Trans. G. E. M. Anscombe. Oxford: Basil Blackwell.

Woolf, Virginia (1983). *Flush.* San Diego: Harcourt Brace Jovanovich.

Wynne-Tyson, Jon, ed. (1989). *The Extended Circle: A Commonplace Book of Animal Rights.* New York: Paragon House.

Young, Frances M. (1975). *Sacrifice and the Death of Jesus.* Philadelphia: Westminster Press.

Zeuner, F. E. (1953). *A History of Domesticated Animals.* New York: Harper & Row.

Index